God's Witnesses

Also by Herbert Lockyer

All the Men of the Bible
All the Women of the Bible
All the Kings and Queens of the Bible
All the Apostles of the Bible
All the Children of the Bible
All the Promises of the Bible
All the Prayers of the Bible
All the Doctrines of the Bible
All the Miracles of the Bible
All the Parables of the Bible
All the Books and Chapters of the Bible
All the Trades and Occupations of the Bible
All the Holy Days and Holidays
All the 2s of the Bible
All the 3s of the Bible
The Sins of Saints
The Unseen Army
Dying, Death, and Destiny
Their Finest Hour
Dark Threads the Weaver Needs
The Life Beyond
41 Major Bible Themes Simply Explained

God's Witnesses

Stories of Real Faith

Herbert Lockyer

Fleming H. Revell
A Division of Baker Book House Co
Grand Rapids, Michigan 49516

© 1975 by Herbert Lockyer

Published by Fleming H. Revell
a division of Baker Book House Company
P.O. Box 6287, Grand Rapids, MI 49516-6287

One-volume paperback edition published 1997

Previously published by Baker Book House under the title *Ancient Portraits in Modern Frames, Bible Biographies* (volume 1) and *Church History Biographies* (volume 2)

Printed in the United States of America

ISBN 0-8007-5640-1

To
the saints in pastorates
I held in Dundee, Hawick, and Bradford,
whose pictures still hang on the walls of my memory

Contents

Preface
The Fascination of Biographical Study

One of the most popular and practical, instructive and inspiring methods of presenting Bible truth is to take up a character and study all that is recorded of him. It is likewise one of the easiest forms of Bible meditation. Thomas Carlyle, in his *Essays,* reminds us that—

> There is properly no history, only biography—
> Biography is the only true history:
> History is the garb of biography.

A German proverb has it, "He that would rightly understand a man must read his whole story." Samuel Johnson goes further and says, "Nobody can write the life of a man, but those who have eaten and drunk and lived in social intercourse with him." Although such intimate association with Bible characters is impossible, seeing they died centuries ago, yet we can read their whole story, and live with them as they come before us in Holy Writ until we come to know them very well. If "a well-written life is almost as rare as a well-spent one," then we are fortunate in having many well-written lives in the imperishable record of Scripture.

Some Bible characters, like Enoch, are given a few verses; others, like Ananias are confined within the limits of a chapter; others, like Adam, stretch over the whole Bible. Yet others, like Luke, are hidden under their own work; while a figure like Paul asserts himself on our notice in history and biography. There are those, like Absalom, who warn us by their vices; but others, such as David who inspire us by their virtues. All kinds of characters engage our attention in God's picture gallery—heroes like Samson, villains such as Joab, failures such as Judas. The most outstanding character in the Bible, apart from the Lord Jesus Christ, is Moses, who had a personal conversation with Him in the days of His flesh.

With the aid of a Bible concordance to gather together all the references to a given person we discover, as Augustine stated it, that "the sacred record, like a faithful mirror has no flattery in its portraits." How encouraging this is! Here are men and women of like passions as ourselves, and they appeal to the imagination of the average person today because of a similarity of experience. Like these ancient characters, we triumph by faith, as some of them did, or fail through disobedience, and unbelief, as others did. Thus, while all biography is fruitful, Scripture biography is singularly so. The lives of men and women of old may be a continual inspiration or warning to us in these modern times. Allowing for differences of time and place, their temptations and potentials are ours. Their God is our God; but we have a spiritual armory and resources of which they knew little, and thus their defeats should not be ours.

Biography also enables a preacher to deal with doctrinal themes in an interesting way. For instance, dwelling upon Joseph's life, one can emphasize the overruling providence of God. If the study is David, then he can be used as a living object lesson of divine forgiveness of sin. That popular Professor of Homiletics at Princeton Seminary, Dr. A. Blackwood, tells in his most valuable treatise, *Preaching from the Bible*, of an incident in a church he knew of, where the pastor had died, and the members came together to pray for a younger man to take the place of the aged leader who had been taken from them. A visiting preacher during the vacancy spoke about Apollos, the eloquent preacher in the early

10

church, and a layman in the church was so impressed with the sermon that he had it printed for free distribution. This led the church to pray for a minister after the pattern of the one the sermon presented. Soon a young preacher was found who answered to the main points of that sermon on Apollos—

> He is eloquent, but accurate.
> He is cultured, but ardent.
> He is dogmatic, but docile.
> He is evangelistic, but educational.

If a character is studied for his outstanding feature as a type, Stephen could be profitably used. He was the church's first martyr, and as *martyr* means "witness," material could be gathered around these points—

> The witness of his life, Acts 6:3, 5
> The witness of his labors, 6:8
> The witness of his lips, 6:10; 7:2-53
> The witness of his looks, 6:15; 7:55
> The witness of his love, 7:60

Biographies, not only of Bible saints, but saints—and sinners—all down the ages are often surpassingly instructive. Facts relating to an individual life can often be more readily stated than those of general history. Early preachers made much use of biographical illustration in their sermons. In my own volume, *All the Men of the Bible,* the student will find in the bibliography a list of authors who have given us some very profitable help along the line of biographical preaching. Further illustrations of this appealing form of presenting Bible truth can be found in other works of mine, namely—

> *All the Women of the Bible*
> *All the Kings and Queens of the Bible*
> *All the Apostles of the Bible*
> *All the Children of the Bible*

The following characters, dealt with somewhat fully, were among several biographical sermons and lectures I gave several years ago while in the regular ministry. It is to be hoped they will serve as guides to those who have a desire to pursue such a method of approach whether to Biblical, Church, or General History. In warning the church at Corinth not to court disaster through murmuring against God's providence, Paul, referring to the twenty-three thousand Israelites who were destroyed because of their fornication, wrote, "These things happened unto them by way of illustration, and they were written for our admonition unto whom the revenues of the past ages have descended" (I Corinthians 10:11, literal reading). Borrowing such a statement, we can apply it to the biographies of both Bible and church warriors and say that they were written for our admonition. Emulating their faithfulness, we must, by God's grace, avoid their failures. Longfellow, in "A Psalm of Life" advises that the—

> Lives of great men all remind us
> We can make our lives sublime,
> And, departing, leave behind us
> Footprints on the sands of time.
>
> Footprints, that perhaps another,
> Sailing o'er life's solemn main,
> A forlorn and shipwrecked brother,
> Seeing, shall take heart again.

Part 1
Bible Biographies

What a marvelous portrait gallery God has given us in the Holy Word He inspired! The strength and fascination of such a gallery "lies not in the number but in the variety of its representations," says George Matheson in his *Representative Men of the Bible,* "and its highest artistic claim must ever be, that as the canvas of human life it has succeeded in delineating the manifold wisdom of God." No national gallery, however famous, is comparable to God's ancient gallery with its true portraits of the renowned and renegade, the conspicuous and common alike, for all mankind to study. Here we see people who differ in character. Some are grave, others gay. Some are magnificent, others mean. Some are worthy, others wicked. The stories of all should be meditated upon, for in them we can find our own history, in fact and parable.

Young people delighting in each other's company, and anticipating marriage, should read the love stories of Ruth, Rachel, and Rebekah.

All who face severe reverses or bankruptcy should read Job who lost all, and learn from him the blessing of adversity. "The Lord gave, the Lord hath taken away. Blessed be the name of the Lord."

Girls who have a desire to dedicate their precious lives to the Lord will find much to stimulate them in stories such as the captive maid, or in the rise of Esther from obscurity to fame, or in Lydia.

Boys, haughty and indifferent, demanding independence and freedom from home ties, can learn an illuminating lesson from the prodigal son who paid dearly for his decision to live as he pleased.

The affluent, who have plenty of this world's goods can find warning beacon lights in the histories of the rich farmer, the rich young ruler, and the rich man in hell.

The poor and straitened in circumstances will find a companion in Lazarus who, although he lived on crumbs, yet went to Paradise. Consolation will also be theirs as they think of Jesus who had nowhere to lay His head.

Here are ten portraits we have chosen from the divine gallery to look at from every angle in order to discover wherein we resemble them.

1

Enoch

The Companion of God Who Never Died

Enoch has one of the shortest yet sweetest biographies in the Bible. There are only two men in heaven who never died —Enoch and Elijah. George Matheson speaks of him as Enoch the Immortal. A reading of Genesis 5 is like taking a walk in a cemetery and reading the names inscribed on the tombstones. But this graveyardlike narrative has this peculiarity: the facts of each person are related in the same way. So-and-so lived so long before so-and-so was born, and lived so long after, and then died. But when we come to Enoch, the somber monotony is broken, for while his record begins in the usual way, there is no account of his death, simply because he did not go the way of all flesh. One day he was missed and could not be found. God took His walking companion home to be with Himself forever, robbing the undertaker thereby of a mournful task.

His History

Because of the uniqueness of his life, books, articles, and sermons about him abound. The Bible condenses all it has to say about Enoch in eleven verses, or some 150 words (Gen. 5:18-24; Heb. 11:5; Jude 14-15), yet here I am writing almost ten times that amount about this figure in the cradle of the human race. As we bring together the scanty material we have, the following facts are evident.

15

First, the name he bore proves that Jared his father was rightly guided in his selection of a name, for *Enoch* means "teacher, disciplined, dedicated"—a name fittingly corresponding to his life and witness. His character reveals him to have been a dedicated man whose life was disciplined and whose habits were regulated by the guiding hand of God. His unbroken walk with God made him the effective prophetic teacher Jude declares Enoch to have been.

Second, he was born and lived in a time of social and communal moral declension, proving that God never leaves Himself without witness even in the darkest days of national history. Perhaps somewhere in the world today a child has been born destined to accomplish great and mighty things for God. In these modern times of ever-increasing degeneracy and apostasy, may He raise up many Enochs to declare, as the patriarch did, divine wrath and judgment upon sinners if they fail to turn from their sin.

His father's name, *Jared,* means "descending," a word associated with Jordan's springs, implying, "rapid descender." Thus his name was descriptive of the times, which were characterized by the gradual spiritual deterioration of the human race culminating in the tragic Flood. In such a putrid age Enoch was an arrestive force, for in the midst of increasing corruption and violence he functioned as the salt of the earth and was doubtless hated because he despised the paint and varnish used to cover up the sin of his age.

Third, Enoch's record is the shortest in the narrative, as was his life, whereas his son, Methuselah lived the longest— 604 years longer than his godly, illustrious father. Enoch lived for 365 years—a year for every day of our normal year. The only thing his son was renowned for was his old age—969 years—hence the proverbial saying, "As old as Methuselah." Taking these two characters together they teach us that one's life is not to be judged by its length, but by its quality. Often the shortest life is the most fruitful and influential. Jesus was only 33 years old when He died. The question, whether our

journey is long or short, is, Is our life telling
the world around? Because we "live in dee(
thoughts, not breaths," how important it
utmost for the highest.

> He liveth long who liveth well-
> All else is being flung away:
> He liveth longest who can tell
> Of true things truly done each day.

Fourth, another startling innovation, Enoch did not die as
did the others who are mentioned in this birth-and-death
chapter, with its solemn monotony of a graveyard. When we
reach Enoch there is a startling and blessed break, described
for us in a threefold way: "He was not. God took him." The
first phrase suggests how the world regarded Enoch's mysterious disappearance; while the second reveals the divine account of his removal from his home circle. Because he belonged to God, God had every right to take Enoch to be with
Himself (see John 17:24).

"[He] was not found" (Heb. 11:5). Do not these words
conjure up a massive search for a man of such godly character? If no one saw him vanish, family and friends missed him,
and sought for him without avail. "He passed away, and, lo,
he was not; Yea, I sought him, but he could not be found"
(Ps. 37:36). Saints like Enoch are always missed. Are we
living so that when we have died, we, too, shall be missed?
Robert Murray McCheyne's motto was "to live, so as to be
missed when gone." The alarm of the sudden removal of
Enoch can illustrate the consternation over the removal of
believers at the return of Christ in the air.

"God translated him . . . that he should not see death."
This further account of Enoch's mysterious disappearance
suggests precious truths. First of all, the word *translation*
means to remove from one place or position to another. Paul
uses the term to indicate the sudden change in the religious
attitude of the Galatians (Gal. 1:6). When Enoch was trans-

ne found himself immediately transferred from earth to ven. In his miraculous and supernatural ascension he was ʒmoved from the position of an earth-dweller to that of a companion with God in His high and holy temple.

Perhaps this is what might have happened if Adam had not sinned and his descendants had remained sinless—perhaps they would have been suddenly translated from an earthly existence to a heavenly one at God's command. As we shall later see Elijah shared the unique experience of Enoch of going directly to heaven in his body. If Christ should return today countless thousands of regenerated men and women would likewise go to heaven without dying.

> Oh, joy, oh, delight,
> Should we go without dying.

The purpose or result of Enoch's translation was that he should not see or undergo death before the judgment of the Flood. As such he was a type of the true church translated before the Great Tribulation overtakes a godless, guilty world. For some three hundred years he had habitually walked with God, and heaven, therefore, was in his heart, and his body had no need to rest in foreign soil before its resurrection. Because Jesus was perfect in creation, in character, and in probation He could have gone straight to heaven from the Mount of Transfiguration. But, for the joy of having myriads of redeemed hearts sharing His glory, He turned from the mount and endured the cross. One devotional writer has suggested that as very close friends, God and Enoch were in the habit of walking together each day, and that one day God said, "Enoch you have walked a long way with me today, why not come home with Me?" Thus, God took him to His abode, thereby extending an earthly walk into eternal companionship.

The historian tells us that "*before* his translation" Enoch had the indisputable testimony "that he pleased God." Walking with Him, and getting to know His will, it was his delight to do His will. Oh, that it might be said of each of us, "He pleased God"! Are we well-pleasing to Him? "Without faith it is impossible to please Him," but faith was exhibited by Enoch in his walking with God, and in his passion to please Him. Faith alone can create such a close, personal relationship as existed between God and Enoch. The phrase "had this testimony" preserves the force of the perfect tense, "He *hath had* witness borne to him," and such a testimony still stands on record. At the heart of Christ's gospel is His declaration, "He that liveth and believeth in me, shall never die."

His Character

From the passages associated with the career of Enoch, we can glean one or two lessons regarding the divine ideal for our witness here on earth. First of all, it is interesting to observe how and when he was called to work and walk with God. We have no way of knowing whether Enoch was a man of faith *before* the birth of Methuselah which took place when Enoch was sixty-five years of age. What is clearly evident is that his walking with God commenced *after* the birth of his son. Perhaps before the child was born he may have believed and worshiped God, as Abel had, but that *after* Methuselah's birth something happened in Enoch's heart and a closer walk that continued for three centuries commenced. From that time on God and he became agreed companions as never before (Amos 3:3).

The inference then is that the coming of this child into his life and home marked a spiritual crisis, and awakened Enoch to a sense of his responsibility to Him who had given him a son. Often spiritual experiences are associated with various circumstances. With Enoch it was the birth of a child. But with Isaiah it was the death of a king. "In the year that King Uzziah died, I saw also the Lord" (6:1). Both the cradle and the grave have been used of God to draw those standing around them nearer Himself. Crises have resulted in many conversions.

19

Twice over we are told that Enoch "walked with God," or "lived close to God," as Moffatt puts it. The word used for "walked" means, "to go on habitually." Do you not covet such a short and signal biography? There was nothing intermittent about this marvelous friendship between the Creator and one of His creatures. There was no break in this remarkable companionship. Enoch lived a life of continual—full and unbroken—communion with his heavenly Companion. The lost privilege and forfeited position of Eden was regained and held by Enoch who did not have Adam's perfect environment. In spite of the increasing godlessness of the time in which he lived, this friend of God did not yield to the seductive enducements of his age.

At the end of each day's walk, Enoch found his difficulties surmounted, conquests gained, and new songs of triumph to sing. Although compassed about with iniquitous contemporaries, this companion of God went on from strength to strength. His character was deepened, and his pure soul mounted to experiences still higher and broader and more satisfying and spiritual. There was, of course, a goal to crown the exercise of walking with God for three centuries. At the close of his earthly walk the Celestial City was reached, and Enoch entered the perfect life his heavenly Companion of the road had treasured up for him.

That memorable walk, then, was gloriously maintained in spite of a corrupt and degenerate civilization. What was possible for this seventh man from Adam in the dawn of human history may be deemed impossible in the cesspool of iniquity surrounding us today. Yet we have provisions to draw upon that Enoch did not have. We live on this side of the cross and in the dispensation of the Holy Spirit, making vast resources available to us to become more than conquerors over the world, the flesh, and the devil.

Enoch's walk with God was maintained in spite of family ties and home cares. Such responsibilities should not interfere with our walk with God. Our home life can be peaceful and fragrant only as each member strives to live in uninterrupted fellowship with Him who "setteth the solitary in families."

Enoch's walk with God was sustained even amid the obligations of his secular employment. In all probability he was a proprietor of cattle and lands and a master of servants; yet in spite of the trials and problems that must have arisen, his life was unspotted. Because of the boundless grace and power of God there is no legitimate sphere in which it is too hard to be a Christian. Saints could be found even in Caesar's household. Too often businessmen fail to put the principles of Christianity into practice. They shrink from the cost of true discipleship.

Enoch's walk with God was not hindered in any way by the growing spiritual deterioration of his times. Jude reminds us that Enoch was a prophet who was not afraid to declare to the ungodly the wrath of God they would experience. Although he lived in a vitiated atmosphere, breathing the purer air of heaven he rebuked the works of darkness. Thus his record gives the lie to the idea that it is impossible to be a Christian after the New Testament ideal in a complex and Christless world like ours. If anything, the world today is more degenerate than it was in Enoch's time, yet it is easier for us to wear the white flower of a blameless life. Do we not have a fuller knowledge of the will and program of God, and a fuller measure of the grace of Christ and power of the Holy Spirit than Enoch had?

As the shadows of Enoch's predicted judgment are gathering around our godless world, there are two perils we can easily glide into if we are not prayerfully watchful.

1. The peril of being influenced by our surroundings

Beyond doubt Enoch was counted odd or antiquated by those of his generation because of the saintliness of his life. His striving to please God, we can be assured, displeased men. Having chosen to walk with God, he could not walk with the

21

ungodly. It takes a living fish to swim against the stream, and rather than be caught in the whirlpool of corruption Enoch lived a life contrary to others. He preferred divine company to worldly companions. It is to be feared that we often find it easier to float with the stream, to accommodate ourselves to our environment, or refuse to separate ourselves from worldly pleasures and pursuits. Some there are who, chameleonlike, try to be at home in their surroundings, religious or otherwise. They think it clever to be "good mixers."

2. The peril of thinking it is too hard to live for God

What God has enabled one to do, He can enable another to do, for His grace and power are for each and all. Like Enoch, we too can walk with God by faith, and like him throw into greater contrast, by our holiness, the evil of the day in which we live. If we follow Enoch's example and walk habitually with God in spite of uncongenial and unresponsive surroundings, then, ere long, we too shall not be found. At the return of the Saviour we will be translated from the dusty lanes of earth to the golden street above.

> Walk in the light, and thou shalt own
> Thy darkness passed away,
> Because that light hath on thee shone
> In which is perfect day.

2

Lot

The Compromising Mayor of Sodom

The story of Lot is one of the most tragic in the Old Testament. What a blemished biography Scripture gives us of this pioneer of faith who made a wrong choice! From the portrait Peter gives us of Lot, it would seem as if he had never compromised with the wicked ways of Sodom, for the apostle speaks of him as "a just man," a "righteous man" whose "righteous soul" was vexed by the filthy, unlawful deeds of the Sodomites (II Peter 2:7-8). The American Standard Version repeats the word "righteous" three times. "[God] delivered righteous Lot, sore distressed by the lascivious life of the wicked: (for that righteous man dwelling among them, in seeing and hearing, vexed his righteous soul from day to day with their lawless deeds)." Such an evaluation of Lot's character presents him as one who was not such a "bad Lot" after all. But let us see how this so-called righteous man is presented in the opening book of the Bible (Gen. 13; 14; 19).

Both Abraham and Lot, as well as Sodom, are typical of many aspects of our spiritual witness and experiences.

Abraham is conspicuous as the man of faith, separated from the world, and separated unto God, and whose eyes looked for the things unseen and eternal.

Lot, unlike his uncle who was spiritual, was a man of the world and of sense; a selfish, carnal, compromising character, who looked only at things seen and temporal. Therefore, Lot has no place in the catalog of the heroes of faith in Hebrews 11.

Sodom is a fitting type of our sinful, wicked world. David Thoreau, the American writer and philosopher of the eighteenth century wrote, "Wherever men have lived there is a story to be told," and what a story of sordidness and of destruction Sodom tells! All cities—and citizens—Sodomlike in character face a doom similar to that city of old from which Lot was divinely rescued.

Two things are prominent in the portrait given of Lot, namely, the gain of position and the loss of power.

The Gain of Position

Lot, as the sacred record tells us, was the son of Abraham's brother Haran, who died before Abraham and Lot left the Ur of the Chaldees. Being childless, Abraham was drawn to his fatherless nephew, and possibly looked upon him as an heir to his possessions. Although "there was nothing of the originality and the initiative of Abraham in Lot," yet the young man did believe in his uncle's God, and was one with him in the great venture into the unknown. Under divine inspiration, Peter called him, "righteous Lot," which implies he had had some knowledge and experience of God. "The righteous man" of the Old Testament would be the equivalent of a "Christian" under grace.

Lot, then, started well. Left with his father's inheritance, and then with his grandfather Terah's possessions (Gen. 11:31), after his father's death he followed his uncle out of Haran into Canaan (Gen. 11:32; 12:4-5). When in disobedience to the divine call, Abraham went into Egypt, Lot went with him, and returned with him to the place where their tent had been at the beginning (Gen. 12:10; 13:4). Lot, then, ran well at the beginning, but he was hindered in the race

(Gal. 5:7). He began in the Spirit, but, as we shall see, he ended in the flesh.

The first stage in Lot's downward career came when he made a selfish choice. What and how man chooses when opportunities and alternatives are put before him often discovers what kind of a man he is. There are three marked steps in the journey toward Sodom: *Lot chose; he pitched his tent toward Sodom; he sat at the gate* (Gen. 13:10-11; see Ps. 1:1). Because Lot willingly followed his uncle when the call came to him to leave the land of their nativity for the land God was to show him, he shared the prosperity of Abraham. "*Their* substance was great," and because of this they could no longer dwell together (Gen. 13:5-6).

Then there came the strife between their respective herdsmen, leading Abraham to offer Lot his freedom and also the choice of the whole land before them. How magnanimous it was of Abraham to give Lot the first pick, which by right of seniority should have been his (13:7-9)! Greedily Lot chose the well-watered plain before him where Sodom was situated, and in so doing he separated from his revered relative and friend, whose assistance he was yet to need. Lot should never have severed such a strong link with a God-chosen man like Abraham, and thus remove himself from the sphere of spiritual and moral influence that had nurtured him up to this time. If God has given us the friendship of a godly, strong, and stalwart person as a companion, let us see to it that nothing comes between to mar such beneficial companionship.

The gospel of the world is, Take care of No. 1—each man for himself and the devil take the hindermost. When Abraham gave Lot first choice, the honorable thing would have been to say, "No, Uncle, because you are my senior, you make the choice. I am here with all this substance because of you. I am reaping part of the blessing God pronounced upon you before we left home." But such nobility was not characteristic of Lot, who appears as a "mean Lot" in his selfish

25

choice which, ignorantly, he thought was the better choice as he pitched his tent toward Sodom, or "near to Sodom," as the Revised Version expresses it.

The citizens of Sodom were "wicked and sinners before the Lord exceedingly" (13:14-15). Isaiah speaks of the shamelessness of the men of Sodom (6:9). Jeremiah condemned them for their evil influence and idolatry (23:14). Ezekiel exposed their pride, satiety, idleness, and neglect of the needy (16:49). Peter wrote of their filthy conversation (or manner of life) (II Peter 2:7). Jude singles out their fornication (v. 7). If only Lot had seen the putridness of this city in that well-watered plain, and had taken a different road, what a different story would have been his.

Pitching *near* Sodom, it was not long before Lot was *in* it, only to experience the disaster of his selfish choice, for he was plundered of his goods and taken prisoner by warring and avaricious kings. Word reached Abraham as to his nephew's tragic condition and he hastened to deliver him from his predicament. Freed by Abraham who recovered all his goods, one would have thought that Lot would have come to his senses, and after thanking his aged uncle for rescuing him, confessed how he needed him. But no, graciousness and gratitude were not in his make-up, and so the breach between the two was not healed (14:1-16).

The gain of public office

Once settled in sinful Sodom, Lot was not long in becoming a prominent figure in civic affairs. The world is ever ready to engulf and honor the carnal Christian. "Lot sat in the gate of Sodom" (19:1). "Sitting in the gate" is an Eastern phrase used of one with an office equivalent to our judge, or mayor, one whose responsibilities were the settling of disputes between inhabitants and the reception of visitors as the representative of the city's hospitality. It was in the latter capacity

that Lot welcomed and entertained the two angels sent by
God to warn Sodom of its doom. Thus the one-time pilgrim
became the provost. One wonders whether Lot thought he
could change the morals of the city by living in it and taking
office in it. If so, he embarked on a futile and dangerous
policy. The man who had the most influence upon Sodom
was the man outside it (14:16), who, as a good soldier, did
not entangle himself with the affairs of this life (II Tim. 2:4),
and believed that the friend of this world is an enemy of God
(James 4:4). Abraham was a "separated man."

Oh, the peril of position! Too often when a professed
believer gets on in the world, he goes backward in his spiritual life; yet this should not be. Consecrated, good men are
needed in all public offices; but, alas! because of the corrupted ways of life and of society, it is well-nigh impossible
for a spiritually minded person to retain his spirituality.
Satan tried to lure Jesus with the promise of position. "All
these will I give thee." But the proffered possessions were
strongly despised by Him who was tempted like as we are.
Many have found ambition to be ruinous! So much has been
sacrificed to be somebody and have something. Is it not far
better to be a nobody here, and a somebody over there? Too
often a coveted career ends in an early coffin.

The gain of a wife

In Luke 17:32 our Lord refers to Lot's wife, who is not
referred to in Lot's story until he was commanded to take his
wife and daughters out of the cesspool of iniquity (19:15).
Her presence in the home is, of course, inferred in the conversation between Lot and the angels (19:8, 12, 14). When
Abraham left his country, Sarai his wife accompanied him,
but nothing is said about Lot's wife. It would seem as if he
was a bachelor until he settled in Sodom and that he took a
Sodomite to wife and that she is one of the unnamed women
in the Bible. Perhaps it was she who gradually brought Lot

27

over to the life and ways of the Sodom she dearly loved—and died in because she was too reluctant to leave it.

If Lot did marry a Sodomite woman then this was a further step in his continually compromising journey. Uniting with such a godless woman was an act of disobedience to the revealed will of God. By yoking himself to an unbeliever, Lot, as a professed believer in God (19:18-19), courted disaster. The kind of daughters Lot's wife bore, proves her evil influence as a mother. When two marry it should be in the Lord. But when a Christian marries a non-Christian, such a union is *not* in (or of) the Lord. Often the Christian loves the non-Christian, and thinks that by marrying the unbelieving partner he/she can win her/him over for the Lord. While this has been known to succeed, in the majority of cases there develops strife and trouble and constant friction, with one pulling one way, and the other, the opposite. Compromise in respect to marriage, then, can prove disastrous, as it did in the case of righteous Lot who should have chosen a righteous wife and the two have lived together as one in the Lord.

The gain of material possessions

Like Abraham, Lot lived in a tent as they journeyed from Haran into the land of Canaan (13:5; 19:1). But once in Sodom he no more experienced the confinement and lack of facilities of a rough outdoor life, for Lot now possessed a house. It must have been a large one to hold his family, give shelter to his servants, and to entertain strangers (19:2-3). Once a sojourner, Lot is now a comfortable settler, living no longer by faith but by sight. Having brought considerable wealth with him in flocks, herds, tents, and herdsmen, trade with the Sodomites must have added to his riches. But, unlike his uncle, Lot's investments in God were not very large. Pitching his tent toward Sodom he soon lost the pilgrim life, and as the city's mayor, added to his possessions.

It is not wrong, of course, to have earthly possessions. The sin comes when such possessions have us, and dominate our life. Too often, spiritual impoverishment follows the enlargement of our borders. The warning is, "If riches increase set not your heart upon them" (Ps. 62:10). It is somewhat surprising what airs even professing Christians can cultivate if they rise a few steps on the social ladder because of the acquisition of greater wealth. A Christian in the world is necessary and God-designed, but the world in a Christian is wrong and disastrous. What truth is wrapped up in the old proverb that "more men are killed by meat than poison." How we have to guard against the peril of gain! When gold is substituted for God, and faith is forfeited for fame, and desire for gifts kills love for the Giver, barrenness of soul is bound to follow. Lot's prominent place in the questionable society of Sodom cost him his spirituality. He found that the corruption of a city was the wrong kind of soil in which to cultivate the flower of holiness.

The Loss of Power

How paltry the material gains of Lot in Sodom appear when balanced against the spiritual losses he sustained! Paul could triumphantly declare, "What things were gain to me, those I counted loss for Christ" (Phil. 3:7). It is said of Moses that he esteemed the reproach of Christ greater riches than the treasures of Egypt (Heb. 11:26). But poor Lot esteemed his position and possessions in Sodom greater riches than the unclouded vision of God's face, and consequently he lost so much of imperishable value.

He lost the power of his spirituality

Being an important figure in Sodom, Lot must live like a Sodomite although inwardly he knew that such a course was not right, for Peter says that his righteous soul was vexed by all he saw and heard. Yet the fact remains that he sur-

29

rendered the altar of God at Bethel for the idols of Sodom. What a tragic exchange! When the angels forced him to leave the doomed city we read that "Lot lingered." What kept him back? Was it that which led him there, namely, material advantages? The deeper into the life of Sodom he plunged, the firmer its grip on him became. How imperative it is for us to learn how to sit loose to things of earth, having little to bind us to a doomed world!

Some idea of Lot's spiritual loss can be judged by the actions of the angels who came to warn him of Sodom's destruction. They would not accept the offered hospitality of his home, but preferred to stay out in the street of the city. The kind of home he had made lacked the atmosphere necessary and congenial for the entertainment of visitors from heaven. "Lot knew too much about Sodom to be happy with it: and he knew too much about God to be fully happy in Sodom, and so he let his life be spoiled."

He lost his power with Abraham

Had Lot kept near his uncle, a more commendable story would have been his. How fortunate he was to have had a grandfather like Terah, and a relative like Abraham! But, having made a good start with the mighty patriarch, now that he is somebody in Sodom, he has no further use for the wise old man whom the Lord blessed in all things. How heartless it was to separate from Abraham, and sever himself from the safeguard of such a holy relationship! Now in Sodom, Lot must have companions corresponding to his ambitions, so he mingled freely with the men of Sodom, just as backsliding Peter sat down among those who were crying out for the blood of Jesus.

Have you noticed how carnal Christians shun the fellowship of true Abrahams? Becoming more at home with those who are worldly minded, they shun the company of those who are separated unto God. When Lot turned himself adrift from Abraham, he deliberately cut himself off from godly influences that would have made him, like his uncle, "a friend of God." We say that "a man is known by the company he keeps." How true! Show me the kind of company you like best, and I'll tell you how near to, or far from, Christ you are. Are you glad when spiritually minded friends say to you, "Let us go into the house of the Lord"? The well-known hymn reminds us that if we would "take time to be holy," we must—

> Make friends of God's children;
>   Help those who are weak;
> Forgetting in nothing,
>   His blessing to seek.

He lost his power with the Sodomites

In coming down to the level of their unlawful deeds, Lot surrendered what influence he had had over them. When he tried to prevent the men of the city from committing sodomy with the two angels—*sodomy,* being the legalized homosexuality of today, or to put it as Paul did in no uncertain terms, "The men, leaving the natural use of the woman, burned in their lust one toward another; men with men working that which is unseemly, and receiving in themselves that recompence of their error which was meet"—when Lot tried to protect his guests, the corrupt men of Sodom rebuked Lot by saying, "Stand back. . . . This one fellow came in to sojourn, and he will needs be a judge: now will we deal worse with thee, than with them" (19:9). What an unbecoming way that was to treat their magistrate who had sat in the gate! But those men knew that Lot, in spite of his professed faith in the Lord, was a compromiser trying to make the best of both worlds, and his appeal to them not to commit a foul deed, therefore, carried no weight. So destitute was Lot of spiritual influence that he was not able to take one convert to God out of the city. All the Sodomites, with the exception of his two daughters, perished in the doom overtaking the city. Had it not been for Abraham's intercession for the city in which it was impossible to find ten righteous men (18:32), Lot himself might also have perished in the destruction of Sodom. The further removed we are from the ways of the world, the greater is our spiritual influence over those who are of the world. As Mary Slessor once put it, "Complete separation from the world spells power from God."

He lost his power with his wife

Lot suffered much because of his compromise in entering into an unholy union with a woman of Sodom. The kind of wife and mother she was can be seen in the gross immorality of the two daughters she had brought up. As for Lot, we can see how far he had fallen from grace, when he was willing to hand over his two virgin girls for the men of the city to rape, in order to protect his visitors. When, ultimately, the brimstone and fire from the Lord out of heaven fell upon Sodom and Gomorrah, and the angels hastened Lot to flee with his wife and daughters, and they escaped, they said to Lot, "Look not behind thee." But the wrench was too much for Lot's wife who, although she was forced to flee from Sodom, had Sodom very much in her heart, and "looked back . . . and became a pillar of salt" (Gen. 19:26). Lot had no influence over her in such an hour of crisis.

How different it was with Abraham when it came to the choice of a wife for his beloved son Isaac! Although he was living among idolaters, he did not look for a partner among their eligible young women, but made his servant swear that he would "not take a wife for my son of the daughters of the Canaanites, among whom I dwell; but thou shalt go into *my* country, and to *my* people, and take a wife for my son Isaac" (Gen. 24:3-4). And we know the rest of the story, how the servant was led of God to Abraham's own brother, Nahor, whose beautiful virgin daughter, Rebekah, proved to be God's choice for Isaac.

When our Lord used the catastrophe overtaking Sodom as a type of the divine judgment that will overtake a guilty, godless world, He said, "Remember Lot's wife" (Luke 17:32). This exhortation of His was a warning that to look back may have fatal results. The phrase "standing pillar of salt" is given as "a monument of an unbelieving soul" (*Wisdom* 10:7). Those who put their hands to the plough and look back are not fit for the kingdom, said the One whose eyes were set steadfastly towards the cross at Calvary.

What a tragedy it is when a professing Christian husband because of his worldly compromises has no spiritual influence over the one nearest to him, and vice versa. Ruth was so swayed by the religion of Naomi that she said, "Thy God shall be my God, and thy people, my people."

He lost his power over his children

Lot's two daughters, born in Sodom, married Sodomites who perished in the flames. If his righteous soul was vexed over the ungodliness of the men of Sodom, he had no influence in preventing his daughters marrying two of the men who must have been very corrupt, seeing they were not allowed to leave the doomed city with their wives. Having such husbands, one can judge the kind of women they were. That they were thoroughly immersed in the evil morals of Sodom is seen in what happened in that cave when they made their father drunk, and committed such a dreadful sin (19:33-38) and made their own father the father of their children. This terrible episode abruptly ends the dark story of Lot's compromising life.

What a tragedy it is when religious parents lose the power to influence their children for God! Inconsistency, worldly compromise, lack of affection and understanding, or too rigid a discipline often drive children away from the true life God

33

would have His own to live. If Lot was vexed over the way his children grew up in such a mire of iniquity, he could have saved himself the vexation of his righteous soul Peter said he had by leaving Sodom and its corrupt ways and joining up with godly Abraham again. Alas! however, he was too deeply immersed in Sodom's life and ways, and stayed there until destruction fell. "Come ye out from among them, and be ye separate," is the only way spiritual influence that has been lost can be regained, as many carnal-minded Christian parents have proved. When a truly spiritual home is created, what a joy it is to see children growing up in the fear of the Lord, and "like olive plants round about the table" (Ps. 128). There is beauty all around when godliness pervades our home life.

He lost his power over his relatives

What a bitter experience it is when one loses the reverence, respect, and love of relatives! This, also, was part of the price Lot paid for his compromising weakness. When he received the angelic warning regarding the overthrow of Sodom he sought to impress his sons-in-law with the extreme gravity of the situation—but with what effect? "He seemed unto his sons-in-law as one that mocked" (19:14). They looked on him as a sorry old man who was unnecessarily scared. The life of their father-in-law contradicted his professed faith in God and in His hatred for sin; thus his declaration of the doom of the city fell on deaf ears and as a result these two young Sodomites perished with the rest.

In his despair, Samson cried unto the Lord, and his prayer was heard and power was restored. Not so with Lot. He had lost his life in worldly gain, and left God, and his urgent witness was spurned and treated with contempt. The godless never heed, or believe, the warnings of those who live a compromising life. Parleying with sin and the world, any pleading on their part for sinners to repent is scorned. Let us beware, lest in the gain of position, possessions, and influence we lose our power to warn others to flee from the wrath to come.

Lot may have added greatly to his riches and prestige in Sodom, but in the end he left it a pauper, both materially and spiritually. Escaping for his life, all he possessed was destroyed, save the two ungodly daughters who left with him. He had lost his goods and his godliness, as well as his opportunity of turning any of the Sodomites from the evil of their ways. For the spiritual welfare of the city "righteous Lot" did absolutely nothing. Even when he broached religion, the people would not listen. What a sorrowful story!

He lost his power with God

Among Lot's spiritual losses through material gains one was the most tragic of all—the severance of fellowship with God. In all Old Testament references to Lot there is not a single word from him about God or of any faith he had until any intervention or intercession on his part to save Sodom from its doom was too late. Lot was commanded to escape for his life to "the mountain." Lot then utters his first recorded reference to the Lord who had been so merciful to him—and it was in the form of a protest! "Oh, not so, my Lord!" (19:16-18). Pleading the grace and mercy of the Lord, he tried to trade on His goodness in delivering him from the burning city.

This worldly wise, unspiritually minded man argued with the Lord about severing him completely from the wicked city. Being exiled to a mountain was too dreadful to contemplate, for some evil might befall him there! So he blatantly asked, "This city is near to flee unto, and it is a little one: Oh, let me escape thither (is it not a *little one*?) and my soul shall live" (19:20). Mercifully, the Lord responded to this request, and Lot fled to Zoar (which means *little one*), and although the sun rose as he entered the small city within easy distance of Sodom, it does not seem as if the Sun of Righteousness had risen in his heart. Still the compromising Lot, he did not want to go too far from the city. There is no record of any return to the altar, or to Bethel where along with Abraham he had called upon the name of the Lord (13:3-4). If Lot died "a righteous man," he was saved yet so as by fire (I Cor. 3:13-18).

There is a pathetic touch to the phrase, "Abraham gat up early in the morning to the place where he stood before the Lord: and looked toward Sodom and Gomorrah." As he saw the country enveloped with "the smoke as of a furnace," the old patriarch must have had painful thoughts about his nephew who had started out so well on the pilgrim journey but did not choose to finish it.

The sad story of Lot is a beacon light to all who name the name of the Lord to beware of compromise in any shape or form. They must be on their guard about taking the first step, which, if taken, leads to another and on to a disastrous end. In the goodness of God, the angels delivered Lot out of Sodom, and He alone can take us by the hand and bring us out of the pollution of the world, if we have succumbed to it, and restore our soul. Peter tells us that God is able to deliver us out of temptation. Backsliding, carnal Christians must return to Bethel, and renew their covenant with God, if, like Abraham, they would have God as their "shield, and exceeding great reward."

If, like the angelic messengers, we are sent into Sodom to warn sinners of their doom—that if they linger they die in their sins—then He will keep us safe from its filth and iniquity. The sole mission of those angels was to declare the mind of God as to the destruction of the city, and to pluck four out of it before the fire fell. Separated from the world, our constant message to it must be, "Escape thou for thy life! Flee to the mountain of Calvary before judgment overtakes such a godless world!"

3

Rachel
The Wife Who Wept Because She Was Barren

Any student of Homiletics knows that there is a tendency on the part of some preachers to widely and wildly spiritualize Scripture. Origen, one of the Church Fathers of the third century, is said to have been the originator of Christian allegorizing, and from then on fanciful treatment of Biblical themes became popular. Some of the titles early preachers gave to the sermons were ludicrous, while the sermons themselves were often imaginative flights of oratory. Even today there are those who, most ingeniously, can find types of Christ and emblems of the spiritual life in almost every part of the Bible.

That there is a sane and warrantable spiritualizing of Scripture is clear from Scripture itself. The writer to the Hebrews tells us that the ordinances and offerings associated with the tabernacle of old were illustrations of spiritual truth or "figures of the true." The same applies to persons as, for instance, Melchizedek and Christ. In effective Scripture preaching and teaching the first principle is *interpretation,* then *application* within reason—a principle our meditation of Rachel is meant to prove.

As a pastor stands at the portal of his winter's work, or an evangelist commences a gospel campaign, they find it incumbent upon them to enunciate a few spiritual guidelines for successful soul-winning. What more impressive basis for appeal to devotion to such a God-honoring task can be found than that of Rachel's heart-breaking cry, "Give me children, or else I die" (Gen. 30:1). If there is to be a breath of revival, Christians must have a great passion for souls. All who form a church, or unite in revival effort must cry, "Give us spiritual children, implant within our hearts a passion to save the lost, make us soul-winners, or else we die!" When any church travails like this, she brings forth children. Rachel was not the only woman in the Bible to weep because of her barrenness, but we take her story, seeing it suggests spiritual parallels for those who seek to win the souls around them for the Saviour who died that those lost in sin might be saved.

Rachel herself was the younger daughter of Laban whose great-uncle was Abraham. Laban's sister was Rebekah, who became the wife of Isaac. While caring for her father's sheep at the well of Haran, she saw a young man approaching and soon discovered it was her cousin Jacob, the son of her aunt Rebekah. Fleeing from his brother Esau's vengeance, he followed his mother's advice and came to his uncle as a fugitive. Jacob saluted Rachel with a kiss of frank and fearless affection, for as cousins, their love was unreserved. There seemed, however, to be a deeper love at first sight, and that meeting at the well was the beginning of a deep and long devotion. In the Bible gallery, theirs is the first recorded courtship and it grew out of a cousinly relationship. The surest sexual love is that which begins, and continues, in a mutual friendship.

Rachel Was Greatly Loved

There is no doubt that she was the love of Jacob's life. Dr. George Matheson, in his comparison of Leah and Rachel, comments, "I should say that Leah had the keys of Jacob's house; Rachel had the keys of Jacob's heart. Leah seems to have influenced his judgment; Rachel never ceased to hold his love." The record says that "Jacob loved Rachel" (Gen. 29:18). She was the best loved for she was the first and fairest to be seen. We have Jacob's pronouncement, "Ye know that my wife bare me two sons" (44:27). "*My* wife"— no mention of Leah and her large brood of children. Those two sons, Joseph and Benjamin, were love-children. The deep, mutual love of Jacob and Rachel found fulfillment in these sons. Another evidence of the love Jacob bore for Rachel is in the pathetic phrase, "Rachel died by me," or as the Revised Version expresses it, "Rachel died to my sorrow" (48:7). What a sorrowful allusion to a parting he could not forget! Whenever he thought of her passing, emotion was kindled within his empty heart. "In the heart of Jacob the grave of Rachel remained ever green, and he never ceased in fancy to deck it with flowers." Joseph was also moved with the same deep feeling as an aged father when he referred to his mother, the parting from whom he never forgot.

But the most remarkable proof of Jacob's love for Rachel is suggested by the phrases, "Jacob served seven years for Rachel: and they seemed unto him but a few days, for the love he had to her" (29:20); and "[Jacob] served . . . seven other years" (29:27-28, 30). Fourteen years in all he served Laban for Rachel. How he must have loved her to work so long! As we know, this was occasioned by Laban's deception in substituting Leah for Rachel. Evidently he was not pleased that Rachel was preferred to the elder Leah, and perhaps felt that the plainer daughter would be left on his hands. What a shock it must have been for Jacob to find that he had been cruelly beguiled by Laban! Did he hear in the deception the reverberation of his own sin? Having been guilty of deceiving his own father and brother, he finds himself reaping what he had sown, and found himself the husband of two wives.

Yet in spite of such a polygamous entanglement, Rachel was always first in the mind of her lover, even after her lamented death. Does not the unchanging love Jacob had for Rachel suggest a higher relationship? Are we the Lord's? Then He loves us best of all. He loves us better than any other part of His creation—better than the brown cornfields,

39

lovely landscapes, glorious sunsets, majestic seas, silvery rivers, rippling lakes, starry heavens, beautiful birds, and other masterpieces of His handiwork. He never shed His tears over them, or His blood for them. God loves us better than archangels, or cherubim and seraphim of the angelic and celestial host. His beloved Son served for us as Jacob did for Rachel, and loves us with a deeper, truer love than human love. He served for us not fourteen years, but a lifetime. He toiled, endured, suffered all through those thirty-three years, and then bled and died in shame and nakedness on a wooden gibbet. "Christ loved the church and gave himself for her." What a royal example! Souls are won for Him only by those who share Calvary's love and compassion for them.

Rachel Was Beautiful

Of the two daughters of Laban we read,—"Leah was tender eyed: but Rachel was beautiful and well-favored" (29:17). Rachel had a beauty of form and features giving her a compelling attractiveness which captivated Jacob's heart. The Hebrew suggests "beautiful in form, and beautiful in look." Her name means "the ewe," an animal known for its grace and loveliness. *Leah,* on the other hand means, "langor, weariness," probably because of her droopy look. "Tender-eyed" implies dull, bleary eyes, possibly due to some form of ophthalmia common to the hot sandy region where she lived. Ellicott's comment is helpful, "Leah's blurred eyes would be regarded in the East as a great defect, just as bright eyes were much admired." (See I Sam. 16:12 where David is described as "fair of eyes.") Yet it was not Rachel, with her fair face and well-proportioned figure, object of her husband's lasting love, that was the mother of the progenitor of the Messiah, but the "weary-eyed Leah."

Rachel, with all the beauty of her aunt Rebekah, immediately possessed Jacob, who was dazzled by her loveliness because of the poetic aspect of his own nature. Watching

40

Rachel as she drew water for the flocks, Jacob's eyes feasted upon her attractiveness, her charm of movement, and immediately he fell in love with her. At that moment the red heat of affection was generated in his heart, and its warmth and glow remained throughout their years together.

In ourselves we are like Leah, plain and unattractive, with the eyes of our soul bleared by sin. But in Christ, we are as Rachel, "beautiful and well-favored," or "black yet comely," like the female Solomon depicts. In ourselves we are ugly, unfavorable, distorted. "In us that is in our flesh, dwelleth no good thing," but clad in His grace, beauty, and righteousness we are all fair. How blessed to know that God sees us in His beloved Son, and that we are accepted in Him, seeing we are covered with His robe of righteousness! The beauty of the Lord our God is upon us.

> Thou hast bid me gaze upon Thee,
> And Thy beauty fills my soul,
> For, by Thy transforming power,
> Thou hast made me whole.

Rachel Was Barren

An Oriental proverb assumes that a childless wife is as good as dead, and likely this is the meaning of Rachel's heartbroken cry, "Give me children, or else I die" (30:1). Among Hebrew women it was counted a great affliction to go through life sterile and childless. How heart moving is the vow of childless Hannah, "Look on the affliction of thine handmaid and remember"! Graciously the Lord did look upon her affliction of barrenness and bless her with a son who became the first of the great prophets in the prophetic school of the Old Testament. And here is Rachel's similar request. Oh, the sorrow of it. She was beautiful but barren—favored but fruitless!

Is there not a spiritual truth for our hearts in Rachel's

41

plight? Are we not barren insofar as bringing sinners to a spiritual birth is concerned? The beauty of the Lord is upon us but we are fruitless. We have a name that we live but are dead—*dead* in respect to the Holy Spirit's activity and vitality in our lives, and dead in respect to success in service. If we do not maintain deep love for the Lord and His Word, we will not have a passion to bear souls or rescue sinners. Are we saved—but sterile? How tragic that many have been the Lord's for years, yet through the whole of their Christian life have failed to lead a soul to Him! We have beautiful churches, an educated ministry, interesting sermons—but no children coming to birth. The womb of profession and witness are not producing those born of the Spirit. People are added to churches as members who, in the majority of cases, have never experienced the throes of a spiritual birth. We know so little of the apostolic travailing in birth until Christ is formed in the hearts of the lost.

It would seem as if there were three reasons why Rachel longed and wept to be saved from her barrenness.

1. She wept that she might emulate her sister Leah, for we read that "Rachel envied her sister" (30:1)

As she watched Leah's brood of children increase, Rachel's yearning became more intense to bear children for Jacob. The abounding fruitfulness of her sister stirred up covetous feelings in Rachel's disappointed heart. Can we not draw a lesson from this desire to emulate Leah in child-bearing? Are we possessed with a holy, legitimate covetousness? We have every right to win souls, and in the plan of God every believer should be a soul-winner. No preacher or evangelist has a monopoly on soul-winning. Each of us has the commission to make disciples.

God seeks to use *you,* as much as He uses someone else, if

not more so. You must not let others out-strip you when it comes to soul-winning. Since Pentecost many have been mightily blessed of the Spirit in spiritual births. Peter, and the three thousand saved on that historic day of Pentecost; Paul, with the multitude he brought to Christ; John Knox; John Wesley; George Whitefield; David Brainerd; D. L. Moody; and a host of others have cried, "Give me children, or else we die," and God made them mighty in the salvation of sinners. As we think of others, conspicuous or otherwise, who have borne many spiritual children, do we envy them, and seek to eliminate anything in our lives that would make it difficult for God to reach others through us?

Later on Rachel says, "With great wrestlings have I wrestled, and have prevailed" (30:8). This marks intensity and passion, a mighty, prevailing intercession. For those wrestlings were not in rivalry with Leah but "the wrestlings of God." The phrase "great wrestlings" means "the wrestlings of El," or "mighty wrestlings with God in prayer." Without such passion we cannot prevail. If we would bless, we must bleed. Our spiritual sterility will never depart unless there is Spirit-inspired intercession. Jeremiah could write, "Mine eye runneth down with rivers of water for the destruction of the daughter of my people" (Lam. 3:48-49). No wonder they called him "The Weeping Prophet"! Jesus beheld the city and wept, and the shedding of His tears for His rejectors led to the shedding of His blood to save them.

> Oh, for a passionate passion for souls!
>   Oh, for a pity that yearns!
> Oh, for a love that loves unto death,
>   Oh, for a fire that burns!
> Oh, for a prayer power that prevails,
>   That pours itself out for the lost;
> Victorious prayer in the Conqueror's Name,
>   Oh, for a Pentecost!

2. She wept that she might become more dear to her husband

Rachel had a fear that her continued barrenness might cause her to become despised in Jacob's eyes. She longed for their love-union to be blessed with a child, forging a closer link between them. Much as she loved Jacob, she knew that children would produce a still deeper attachment. Here is another feature of Rachel's cry we can apply to ourselves as professed lovers of the Lord. If we desire to become more precious to our Heavenly Husband, even our blessed Lord Jesus, then we must have a deep and ever deepening love for the perishing. When He hears us making Rachel's request our own, "Give me children, or else I die," then we will become more dear to His heart, and He will embrace us more firmly. When we plead, toil, suffer, and weep for souls, we but reflect Calvary's compassion for a lost world, and our intercession for souls becomes an echo of Christ's own intense cry.

3. Rachel wept because she wanted to share the hope of becoming an ancestress of the Messiah

Every Hebrew woman was dominated by the desire to produce the promised Seed (Gen. 3:15). The covenant made to Abraham brought hope to every loyal feminine heart that the Messiah might come through her. In his salutation to Mary, Gabriel said, "Blessed art thou among women" (Luke 1:28). All God-fearing women had longed for the privilege of bringing the promised One into the world. The poor but godly peasant girl, Mary, was the divinely chosen one to become the mother of our Lord.

As every Hebrew woman longed to be the chosen vessel for the fulfillment of God's purpose, so we must yearn to be used in causing Christ to be formed in those who know Him not. Further, every soul we win for Him brings nearer the completion of His Body, the church and His second coming.

44

Are we reproducing the image of the Lord in other lives, hastening thereby, His glorious appearing? It avails nothing for a person that Christ was born in Bethlehem if He has not been born in his heart by faith. Humbly we must confess that we know so little of what it means to *travail* in birth until Christ is born as Saviour in those who are strangers to grace.

Rachel Became Fruitful

Her tears ended in triumph; her heartfelt cry resulted in conquest—"Rachel bore Joseph " (30:25); "the sons of Rachel; Joseph and Benjamin" (35:24). Said the well-wishers of Ruth when she bore Obed, and thus became the ancestress of our Lord, "The Lord make [thee] like Rachel and Leah, which two did build the house of Israel" (Ruth 4:11). At last, Rachel's longing was appeased and her heart ravished as she held her baby Joseph in her arms. Her barrenness was ended, her husband satisfied, and God was glorified. For her, the promise was fulfilled: "Sing, O barren, that didst not bear!" (Isa. 54:1). How Rachel must have rejoiced over her precious gift of a son—and what a famous son he became in Israel's history! Truly, he was a child worth waiting for.

A fruitless Christian life—what a blight it is! How dishonoring it is to the Lord of life, as well as disastrous to ourselves! Yet no matter how barren we have been, having never won a single soul for Christ, yet we can become fruitful. We can go forth unctionized by the Holy Spirit and function as mighty soul-winners. He who brings souls to spiritual birth can make us like Rachel and Leah—builders of the house of the Lord, even His mystical body. May grace be ours to confess our lack of passion, zeal, intensity, heartache, and soul-travail for the lost! May we determine to put away all known hindrances and strained relationships; may we get right with God and with others and thus be fit and ready for Him to use! When Rachel left home she took with her the gods of Laban's home (31:19-20, 34), which implied that she had tried to serve God *and* her idols. We must tear any idol from the throne of our heart, and enthrone Him Lord Supreme. Then we can go out as effective winners of souls. If we would be neither barren nor unfruitful, then we must manifest the virtues Peter reminds us of (II Peter 1:4-8).

Further, if we desire to be used in the salvation of souls, we must be willing for God to lead and guide us into right avenues of service. Rachel's name, as we have seen, means "The Ewe," and is from a word signifying "to be gentle." Perhaps the name was suggestive of Rachel's disposition. If we would follow the Lamb whithersoever He leadeth, then we must be lamblike, or gentle—kind and loving in our approach to those we seek to reach for the Saviour. We must be winsome if we would "win-some" for Him. Whether pastor, preacher, or worker, our preeminent task is that of rescuing the perishing. At the Judgment Seat, we shall be judged not by our scholarship, but by souls won for Christ; not by our eloquence, but by our entreaty; not by our preaching, but by our passion; not by our writings but by our wrestlings; not by our ability to raise money and build churches or to draw and influence crowds, but by the power we expended to agonize men and women into the kingdom of God. Without the cry of Rachel continually prominent in any church, it is but a well-dressed corpse. Its architecture, music, and order of service may be attractive, but so far as God is concerned such a church is dead. Christ builds His church by using her to win the souls He can make as "lively stones" to complete such a mystic fabric. The first and paramount obligation, then, of any church or Christian is to pluck souls out of the fire (Jude 23).

Rachel Died in Travail

What a moving spectacle we have in the record of Rachel's painful death in childbirth!

"Rachel travailed, and she had hard labor . . . she called her son Ben-oni [meaning, "son of sorrow"], . . . (for she died)" (35:16-18).

She passed out of her sorrow and pain near Bethlehem, and her heartbroken husband buried her there and erected a pillar over her grave (35:19-20; I Sam. 10:2). To his mother, who died bringing him to birth, the child was Ben-oni, son of sorrow, but to his father, he was Benjamin, meaning, "son of my right hand." Benjamin became the one especially honored among the Gentiles (Gen. 45:22).

In this tragic episode, death and life throes meet. A mother goes down to death in giving life to a child. There are at least two thoughts we can gather from this sorrowful scene.

1. Death leads to life

Rachel dies, Benjamin is born, and so life springs from death. Our Lord taught that unless the corn of wheat dies it cannot bring forth fruit. Such an illustration was a foregleam of His cross. Fairer and more beautiful than Rachel, Jesus died at Calvary, but out of that death countless myriads have been spiritually born, and in their salvation He sees of the travail of His soul and is satisfied. How slow we are to learn that life can only spring from death; that we cannot win the lost unless we die to self with all its wretched forms of ease, indulgence, and self-glory! It is only as we "lay in dust life's glory dead" that there can rise from the ground "life that shall endless be." Are we willing to "die daily" that others might be brought to life?

2. Second, Rachel died in anguish at Ephrath, which means "fruitful"

This beautiful woman died in the place of fruitfulness as she bore another son. Thus would I live, and thus would I

47

die, winning and saving precious souls! If I should go home to heaven by the way of a grave, I pray that I may be privileged to die pleading with God for souls, and pleading with souls for God. Countless numbers have been born anew by the Spirit through the dying, triumphant witness of the saints of God. Saul of Tarsus watched Stephen die a terrible yet victorious death and he was never the same man again. May we be found burning out for God—consumed with an undying passion to win others! The church's deepest need today is for those who live for souls, plead for souls, yearn for souls, die for souls; to concentrate every breath, word, thought, and action upon this supreme service.

Because the sands of time are sinking it is incumbent upon each of us to make Rachel's cry our daily prayer—"O Lord, give me children, or else I die." We must not shrink from travail-pains, for when Zion travailed she brought forth. Bringing Benjamin to birth is most costly, but wonderfully rewarding. Let us not forget, then, that in the plan of God, *every* believer should be a soul-winner. Bringing men to Christ is not the prerogative of professional evangelists. A church in which every member seeks to win others for the Saviour has no need of an evangelist. May God help us then to—

> Seek the coming of His Kingdom,
>   Seek the souls around to win them,
> Seek to Jesus Christ to bring them,
>   Seek this first!

48

4

Elijah

The Prophet Who Was Conspicuous for His Solitude

As the Bible is largely biographical it carries an irresistible charm for our hearts, seeing that the characters portrayed reflect human nature in every age. Within its portrait gallery we find those who experienced trials and triumphs similar to those we face in this twentieth century. We now consider another of its unforgettable personalities—the strong and rugged prophet of the desert, Elijah the Tishbite, who, in some respects, is the greatest of the prophets in the Old Testament. So great was he that we can approach his remarkable life from different angles, all of which are profitable for our own spiritual life. We choose to concentrate, however, on the most outstanding fact of his career—his *solitude.* Shelley wrote of loving "tranquil solitude," but Elijah's solitude was not always of the tranquil kind.

Had we the space we could dwell upon the following features of the life of this miracle-working prophet:

Elijah has been twice upon the earth, and if, as some prophetic students affirm, he may be one of the two witnesses John speaks of, then he will be coming back to earth again (I Kings 17:1; Matt. 17:34; Rev. 11:3).

Elijah was a man who never tasted death. Like Enoch, his body was never buried in a grave. If he is to return to earth as one of the two witnesses, he will be slain, and along with his companion martyr, his dead body will lie in the street (Rev. 11:8).

49

Elijah accompanied a man born some one thousand years before him, namely, Moses, when he came down from heaven to the Mount of Transfiguration to speak with Jesus about His death at Calvary.

Elijah, like Enoch, experienced miraculous translation. Although these two worthies were not able to sing "Oh joy, oh delight, should we go without dying" both of them knew what it was to be caught up to meet the Lord.

Elijah, under God, had power over two of the greatest elements in nature—fire and water. He could bring fire down and keep the water up.

Elijah was a miracle-worker, as his many miracles in various realms prove. He knew that of himself he had no might, but that his power was of God.

Elijah was a man who, in spite of his grandeur and greatness, and mighty works and preaching, was a man of like passions as ourselves.

The commanding feature, however, of his sojourn on earth was his solitude. Above all else, Elijah was the man who experienced "the self-sufficing power of solitude," as Wordsworth put it. Perhaps no other Bible saint lived a more lonely life than this prophet whose career was one of aloneness and aloofness. Because of his sensational, dramatic, and miraculous experiences, unshared by others, Elijah stands out as a man shut off from men but shut up with God.

This stern, righteous stalwart for God was essentially a man of the desert. He stepped abruptly upon the stage by divine plan, coming from some quiet country, some rural sphere, and he remained a man of the open spaces. Like many other champions God raised up out of obscurity for a conspicuous ministry, Elijah was a nobody who became a somebody. God called Moses from the backside of the desert, David from the sheepfold, John the Baptist from the wilderness, Jesus from His quiet, country home.

Elijah owed his prominent position as a prophet not to his high birth or station, not to a native place of renown, nor yet to his courage. He was born in Tishbe, probably a mean and obscure village among the mountains, of a poor, banished Jewish family. We have no record of his parentage and early life. It would seem as if he knew nothing of schools of learning and worldly grandeur, which men court and count as necessary to a position in the world. God has often delighted to choose the weak things of the world to confound the mighty, to prove that His choice is not of flesh and blood. He bears the title, "Elijah the Tishbite"—*Tishbite* meaning "converter"—and the name befits his life and labors, for under God he was the means of reclaiming multitudes out of the dark idolatry and apostasy of his time.

Alone with Heaven: Dependence (I Kings 17:1)

Elijah did not live in a little world all his own. William Cowper writes, "How passing sweet, is solitude." And the prophet's solitude *was sweet* because it was shared by God: "The Lord God of Israel before whom I stand." The secret, then, of his remarkable power was his aloneness with God, for in the divine Presence he allowed God to search, penetrate, and command him. Communion with God in the desert was the sublime secret of Elijah's spiritual character. Ever conscious that he was nothing in himself, he could yet seek divine authority and power to open and shut the heavens, raise the dead, cause the living to die, and bring judgment upon the enemies of God.

The name of this unique man is suggestive, for *Elijah* means, "My God of Power," or "Jehovah Is My Strength." Such an excellent name must have been chosen by godly parents. He lived out its meaning in deed and in truth. Like you and me, he was nothing in himself, but invincible when girded by divine strength. Of himself, Elijah could do nothing, yet deeds of omnipotence proceeded from his hands because in his solitude, he had traffic with heaven. In "A Poet's

51

Epitaph" Wordsworth has a couplet we can apply to Elijah the prophet—

> Impulses of deeper birth,
> Have come to him in solitude.

Alone at the Brook: Dearth (I Kings 17:3-6)

According to Elijah's divinely inspired command, the heavens closed and became as brass, the fountains failed, the brooks dried up. The sun fiercely shone upon the earth, burning all verdure by its scorching beams—a symbol of the eyes of the Lord as a flame of fire destroying man for his gross iniquity. Every day Elijah saw the famine of food and water approach, and he wondered whether he was to share in the common calamity pronounced upon the guilty nation. Then came the command to go to the brook at Cherith where God said He would take care of the fearless prophet and feed him in unaccustomed ways. The prophet was indeed a man of faith—he could stand alone when his sustenance was cut off and trust God absolutely and entirely to meet his every need. This is where Elimelech failed. He forgot the promise, "In the days of famine ye shall be satisfied" (Ruth 1:1).

Think of Elijah as he dwells near the banks of Jordan where dead silence reigned, and no human footsteps were heard or seen in all that wild and solitary country. Yet here sits this man in his hairy mantle, reflecting on God and His ways. To quote Wordsworth again—

> On Man, on Nature, and on Human Life,
> Musing in Solitude.

When solitude seemed to weary him and the surrounding rocks cave in upon him, faith and hope would be strengthened as he was shut in with God—a prisoner for His sake. For twelve months he lived in the rocky vale at Cherith with no one to serve him but the ravens, those black livery waiters who came to the hungry prophet morning and night laden with meat and bread. God is elsewhere pictured as feeding the ravens—here He uses these birds to feed His lonely servant. Few of us, I fear, know what it is to be alone in this respect, shut off from all sources of supply and to experience that God with that magnificent omnipotence of His is able to meet all our need. How wonderful He is at spreading a table in the wilderness!

Alone with a Poor Widow: Destitution (I Kings 17:9)

Because Elijah believed that "solitude is the mother-country of the strong," he was a man ready for any crisis or emergency. A good servant obeys the moment the bell rings, and when God called the prophet to go out to an almost impossible task, he went. Without question or demur he fulfilled the divine will, although at times what was asked seemed to be contrary to the accustomed order of things. Elijah was ready for sacrifice or service, pain or poverty, suffering or success, trial or triumph. Here is a picture of an ox before a plough (service) and an altar (sacrifice) with the caption, *Ready for either!* The solitary prophet, like his New Testament counterpart, John the Baptist, stands clothed in camel's hair, unafraid of the face of man, and ready to do God's will.

Destitution is a terrible test of faith. It requires plenty and prosperity to keep some people contented as well as consecrated. If you have an innate passion for independence, how would you like to be beggared of all and made dependent upon the scanty provision of a poor widow woman? But Elijah's greatness was of such quality that he was able to go into this phase of solitude and, alone with a widow, prove that God was able to feed him in a destitute home, just as He had done by the ravens at the brook. At Zarephath Elijah proved that the barrel of meal wasted not, and the cruse of oil did not fail. When the barrel was almost empty, God heard the scraping at the bottom, and provided a fresh supply. *And the God of Elijah still lives.*

Alone with the Dead: Death (I Kings 17:17-24)

What a poignant scene for some artist to depict is the house of mourning the historian describes! The bereaved widow is bowed down with grief as she sits with her dead child clasped to her heart, her face bathed with tears both over her dead son and her sins. But Elijah, so grateful to this woman at Zarephath for her care of him and sure that God was able to raise up the child, takes the corpse from the mother's arms and goes upstairs to his own small chamber to which he often retired for prayer and meditation. Closing the door, Elijah fell to his knees to pour out his heart before God. There was the prophet, alone with the dead! Perhaps this was the climax of his loneliness. In describing such a lonely experience John Keats wrote—

> A solitary sorrow best befits
> Thy lips, and antheming a lonely grief.

Who can express the feelings of the solitary grief of a crushed heart alone with the dead before burial? But the solitary sorrow of the weeping widow and the lonely grief of Elijah soon vanished, for God heard the voice of the prophet pleading for the dead child and restored him to life. Carrying the boy downstairs to his sorrowful mother Elijah uttered the joyful news, "Thy son liveth." Such a miracle confirmed Elijah as a man of God and as a faithful messenger of truth.

For those of us whose supreme task is that of soul-winning, how urgent it is to carry into the presence of God those who are spiritually dead among our relatives and friends and among the masses at home and abroad, to plead in agony over them until we see them rise again in newness of life. Eternity alone will reveal how many were brought to a spiritual resurrection because of those who, in the solitude of their prayer-chamber, continued in intercession until those they held up to God were raised from their grave of iniquity. God's choicest wreaths are often wet with tears of intense intercession (Heb. 5:7).

> Though sown in tears through weary years,
>   The seed will surely live;
> Though great the cost, it is not lost,
>   For God will fruitage give.

Alone with Ahab: Defiance (I Kings 17:1; 18:1)

Elijah was the most uncompromising of men. Bribery did not tempt this bold man whose iron will knew no yielding to expediency. At times it may seem as if he was hard in his holiness, but although he manifested severity, he was a stranger to temerity and trickery. How his character throws into relief these loose, vacillating, compromising men in our decadent days when equity has fallen on the streets! The righteousness of this lion-hearted prophet is as a plummet. What unflinching loyalty to the God of truth and to the truth of God were his as he confronted Ahab, son of Omri, who did evil in the sight of Jehovah above all that were before him!

No true man of God can escape a feeling of loneliness as he stands before a person he does not like because of his wrong-doing and sin. It is human nature to follow the crowd, to go with the tide. But it is Godlike to stand alone in defiance of Satan and his works. But defiance without depending on God is fruitless, for it has no inner strength. If we know how to live alone with the God of power, then we will not fear as we seek to rebuke the world's mad strife.

Ahab was a man of sin who had set up the satanic trinity of the Calf, Baal, and Ashera—the most awful of the three. Against this dark background of idolatry Elijah the fearless prophet is displayed. Gloomy idols and temples rose on every hand; profane altars stained with the blood of holy men were common; and an arrogant defiance of the most High God called for divine vengeance. It seemed as if Satan had transferred his residence from hell to earth, and strove to obscure the light of heaven by the smoke and vapor of the most horrible forms of idolatry. But amid it all the defiant figure of Elijah the Tishbite poured out denunciations upon the profligate until they trembled beneath his terrible words.

What our idolatrous world needs is an Elijah on every Mount Carmel, a John the Baptist in every Herod's court, an apostle John on every Isle of Patmos, a John Knox in every pulpit to expose and defy the rules of the darkness of this age.

> Many mighty men are lost,
>   Daring not to stand.
> Who for God had been a host,
>   By joining Daniel's band.

There are two occasions when Elijah heard God issuing instructions, and the first time seems to contradict the second. "Go hide thyself," "Go show thyself" (I Kings 17:3; 18:1). Let us note the significance of these two commands, and the connection between them.

"Go hide thyself by the brook"

The various phases of aloneness already considered form a fitting commentary on this stern word Elijah heard God utter. It teaches us that privacy must precede publicity, that solitude determines our power in society, that aloneness is essential to activity. We live too much in the company of others—we need more of the hidden, solitary life. It was only when Daniel was alone with God that he received His secrets, and such a law operates throughout Scripture. "I was alone and saw this great vision." God must have His Josephs in prisons before He can place them in palaces; and His Abrahams alone with Himself before He can make great nations of them; and His Daniels cast into a den of lions before they can move with royalty in Babylon; and His Pauls left as dead before they can stand before kings and rulers to testify of His grace. Our blessed Lord Himself spent thirty obscure years in the village of Nazareth before His brief but dynamic ministry which gave birth to Christianity. Often during His public appearance "He departed to a solitary place and prayed."

God's "Go hide thyself" is equivalent to the Master's "Come ye apart." We need more of the shut door, for in spiritual photography the darkroom is the fitting place for the development of the image of God on life and in service. Jesus "trod the winepress *alone.*" The hiding of himself that God commanded for Elijah was necessary for the prophet's well-being at that stage in his career. The victory to come when he stood before Ahab demanded that he be called apart to isolation and separation to store his spiritual battery with power to call fire down from heaven. It is only as we come apart from the world to make contact with heaven that we can, in turn, go into all the world and preach the converting gospel.

> Go hide thyself—ere Carmel's triumph come,
> A deeper life in Him we all must know.
> We must all come apart with Christ alone
> Ere He can use us, He must keep us low—
> Go *hide* thyself.

"Go show thyself to Ahab"

When we allow privacy to do its perfect work, then we are ready for the service God has prepared for us in public. In his solitude at Cherith, Elijah had access to God through opened heavens, but see what happened as he came from his hiding place. Mantled by God, he made the heavens as brass and the earth as iron. Essential to both man and beast, dew and rain were restrained. The word of the prophet struck like a fever the heart of the earth, withering and scorching all that was fresh and green. Streams and rivulets dried up, and all that had breath languished for the space of three-and-a-half years. Such miraculous, disastrous effects were produced by the voice of a man who in loneliness was a man in accord with the Almighty, hearing only His commanding voice. Having power with God, Elijah prevailed.

There is a time to leave solitude and stand before society, to go from the closet to the crowd and declare publicly what God revealed in private. May we be saved from the folly of trying to speak to Ahab before speaking to the Almighty, and from standing before others before standing before Him. John the Baptist, we read, remained in the deserts *until* his showing unto Israel—and what a "showing" it was because of the training of the dreary desert with its solitude! When God says, "Go show thyself," then we can go and run through a troop of difficulties and leap over the wall of seeming impossibilities. After those days, away from the world, spent in the upper room praying, the disciples went forth to a mighty Pentecost, and became ambassadors with power and authority as they proclaimed the evangel of grace. They became invincible messengers of the invincible God, and earthen vessels filled with heavenly treasure. May we learn to *hide* ourselves when God says, "Hide thyself," and show ourselves as His sent ones when He says, "Go, show thyself"!

> Go show thyself ere Carmel's triumph come,
>   The drying brook of Cherith wrought the power.
> The soul that waits alone upon its God
>   Is fitted for His use in danger's hour,
>   Go *show* thyself.

Alone with Himself: Disgust (I Kings 19:1-7)

After Elijah's courageous defiance of King Ahab, and the marvelous display of divine power on Mount Carmel, he wilted before the blatant taunt of Jezebel to slay him even as he had slaughtered her godless prophets. Elijah stood bravely before the king, he unashamedly "showed himself." But he ran away from a woman and lost himself once more in the solitude of the desert. The conflict on Carmel had been a great strain on Elijah; it exacted a physical toll of even his strong, rugged frame. The torch was badly shaken, but afterwards it glowed brighter.

How pathetic it is to see this strong, courageous man sitting under a juniper tree like an exile in fearful solitude, wishing he might die! Alone with himself, he was filled with disgust and contempt, as Job was when he said, "I am vile," and Isaiah also when he cried, "I am unclean." Elijah sighed, "Take away my life: for I am no better than my fathers." If, at any time, we feel despised, and sigh because of the burdens and trials of life, let us not flee, as Elijah did, and sit under a juniper tree thinking all is lost, but sit before another tree where the incarnate Son of God was made a curse for us, and there find refreshment for our weary, distracted spirit. God understood all about the reaction of His faithful prophet and took tender care of him, even to sending an angel to prepare the overwrought challenger of Ahab a most hearty meal.

One wonders if Elijah would have been so lonely a man if he had had a dear companion to turn to in the hour of physical strain. It was Bacon who expressed the sentiment that "the worst solitude is to be destitute of sincere friendship." As there is no mention of Elijah's wife, the inference is that he did not have such a close companion to turn to for comfort. It is not without significance that after his flight from Jezebel and his despair, that God raised up for His lonely servant a close friend in Elisha, his successor, who never left the prophet's side until the end of his service.

Alone in a Cave: Defeat (I Kings 19:7-18)

From his feeling of despair, Elijah went on to defeatism.

"I, only I am left." After a journey of forty days this solitary traveler came to Mount Horeb and took up his abode in a cave where God's ways with him led to further self-mortification and self-denial. Here we see the man of God in circumstances overruled to increase his humility and the expression of the life of God in his soul. Silently and mournfully he contemplates the decay of his last and fondest hope. Then, out of the deep silence of his solitary abode, a loving voice reaches his ear, "What doest thou here, Elijah?"

The prophet was to learn that his was a defeat spelling victory, for when God gets us to the end of ourselves, He is ready to show us His beginnings. Elijah had been conspicuous as an agent of fire and thunder, but in the divine unfolding he came to learn that grace alone can soften, melt, and convert the heart. He received the revelation that the results which he anticipated from the thunders of the law and the divine judgments could only come through the loving kindness and tender mercy of Jehovah. Following the "Go hide thyself" and the "Go show thyself," there came the "Go, return on thy way to the wilderness." And forth from the lonely cave he went to fulfill a divine commission. Whittier, in his wonderful poem, "Dear Lord and Father of Mankind," has the verse—

> Oh, Sabbath rest by Galilee;
> Oh, calm of hills above,
> Where Jesus knelt to share with Thee
> The silence of Eternity,
> Interpreted by love.

In the calm of that cave, Elijah came to share with God "the silence of Eternity," and to understand its loving interpretation by the still small voice.

Alone at the End: Delight (II Kings 2:1-11)

The sons of the prophets had a foreboding that the end of Elijah was near, and expressed their fear to Elisha who told them to say nothing about such a somber event. There was, however, no need for them to be quiet about the matter, seeing that Elijah knew that the closing scene of his life was at hand. Further, no matter in what form his end was to come, he wanted to meet it even as he had lived—*alone*. But Elisha was bound by an oath not to leave his master, so we have the dramatic episode when Elijah divided Jordan with his mantle and, like Israel before them, they went over on dry ground. Elijah requested Elisha to ask for a parting gift, "Ask what I shall do for thee, before I be taken from thee." All that Elisha desired was for a double portion of his remarkable master's spirit to rest upon him, which was granted, for he performed twice as many miracles as Elijah.

The day dawned when the Lord was to take Elijah up to heaven by a whirlwind. What a fitting exit for a man who had had a whirlwind career! Chariots of fire and horses of fire appeared and parted the two prophets, and Elijah's solitude was thus terminated by a whirlwind translation to heaven where he would be solitary no more. But does he not remain a pattern for your life and mine? As he was a man of like passions as ourselves, his experiences teach us that spiritual solitude is better in every way than the society of the world. His entrance into history was like his entrance into heaven— dramatic; and our end may be as his.

Elijah did not go to glory by the usual way of the grave. Like Enoch before him "he was not, for God took him." He had the delight of being caught up without dying, and God took him in his old, wrinkled, desert-hardened body to Himself. The wonder is that he appeared with it again, glorified, when he came down from heaven with Moses to meet Jesus on the mount. The blessed hope is that if Jesus should return today, as He may, that our translation would be as sudden and dramatic as Elijah's, even though ours will not be with the accompanying chariots and horses of fire. We are to be caught up in clouds—clouds of believers—a vast translation host of the redeemed from every nation, to meet the Lord in the air, and then to be with Him where He dwells forever.

5

Saul
The King Who Forsook God for a Witch

One sign of the reality and truthfulness of Scripture is that it sets up as beacons of warning, not only those whose lives were conspicuously bad, but persons in whom there was a conflict between good and evil, with the evil ultimately prevailing. Men who were entrusted with high privileges and responsibilities fell back into a baser life, despising their loftier calling. Thus it was with Saul, Israel's first king, whose true character is brought out by various experiences in his life. This son of Kish is an outstanding example of those whose character faults appear the greater when contrasted with those of noble characters who surround them.

Saul had close contact with the prophet Samuel, the man of prayer. If only he had prayed as Samuel did, what a different story would have been his! David, the young champion Saul was so jealous of, was a man after God's own heart. If only Saul had been as noble, true, and God-fearing as the son of Jesse, what lapses of faith and obedience Saul would have been spared. Jonathan, Saul's son, was a most lovely character. Had the father only emulated the largeness of heart and sweetness of temperament his son manifested, how loved he would have been. Alas! when it comes to the roll-call of the heroes of faith, Saul's contemporaries, Samuel and David, find honorable mention, but the king who ruled Israel for forty years is excluded from this chapter of remembrance (Heb. 11:32).

Saul's story is a tragic one of regression of soul. His life was made up of a series of gradual changes for the worse, evil always prevailing over the good. In many respects he is the most pathetic character in the gallery of Old Testament men. His career began magnificently, but what unutterable pathos at its consummation! The warning is, "Take heed lest ye fall." The Son of Kish and a Benjamite, Saul, when he was anointed king, was "a choice young man, and a goodly: and there was not among the children of Israel a goodlier person than he: from his shoulders and upward he was higher than any of the people" (I Sam. 9:1-2; 10:21). If he had remained the "goodliest" person in Israel, what a worthy record would have been his. But, "behold, how the mighty have fallen!" The following episodes enable us to evaluate the virtues and vices of this king whom God chose, but had to reject.

With the Donkeys (I Sam. 9:3-27; 10:2)

The first glimpse we have of this well-built young man of remarkable height is out on the mountains seeking a drove of donkeys that had strayed from his father's farm at Gibeah. After a three-day circuit he arrived at Zaph where Samuel lived. His servant advised Saul to consult the seer about the animals he could not find. A day before his visit, Samuel had received a divine intimation as to the approach of this striking Benjamite, and of his future destiny as the king for which the people clamored. There is a precious thought in the phrase "Now the Lord had told Samuel *in his ear* a day before Saul came." The original suggests the lifting up of the curls covering the ear, and the Lord whispering His secret into it.

After Samuel and Saul met, the prophet revealed the plan of God, poured the consecrating oil on his head, and with a kiss of salutation told Saul he was to be the ruler and deliverer of the nation. Though he still wore the outward garb of his domestic vocation, a highly privileged office was his.

Each stage of the return journey was marked by incidents confirming Samuel's predictions as to his coming fortunes: As he passed Rachel's tomb (Rachel, the mother of Benjamin of whom Saul was a descendant) he met two men who told him that the donkeys were safe, but that his father was sorrowing, not for the animals but for Saul himself. Pursuing his journey, this newly anointed king had a vision of the tremendous work he had been called to do. How many there are, born to be kings or to do great things for God, who spend their whole life in the pursuit of donkeys for want of some kind prophet to tell them that they are head and shoulders above others! It is interesting to note how many received a call to follow and serve God while they were busily engaged in secular vocations. Amos, for instance, was a herdsman and a gatherer of sycomore fruit when God came and took him from the flock to function as a prophet to Israel (7:14-15).

Among the Prophets (I Sam. 10:9-13)

The first call, the private, inner call, his anointing as king, was thus far a secret known only to Samuel and Saul. There came another call when he met the prophets on the hill of God, from which he caught an inspiration of the loftier life, one he had never before conceived. The Holy Spirit came upon him and he was given another heart; and he received the promise, "God is with thee." Saul came down from the mountain with his whole character changed as the result of such a noteworthy experience. This was equivalent to regeneration. Under the Spirit's power, he prophesied, which gave rise to the proverb, "Is Saul among the prophets." We learn from this episode that we can never achieve the plan of God for our lives unless we receive the divine enduement to accomplish it.

Saul had many natural qualities. When he commenced his reign he was a stalwart, handsome, and attractive young man. He was also outstanding for his strength and activity, and because of his gigantic stature he was a striking figure all looked to as he passed by. His beauty caused him to be "compared to the gazelle of Israel." In addition to his external appearance, he was a *chosen* one. "See him whom the Lord hath chosen." Over and above all his natural gifts and endowments, divine choice and equipment were necessary for him to succeed. You may be head and shoulders above others in respect to talents, gifts, and personality, but without a change of heart and the anointing with the Spirit, power will never be yours to reign in righteousness.

On the Throne (I Sam. 10:17-27)

The next crisis in Saul's transition from a farmer to a king took place at Mizpah where Samuel had convened an assembly of the tribes of Israel. There lots were taken to choose the king they demanded. The tribe of Benjamin came up trumps, and out of it the family of Matri was taken and the lot fell upon Saul, the son of Kish. He was elected—but he could not be found. His hiding place was discovered, and Samuel presented him to the people with the acclamation, "See ye him whom the Lord hath chosen, that there is none like him among all the people." Then, for the first time in Jewish history the cry rent the air, "God save the king!" The national election was but the acceptance of a divine choice.

Up to this time, Saul had been a shy, retiring youth. "Am not I a Benjamite?" Willingly, he would have retreated to private life, happy in the fields with his yoke of oxen. But, yielding to a divine and human choice, he gathered around him "a band of men whose hearts God had touched" and led the people out to a remarkable victory over the Ammonites. Then, taking up his proper place as king, he became resolute and ruled with equity. For a while Saul's reign was satisfactory and successful. In his cabinet was Samuel as chaplain, or spiritual adviser; Abner, his secretary of war;

Abiathar, the high priest; David, his lieutenant and confidential friend.

Among the high, kingly qualities Saul possessed were his reluctance to accept office, equaled only by the coolness with which he accepted it (10:22; 11:5); the promptness with which he responded to the first call of duty (11:6); the lasting gratitude of the people of Jabesh-Gilead for the timely aid he gave as king. Then, as Thomas Hunter Weir expresses it, "If we remember that Saul was openly disowned by Samuel, 15:30, and he believed himself to be cast off by Jehovah, we cannot but admire the way in which he fought on to the last. Moreover, the fact that he retained not only his own sons, but a sufficient body of fighting men to engage a large body of Philistines, shows that there must have been something in him to excite confidence and loyalty."

Chief among Saul's honorable and noble qualities as king were his prowess in war and his generosity in peace, which David, the man who knew him best, set down in his elegy (II Sam. 1:19). There is no need to linger over all his exploits. Suffice it to say that gradually Saul gave way to passion and eccentric impulses. He became jealous, cruel, and vindictive. When he intruded on the priests' office, he was guilty of self-presumption. His disobedience over the slaughter of the Amalekites resulted in his rejection by Samuel who "came no more to see him," and by God who "repented that he had made him king over Israel." After the first two years of his prosperous reign, Saul's life was one long tragedy in which he went from bad to worse.

"Oh," exclaims Thomas Shepard, "the grievous shipwrecks of some great ships! We see some boards and planks lying in the mud at low water, but that is all!" Just so does Saul's subsequent, disappointing history read. In fits of violence and frenzy he massacred the priests, and hunted for slaughter his own son-in-law, David, although in his better moments he manifested a strong affection for him. Ultimately, he received the stern rebuke of heaven, the death warrant of the royalty

66

of his own house: "Thou hast rejected the word of the Lord, and the Lord hath rejected thee from being king." What an ignoble end to a noble beginning! For us the warning is clear, "Let him that thinketh he standeth take heed lest he fall" (I Cor. 10:12).

At the Witch's Cave (I Sam. 28:7-25)

Rejected by God, possessed of an evil spirit, at war with the Philistines, and no Samuel in the flesh to guide him, Saul felt the chill shadow of disaster facing him and dared not go into battle without some kind of light from the other world. With the loss of the usual means of consulting the divine will, he turned to a necromancer. What a lamentable decay of character! From God to a witch—from heaven to hell, but it is always thus with those who leave God out of their plans. Saul's courage had gone, and he could not pray, for he felt that God had departed from him. And so, in his extremity he turned to forbidden quarters—to an evil source he himself had previously tried to expel from the land. He had forbade all witchcraft, but now in his desperation and melancholy, he turned for guidance in the hour of gloom and agony to the very practice he had sought to stamp out.

The wretched witch, or medium, and the more wretched king stand face to face. But the occult advice brought no relief to his distraught heart, for Samuel's voice only reiterated Saul's fears, and pronounced his doom. He received no gleam of hope, only his death knell. "Tomorrow shalt thou and thy sons be with me." In silence the dejected monarch wrapped his robe around him and passed out into the dark night. His name, *Saul,* means, "the one who asked insistently, or importunately," or "the beggar." If only he had always sought God, prayed always as a beggar dependent upon Him for all things, how different his end would have been.

On Mount Gilboa (I Sam. 31)

From the witch at Endor, Saul went forth to meet his doom at Mount Gilboa, a God-forsaken man. On the heights he met the Philistines, and in the midst of a shower of arrows the end came. Standing at bay before his foes, he had to witness the death of his three sons, including his beloved Jonathan. By his side lay his own armor-bearer, dead. Weak from the loss of blood, he leans upon his spear, and dies by his own hand. Saul ended his sovereignty by committing suicide. The next morning his armor was fastened above the pagan altar of Ashtaroth. His head, that had always been visible above those of his fellows, was severed from his shoulders and deposited in the house of Dagon. As for his body, it was strung up on the walls of Beth-shan like a captured bird.

With the fall of Saul, Israel lost a hero who began his career with brilliant promise. He had been called to do great things, was naturally talented, was richly gifted, bold, valiant. At the outset he displayed a reverence for God. But he thought of God less and less and became self-reliant until, God-forsaken, retribution fell and he died disgraced. Under cover of night some of his valiant men took down his body, and the bodies of his sons and, cremating them, buried the bones under a tree at Jabesh. What a terrible end for a king!

David, receiving news of Saul's tragic death, lamented over the passing of Saul and Jonathan, and uttered one of the most beautiful and eloquent eulogies in literature—"Saul and Jonathan were lovely and pleasant in their lives, and in their death they were not divided: They were swifter than eagles, they were stronger than lions" (II Sam. 1:23; see 1:17-27).

Let us reflect on Saul's sad story, for there are lessons we can glean from it for our own safety.

1. We are reminded of the probationary character of life

Saul was on trial, and as king had tasks to perform and responsibilities to meet and discharge which required certain

68

gifts and endowments. But when God calls He equips, and thus He provided Saul with all he needed. If ever God was patient with a man, it was with this son of Kish, who had such an auspicious beginning. With a wise counselor like Samuel to warn him of dangers, and the inward ministry of the Spirit, he had a fair chance of success. Just so, all of us have a fighting chance of making good. Is it not a mark of true greatness if we can rise above our evil environment? Triumph shapes character, but to yield to forces alien to God's will means loss of soul and exile from God. The span of life is our probationary period, with life as a gift from heaven. The question is, are we using the talent, or are we losing it?

> Not many lives have we,
> One, only one.
> How sacred should that one life ever be,
> This narrow span!

2. Obedience is necessary and important

Obedience is the touchstone of spiritual success. But Saul was determined to go his own way—and he took it, to his own ruin. The turning point in his career came when he disobeyed God in the campaign against the Amalekites; then he lied to Samuel. Such a manifestation of self-will had a destructive ending. "To obey is better than sacrifice," and to obey the will and Word of God at all times earns God's approbation. The Master could say, "I do always the things that please my Father." He was obedient unto death, even the death of the cross.

3. Cognizance can be taken of the remorse rejection brings

Grieving friends by repeated slights, affronts, and inattentions usually ends in separation from them. Saul grieved his outstanding friend, Samuel, and his departure from the prophet was followed by the departure of his inner friend, the Holy Spirit. Saul grieved, insulted, quenched the Spirit. An evil spirit then took possession of him and his character quickly deteriorated. Habitual disobedience to the voice of the Spirit, refusing His invitations and admonitions and persisting in what He hates is suicidal. Coldness of heart, self-accusation, a gradual departure from God, misery, hopelessness, and God-forsakenness ensue.

4. There is a bitter end to it all

The majority of men have a craving for religion of some sort. If it is not for the God of heaven, then it is for the witch of Endor. The soul's thirst must be quenched, if not by the river of life, then by the muddy pools of the world. If we have made a mistake, fallen from heights, sinned against heaven, and feel there is no hope, let us not seek refuge in some God-condemned hiding place. Let us not crave for secret things, for the mysterious, the speculative, and the impossible; but obey the clear command of God to repent and be saved from our sins.

An ever-increasing number, like Saul, are deluded into Spiritism, or Spiritualism, which is strictly condemned by God in His Word as a false refuge. While there may be an element of trickery in some seances, they can be diabolically real and therefore should be shunned. Roaming evil spirits are able to impersonate the dead, and this is where the delusion comes in: Spiritism is a tragic snare, a corrupting influence that draws the soul from God. Man's only hope is to get back to God, to His Word. True forgiveness awaits all repentant hearts. In David's poignant lament over Saul's death, there is no word of revenge or bitterness because of the way he had tried to kill him. God waits to treat those who despise Him in the same way, namely, with overtures of grace and mercy. Many years ago an American artist attracted wide attention by a picture he called *The Return*. It depicted a wanderer in rags and tatters coming to a forsaken home in hopeless anguish, and kneeling by the side of a high bed whereon his father lay dead, and the prodigal cried *"Too late! Too late!"* For him there was no word of welcome and forgiveness. But our blessed heavenly Father above waits to forgive and to restore nobility of character ruined by sin. His arms are ever outstretched to welcome those who turn from their disobedience and despair to Him in penitence and faith. He is a God, rich in mercy.

> Though we have sinned,
> There is mercy and pardon,
> Pardon for you and for me.

6

David and Jonathan
The Two Men Who Loved Each Other

There are many different ways of approaching the Bible, the crown of literature. Variety is not only the spice of life, but the key to an understanding of the comprehensive nature of God's infallible Word. One of the most fascinating features of Scripture truth is its record of charming love stories. We never tire of reading about Jacob and Rachel, Ruth and Naomi, Hosea and his wife, and the matchless love story of God who loves a world of sinners lost and ruined by the Fall. In this present biographical sketch we consider the superb romance of David and Jonathan, which is most unusual because it tells of a love that bound two men together in an indissoluble bond. From the first assertion of their mutual love until the last expression of David's love for Jonathan when he reverently buried his bones, there was never a cloud between them (I Sam. 18:1; II Sam. 21:13). Their counterpart in the New Testament is Jesus and John, the disciple Jesus loved and who became known as "The Apostle of Love." John was Greater David's Jonathan.

We consider David and Jonathan together, seeing they are seldom separated in the Old Testament, and from the wonderful love tie that existed between them, several spiritual parallels can be traced.

The Wealth of Love

Among the many aspects of the noble life of David that

the sacred record presents, perhaps the most outstanding is that of *love*. His name means "Beloved" and is from a root signifying "to love." His name, then, was a true expression of his character and disposition, for he possessed a warm, loving nature. He was the essence of love, and so found himself loved. He drew out the affection of all hearts who came to know him. Is this not so with God? Love is not only one of His transcendant attributes, but an integral part of His Being or Nature—God *is* love!

David was loved by God

If Saul was man's choice as king, David was God's choice. "The Lord hath sought him a man after his own *heart*" (I Sam. 13:14; Acts 13:22). God chose him because he was a mirror of His own warm, pure heart. David had a passion for God, for worship, for obedience. God said of him, "He shall fulfil all my will." Such a love was mutual—God loved David and David loved God: "I love the Lord" (Ps. 116:1; see Ps. 31:23). If this was true of David, it was truer of Jesus, who was of the house and lineage of David. He was a Man after God's own heart, as David could not be. He was the beloved Son, in whom God was ever well-pleased. Could He not say, "He that hath seen me hath seen the Father"? He came as the embodiment and personification of divine love. The same mutual love exists between God and His redeemed children.

David was loved by Saul

When we think of these two contrasting characters, we usually call to mind Saul's jealousy and his effort to kill him. But let it not be forgotten that the Bible says, "Saul loved David greatly" (I Sam. 16:21). This love, however, was not very deep, or of an abiding nature. It was effervescent and could turn to anger. With Saul, love turned to loathing as he witnessed David's prowess and popularity, and thus he sought to slay the young champion of Israel.

Do we not have a picture here of Satan's attitude toward Christ? If Saul loved David at one time, it is evident that the devil, before he became a devil, loved and worshiped the Eternal Son. But as with Saul, so with Satan, admiration turned to anger, and since his expulsion from heaven, he has been bent upon the destruction of Christ, of the cross, of the true church. Saul's change of heart can also suggest the sad plight of those who have lost the love they had for the Saviour. Does not Paul mention those who once loved the Lord but are now enemies of His cross (Phil 3:18)?

David was loved by Jonathan

Longfellow writes,

> All through there are wayside inns
>   Where man may refresh his soul with love:
> Even the lowest may quench his thirst
>   At rivulets fed by springs from above.

The unique and remarkable love-covenant between David and Jonathan is one of these wayside inns where our hearts can be refreshed. No writer is able to surpass the superb description Samuel gives us of the love binding these two hearts together. "The soul of Jonathan was knit with the soul of David, and Jonathan loved him as he his own soul" (I Sam. 18:1). They exhibited the exhortation of the Apostle of Love—"Beloved, let us love another: for love is of God" (I John 4:7). There are two references as to the quality of Jonathan's love for David.

1. It was *deep*

Three times over we have the phrase, "loved him as his own soul" (18:1-2; 20:17). Truly Jonathan loved his neighbor as himself. There was nothing formal, nothing perfunctory about this love pact. Jonathan took David and all his interests into his heart. He lived for and loved David as no other. Does not such a love represent the love of the individual believer for the Lord Jesus? Do His interests appeal as powerfully to us as if they were our own? It is to be feared that too often our love is selfish and shallow. If we loved the Lord as we love ourselves we would find our miserable self-life growing less and less.

2. It was *surpassing*

Hearing of the tragic death of Jonathan, David in his eulogy uttered the beautiful words, "Thy love to me was wonderful, passing the love of women" (II Sam. 1:26). David knew a good deal about the love of women. No doubt he was inspired by the love of his grandmother Ruth for Naomi. He also knew that womanly love can be fickle; that a mother can forget the child she bore. Jonathan's love, however, was neither fickle nor forgetful. Because of its rich quality it surpassed female love, even though that is often the highest form of human love. No matter how others may love us, they can never match God's love revealed in His Son for you and me. "There is no love like the love of Jesus." On the other hand, is our love for Him deeper, purer, and stronger than the affection we shower upon others? There may be a reference to supernatural love in David's praise of his friend's love: that such surging love as he constantly manifested was divinely inspired. The believer's love for God is more than natural love. The natural heart is at enmity with God and alien to His interests. God loved us before we loved Him. Like the Ephesians, our first love for Him wanes—"First-born light in gloom declines." But His love, like Himself, is ever the same.

David was loved by Michal

Although the marriage between David and Michal was arranged by Saul, twice over we read, "Michal, Saul's daughter loved David" (I Sam. 18:20, 28). We are never told that he loved her. Michal was allocated to David because of his famous slaughter of the giant of the Philistines, Goliath. Being a handsome young man, doubtless Michal found David attractive and fell for him. An aspect of her love that we must not overlook is that she professed it in a home antagonistic to David. Further, it was her love that foiled Saul's angry attempt on the life of her husband. True love is always ingenious in the defense of its own. Becoming the bride of the one she loved, Michal can represent the love of the true church for her heavenly Bridegroom. We live in a world hostile to Jesus, one in which men still try to destroy Him, and our obligation is to declare our love to Him and prove it in utter devotion to His cause.

David was loved by all Israel and Judah

The courageous and commendable ways of David created universal attraction. Everyone was drawn to him by love, as filings to a magnet. After Samuel pronounced David heir to the throne, jealousy ensued and two factions arose—those who followed Saul and the others who followed David. But the day came when all the tribes were united and anointed him king over all the tribes and for thirty-three years he reigned over both Israel and Judah. In this reign over all Israel, we have a foregleam of the day when all God's ancient people will unite to recognize, love, and serve Jesus as their king. He came as their king almost two millenniums ago but they would not have Him reign over them and crucified Him. Over His cross was written—"Jesus, King of the Jews." Yet the day is coming when all the scattered tribes will be regathered and fall at His feet and, seeing Him whom they pierced, they will adore and magnify Him.

Thus our blessed Lord, because of His eternal love, draws all to Himself. Jonathan never tired of telling David how he loved him. A thousand times a day may we be found saying from our heart, "I love the Lord." Out of adoration for His sacrificial love may He continually hear the sincere confession—

> Lord Jesus, I love Thee,
> I know Thou art mine.

When He puts the old-time question to us, "Lovest thou Me?" may ours be the instant reply, "Thou knowest all things, Thou knowest that I love Thee." If He has the love of a heart, true and clean, then He will have possession of the lover himself.

The Spring of Love

Having considered the *wealth* of love showered upon David by all who had contact with him, we now come to examine the reasons why such love was manifested toward him. As we have seen, Jonathan is pictured as loving David with a deeper, holier love than any other could give. What was the cause of such untainted, unselfish affection? Well, we must take into account what happened after David's victory over Goliath— "And Saul took David that day and would let him go no more home to his father's house" (I Sam. 18:2). This meant that the two lads were thrown into daily contact with each other; and what a contrast there was between the two. The young, strong, brave, good-looking yet poor shepherd lad on the one hand, and the rich, young prince of Israel on the other. David was taken out of poor, lowly circumstances and made a member of the royal household—a picture of the condescending love and grace of God in taking poor, insignificant creatures and making them members of His royal household. Having entered His banqueting house of love, we go no more to the old haunts.

The loyal and deep love of Jonathan for David was not causeless. How did it spring up? How was it first begotten, or cultivated? Why did he love him as his own soul? Such an effect must have had a cause, although with God's love for us, it is different. The only reason we can give for setting His love upon us is, "because the Lord loved you" (Deut. 7:7-8). Being so unlike Him, there was nothing in His people of old to draw out His love to them. But parallels can be traced in the ways David was loved by those surrounding him.

He was loved because of his love

This reciprocal love is evident in the phrase, "The soul of Jonathan was knit with the soul of David" (I Sam. 18:1). Like answered to like. Each gave what he got. As each had the same divine quality of love, there came the union of two kindred hearts. The phrase "was knit," implies *bound up.* This strong term is also used of Jacob's love for his motherless son, Benjamin—"Seeing his life is bound up in the lad's life" (Gen. 44:30). Aristotle remarked that two true friends were called *one soul.* The old Anglo-Saxon word for "knit" is akin to our English word *knot.* "Knitting" a garment means interlacing or bringing and binding together single yarns, thereby making them one. It was a *love-knot* that made David and Jonathan one.

David's deep, affectionate, warm, and generous heart responded in full measure to the abandonment of Jonathan's love. Each had the same divine quality, which resulted in the union of kindred hearts. The two youths were knit together in their desires and interests as the warp and woof of web. Their vital aspirations were intertwined, producing a wonderful unity of hope and purpose.

The marvelous love of David is seen in his forced parting from Jonathan. "They kissed one another, and wept one with another until David exceeded" (I Sam. 20:41). Those abundant tears proved the abundance of love. Perhaps because David was the younger of the two, his love was fresher. Does not all this suggest our relationship to Christ? As David's tears exceeded Jonathan's, so the Redeemer's tears over us exceeded the tears we shed over our sinful selves. "We love him because he first loved us." Through grace, the Lord and I are knit together and made one. By the Holy Spirit there has been formed a mystical union between us, and we are eternally one.

He was loved because of his loveliness

David was not only loving, but lovely. Many of us are the latter, but not the former. Yet, after all, beauty of character is more commendable and enduring than beauty of face and form. But David was fortunate in that "he was ruddy and withal of a beautiful countenance, and goodly to look to" (I Sam. 16:12). Who could resist loving such a well-built, handsome, fresh-colored youth? At the time when the two first met, Jonathan would have been about forty and David around sixteen or seventeen years of age. David, therefore, had the bloom of beauty, the freshness and fairness of youth, and this called out Jonathan's love. David was a child of nature, living in the fields, mountains, and valleys, and this was reflected in his beauty and the glow of his countenance. The margin gives us "handsome eyes" for "beautiful countenance."

Do we not love the Lord Jesus with a deep and ever-deepening love because of His loveliness? He retained the beauty of His youth for He was but thirty-three years of age when His lovely visage was marred more than any man's. Renowned though he was for his handsomeness, David could say of the Lord that He was "fairer than the children of men" (Ps. 45:2). Solomon said, "My beloved is white and ruddy, the chiefest among ten thousand. . . . He is altogether lovely" (Song of Sol. 5:10, 16). As for Zechariah, he exclaims, "Great is his beauty" (9:17). Such beauty is eternal, for no wrinkles ever gather on His brow, old age does not disfigure Him. He will ever be "the fairest of all the earth beside." The tragedy is that the vast majority see "no beauty in him, that they should desire him," To their sin-blinded eyes "he hath no form nor comeliness." As the Creator of all that is lovely and beautiful in the world, what must He Himself be like? Because of all He is in Himself He captivates our hearts, and with Peter we confess, "Thou knowest that [we] love thee."

He was loved because of his life

"Beauty" we say, "is only skin deep." This is why a beautiful life is more impressive than a beautiful face. Jonathan's heart was captured by the character of this man after God's own heart, for David knew how to "behave himself wisely." It is written of him that he was "prudent in matters and a comely person and the Lord is with him" (I Sam. 16:18; 18:8, 14-15, 30). To friend and foe alike, he manifested nobility of character. Except in the matter of Uriah, he was above reproach, discreet, wise, and kind in all matters. Such a life was not the product of self-culture but of communion, for he lived with the God of nature and of revelation. Love for the Lord elevated his stature and made him gentlemanly.

The very mention of David's name stirred Jonathan's breast. Is this not so with David's Greater Son who was ever prudent, comely, circumspect, and upright? Do we not love Him because He is holy, harmless, and undefiled? He was without fault also during His earthly sojourn, as even His enemies confessed. He is God's spotless Lamb, earth's first perfect gentleman. David's remarkable life made his name precious: "His name was much set by" (I Sam. 18:30). It was an ointment poured forth, and uttered with reverence and loved by all. Our blessed Lord has "a name above every name" (see Isa. 52:13), a name so sweet in a believer's ear. As David's personal attractiveness and fragrant life drew out Jonathan's affection, so may we be found lavishing our love upon a greater than David who lived and spake as no other man.

Let me love Thee, love is mighty,
  Swaying realms of deed and thought;
By it I shall walk uprightly,
  I shall serve Thee as I ought.

He was loved because of his labors

The record says that David was "cunning in playing, and a mighty valiant man, and a man of war" (I Sam. 16:18). He was both musical and mighty. A poet and a player of no mean order, he became known as "the sweet psalmist of Israel." That melody and harmony were in his heart can be seen in the matchless Psalms he composed. In his mad fits, Saul knew how soothing David's playing on the harp could be. That he was valiant as well as vocal, mighty as well as musical, is evidenced by his triumphs over foes, especially his victory over Goliath. Jonathan's love, then, was fed by the rich, musical gifts and marvelous exploits of David. The noble prince could not help loving such a man.

Again we have a comparison between David and our Lord. At the outset of Creation did not the Lord instruct man how to invent musical instruments and play them (Gen. 4:21-22)? Is He not the one who puts a new song in our mouth? As David's harp calmed Saul in his melancholy moments, so, "The name of Jesus is so sweet in a believer's ear, It soothes his sorrows." Into songless lives in a sad world, He comes with the song of salvation, and as the sinner, whose sin causes the harp to hang on a willow tree, repents, His is the gentle voice heard urging the pardoned one to take down the harp and sing a new song unto Him. Then who is as valiant and mighty as He? A man of war, He fought a grimmer contest than that of David with Goliath. At Calvary, He destroyed the works of the devil. When He cried, "It is finished," He meant that He had laid hold of the principalities and powers of hell and robbed them of their power and authority. By dying, He secured a blood-bought victory for us and consequently merits our heart's full love.

What else could Saul, Jonathan, and all Israel do but love David after his great and glorious victory over the giant which raised him above Saul in courage and faith in God? The maidens sang that while Saul slew his thousands, David had ten thousands to his credit. It was this noble deed that bound Jonathan to David until Saul and his sons were finally slain by the Philistines. David met Goliath *alone,* and Jesus met the forces of hell at the cross in the same way. He fought the giant of the caverns of darkness alone, and now enables us to follow Him in the train of His triumph. "All Israel shouted" when Goliath fell. It is easier to shout than to fight. David killed the giant with his own sword. The devil had the power of death, and Jesus defeated him with his own sword. "By dying, death He slew," and we praise Him for His all-glorious deed. David was versatile, having a variety of gifts. He was expert as a shepherd, singer, and sovereign. Job could say of the Lord, "I know that thou canst do every thing" (42:2). And increasingly we love Him because He is able to deal with the giants of doubt, despair, and defeat we meet on our pilgrimage.

He was loved because of his lowliness

Another cause of the warm, deep, and abiding love of Jonathan for his young friend was his *humility.* Lowly, unassuming, and unassertive, David was doubly attractive. Despite the honor heaped on him he remained humble. He never spoke of or bragged about his defeat of Goliath. Others praised him for his bravery, but you will search the sacred record in vain for any explicit reference to the valiant exploit that saved Israel from her foes from his own lips (see I Sam. 18:7; 21:9; 29:5). "Let another's lips praise thee." How David's humility shines in his single-handed combat with the defiant, godless Goliath! He knew that he was only the instrument God used to achieve such a victory, so he gave all the glory to Him. "The battle is the Lord's" (I Sam. 17:47).

When he appeared before King Saul for commendation and reward, there was no boasting. Not ashamed of his lowly estate he said, "I am the son of thy servant Jesse" (I Sam. 17:58).

Lifting our thoughts higher, do not we love Jesus for His lowliness? Was He not "meek and lowly in heart"? A study of His earthly sojourn reveals that He was a complete stranger to a proud or boastful spirit. Certainly in His great I AMS we have His self-assertion of Deity, but His claims were made without any trace of self-assertiveness. After His resurrection He had little to say about the marvelous deed at Calvary. The fact that He was alive forevermore spoke for itself. The apostles could sing His praises as the victor divine, but they magnified Him for His humility: "Rich, for our sakes, he became poor."

The lesson for our own hearts at this point is that if we would attract the love of others we must follow David and David's Lord. Pride is a sin God hates, and boastfulness, self-glory and self-assertiveness must have no place in our witness. "Let another praise thee, not thine own mouth" (Prov. 27:2). To seek our own glory is no glory at all (Prov. 25:27). Lowliness is not only attractive but blessed for "he who humbleth himself shall be exalted."

> Forbid it, Lord, that I should boast,
> Save in the death of Christ, my God;
> All the vain things that charm me most,
> I sacrifice them through His blood.

The Covenant of Love

Having considered the bounteous wealth of love bestowed upon David and his personal qualities responsible for such universal attraction, we now come to examine the wonderful love covenant Jonathan and David entered into. Their mutual love resulted in a sacred vow: "Then Jonathan and David

83

made a covenant because he loved him as his own soul" (I Sam. 18:3). An interesting fact that emerges from such a covenant is that, suggested by Jonathan and willingly and lovingly entered into by David, the Lord was also a party to it. "Thou hast brought thy servant into a covenant of the Lord with thee" (I Sam. 20:8, 16). Scripture records that David consistently fulfilled his part of the covenant, even after Jonathan's death. "The king spared Mephibosheth, the son of Jonathan, because of the Lord's oath that was between them" (II Sam. 21:7).

Such a solemn, mutual covenant suggests two precious thoughts for our redeemed hearts:

1. There is the love-covenant of Calvary

It was because God loved us that He entered into a holy covenant with His beloved Son in eternity past to redeem us from sin, and the cross was the fulfillment on the Saviour's part of such a love bond. Therefore, sinners can be saved in virtue of the finished work of the covenant-keeping Lord. The Lord's Supper is a memorial or covenant feast, and our participation in it is our part of the covenant, "This do in remembrance of me." The table declares Jesus as the covenant-keeping Lord, and the believer, as a covenant-keeping servant. Ere long, He will return to gather to Himself all those with whom He has made a covenant. The nature of this covenant is such that it cannot be broken, for it is eternal.

2. There is the love-covenant of saints

As love is the foundation of all divine covenants with man, so love is the basis of all human covenants Godward. Every holy vow we take upon ourselves is born as a result of our heart's deep love for Jesus. As the mutual affection of two kindred spirits culminates in the sacred marriage bond, or love-knot, so true love to the Lord constrains us to seek an ever closer bond or union with Him, and a fuller allegiance to Him. The love-covenant between Jonathan and David involved three general obligations, all of which have a parallel in a divine relationship.

The protection of David

It was because of Saul's jealousy and his repeated attempts to slay David, the Lord's anointed, that Jonathan entered into such a love pact. "Saul my father seeketh to kill thee . . . hide thyself." "Thou shalt deal kindly with thy servant" (I Sam. 19:3; 20:8). Jonathan acted as a secret spy and, gauging the turbulent feelings of his angry father, knew when to warn David. Thus we have the moving episode in the woods where Jonathan's love for David foiled Saul's hatred, for his part of the covenant was to preserve and protect the precious life of David at all costs. If the love knot has been tied between the Lord and ourselves, the same solemn vow or obligation rests upon us. We live in a world hostile to the claims of Christ. The devil hates Him, and is bent upon the destruction of His cause. But since we are His, our responsibility is to defend His interests at all costs.

What striking contrasts the narrative affords! "Saul spake unto Jonathan, his son . . . to kill David. But Jonathan, Saul's son, delighted much in David" (I Sam. 19:1-2). The one is out to slay, the other to save. Modernists unite to destroy the authority and claims of Christ; as those having been redeemed by His precious blood we delight much in our heavenly Lord. In spite of Saul's persistent animosity toward David, we read that Jonathan always "spake good of David unto his father" (I Sam. 19:4). What a lovely example to emulate! When others speak evil of our Lord, deny His deity, impoverish His infinity, and belittle His beauty, we must be found speaking well of Him, pleading His cause, extolling His greatness, lauding His power. There were moments when the pleading of David's merit by his loving friend changed Saul's

85

feelings toward him. May we always be found, as those in covenant-relationship with the Saviour, singing His praises, pleading His merit, recounting His achievements, and magnifying His grace! Until we "bless in death a bond so dear," let us defend His interests, and proclaim His virtues.

There is a further application we can make of this love covenant. In the noble act of Jonathan defending David there is an example we can follow among ourselves as saints. Jonathan might have withdrawn his friendship from David and sided with his father against the young champion. But, no, he pleaded for David and endeavored to vindicate him against the false and ungenerous conception of Saul by extolling his merits. There are those who would have us join them in the chorus of criticism, jealousy, wrong and harsh treatment of others. They would have us side with them against others who may, or may not, deserve such handling. Included in the love covenant of Calvary was forgiveness, and we should be more desirous of pointing out the kind, loving things that can be praised in those whom others condemn, and forgive and forget the rest.

The preservation of Jonathan and his seed

Another side of the love bond is clearly evident. While Jonathan did his best for his friend, and shielded him all through, David never had an opportunity to protect Jonathan, seeing he was a fugitive, an outlaw because of Saul's animosity. David would have fought bravely at Mount Gilboa to save from death the man who loved him, but he never had the chance. Yet he fully adhered to his part of the covenant, in that he preserved Jonathan's seed and offspring: "David said, Is there yet any that is left of the house of Saul, that I may show him kindness for Jonathan's sake?" (II Sam. 9:1). "The king spared Mephibosheth because of the Lord's oath between David and Jonathan" (II Sam. 21:7). How royally David treated the lame son of the friend to whose memory he was bound by the solemn love bond they had forged!

The spiritual application of all this is evident, is it not? Our Lord will ever honor His part of the covenant He enters into with His people. If He has our best, His best will be ours. If we live for Him, speak well of Him in a hostile world, defend and protect His cause, He will fulfill His side of the covenant and undertake for us, preserving, providing, and protecting until the journey's end. We are apt to miss a precious aspect to the martyrdom of Stephen, who certainly was not ashamed to own his Lord. As this valiant defender of the faith was being stoned to death, he looked up to heaven and saw Jesus *standing*. As the risen Lord, He had taken His seat at the right hand of God, but He rose to welcome the entrance of His brave follower into eternal bliss (Acts 7:55). Stephen had stood up for Him, which defense he sealed with his blood, and now Jesus stands to receive the martyred saint.

If we put Him first, we can trust him to make all that concerns us His concern, and to protect us and ours. If we love Him above others, and strive to follow Him fully, He will show kindness to our seed. Often we fret and worry about our health, business, loved ones, and a thousand and one other things, as if He will not keep His part of the covenant. But,

> They who trust Him wholly,
> Find Him wholly true.

As the covenant-keeping Lord, He will not fail to honor us if we honor Him. If our soul is knit with Him, then the entire responsibility of our life is on His shoulders. Has He not pledged Himself to undertake for us?

The Surrender of Kingship

If only an artist could depict that love episode in the woods, as Jonathan faced his most difficult part in the love covenant David and he were making. Saul was king, and by every right Jonathan should be his heir to the throne. But listen to this noble heart that shared none of his father's jealousy—"Thou shalt be king . . . I shall be next to thee" (I Sam. 23:16-18). Chiding his son, Saul said, "Thou hast chosen the son of Jesse to thine own confusion"—or loss of heirship (I Sam. 20:30). Such a taunt, however, did not influence Jonathan who willingly surrendered any right he had to kingship. In choosing David as his bosom friend, he had forfeited the crown. What charming self-abnegation he revealed by such an act! Willing to be second to David, he entered into a covenant to surrender all claims to the throne, and became a *subject* instead of a *sovereign*. He was willing to decrease, and for David to increase. But dear Jonathan never lived to become the king's "love-vassal."

If we own the Lordship of Christ, then we must surrender all claims to self-government. Part of the love-covenant we make with Him is, that He shall be king, with others next, and ourselves last. If He has the throne of my heart, then grace will exceed Jonathan's desire to be next to David, or near to him to serve him, for He has promised that I shall reign with Him when I come to share His throne (Rev. 3:21).

The Surrender of Love

Without doubt, Jonathan stands out as one of the loveliest characters in the Old Testament. He was the sincere, faithful, and constant friend of David, whose love for him was beyond compare. Unlike his father, Jonathan's excellence shone untarnished to the very last. He is one of the almost perfect men in the Bible. Not a single shameful trait is recorded of his life. His utter love for David, once he knew that the son of Jesse would succeed his father as king, is seen in the complete surrender of all he had to David—"Jonathan stripped himself of the robe that was upon him and gave it to David, and his garments, even to his sword, and his bow, and to his girdle" (I Sam. 18:4). In such a yielding up of all he treasured, he was certainly true to his name, for *Jonathan* means, "Given of God " or "The Lord is a Giver," and comes from a word, signifying *to give*. So the phrase "gave it to David," can be translated as "Jonathaned to David." What this wonderful son of Saul was by name, he was by nature. He proved that love lives to give, and never withholds its best when giving. There are two phases of Jonathan's surrender of his possessions, occasioned by David's great victory over Goliath. We can note in passing—

1. It was voluntary

"Jonathan stripped himself." He was not asked to, nor was he stripped by another, but willingly, freely, and voluntarily he transferred all to David, whose brave deed had captured Jonathan's heart and whose love kept nothing back from the conqueror. Sacrifice is more acceptable when it is willing, joyous, and freely made. Love lives to give, and it ceases to operate when there is no sacrifice. Too often we withhold our possessions from the Giver of them, and He has to come and strip us of them. Christ remains the most outstanding example of surrender the world has ever known. "He emptied himself," "He gave himself." When He came to the end, all He could give was His ruby blood—and He voluntarily gave it for our redemption. In His incarnation, He laid aside the outward insignia of royalty, and at His crucifixion He yielded up His life. When Jesus confronted the rich young ruler, He besought him to sell all he had, if he would prove how real and deep was his desire to be His follower. But he was unwilling to strip himself, and clung to his possessions and carried with them a sorrowful heart.

2. It was complete

Jonathan did not keep back part of the price, as Ananias and Sapphira did. He had no reserves. As Ornan said to

89

David, "I give it all" (I Chron. 21:23), so Jonathan manifested a similar surrender. True love never seeks its own, but gives, and keeps on giving until red with the blood of sacrifice. Jonathan gave David all of his outward garments and accouterments which is significant, for to receive any part of the dress worn by a sovereign, or his eldest son, or heir was deemed in the East as the highest honor conferred on a subject (see Esther 6:8).

He gave his robe

This would be the outer, beautiful and costly tunic worn by people of rank and importance. When the prodigal returned, his father put "the best robe" upon him. Such an imposing robe suggested royalty and meant that Jonathan was *somebody*, but stripping himself of it and giving it to David implied that he was willing to be *nobody*. He felt that the young warrior was worthier of it. Because of David's defeat of the giant, he merited the distinction. Have we learned how to surrender the robe of so-called dignity to our heavenly David? Have we laid in dust life's glory dead that Jesus might have all the glory? Think of the robe of glory He stripped Himself of when He became a baby and was wrapped in swaddling clothes! It is easy to sing, "Oh, to be nothing." Our hindrance to spiritual growth is that we want to be *something*. We love our robe too much to surrender it.

He gave his garments

Doubtless these were the military dress and armor items which Jonathan wore when in fighting uniform and symbolized his power and prowess as a soldier. They represented what he could do. David needed no such outfit. He tried on Saul's armor, but discarded it. All he needed was the garment of divine strength to cover him. If we love the Lord, all the garments of self-effort, self-righteousness, self-strength must go—"filthy rags," God calls them. We are only acceptable to Him when clothed in the robe of His salvation and righteousness.

He gave his sword

The phrase "even to" is impressive for it accentuates this particular surrender. Because the Philistines had denied Israel smiths there were only *two* swords among the people. "There was neither sword or spear found . . . but with Saul and with Jonathan" (I Sam. 13:22). What a treasure, then, this must have been for Jonathan to strip himself of! It stood for his fighting power, and was valued for self-defense. But even this was yielded to David, and he must have treasured it above the mighty sword of Goliath which also became his. For us, the sword can represent self-achievements, self-ability, self-defense. Yet our heavenly David must have our sword, for loving Him we must not be found taking our own way, dealing with our own problems, and fighting our own battles. "The Lord your God, he it is that fighteth for you, as he hath promised you" (Josh. 23:10). Therefore, we must submit and lay down our arms. George Matheson taught us to sing—

> Make me a captive, Lord,
> And then I shall be free;
> Force me to render up my sword,
> And I shall conqueror be.

He gave his bow

This was the famous and favorite weapon among the Israelites, being used both for pleasure and war. In his eulogy of Jonathan after his death, David eloquently praised his friend for his remarkable success with his bow—"From the blood of the slain, from the fat of the mighty, the bow of Jonathan turned not back" (II Sam. 1:22). For us, the bow can **stand**

91

for our favorite pleasures, for that which we count precious, whether a possession or a person. In the revival that swept through Ephesus, the curious arts and books the people valued were burned. We must not murmur if God asks for our "bow," or that which gives us fleshy pleasure.

> Neither passion or pride,
> Thy cross can betide.

He gave his girdle

This beautifully formed article was the chief ornament of the soldier, and was the support around his waist to hold his sword. When worn, it meant that he was prepared for active service. It was also an essential part of the clothing of the priests. "Gird them with girdles" (Exod. 29:7; Ps. 109:19). It was a small part of their equipment, keeping the rest of the armor or clothing bound close to the body, and it can symbolize the small things of life on which so much may hang. Some "girdles" are good for nothing (Jer. 13:10). We are well-equipped for service, if God's righteousness is the girdle around our loins (Isa. 11:5).

When Jesus came to die He had not even a girdle. When prepared for crucifixion, He was stripped of all. But His surrender commenced when He left the ivory palaces for a world of woe. Rich, so very rich, for our sakes He became poor.

He parted with His robe, with all outward aspects of royalty and majesty, and was found as a babe in infant's clothing.

He parted with His garments. He died to all self-defense. "They parted his garments among them." The taunt was "Himself he cannot save."

He parted with His sword. He could have smitten His foes who spat upon Him and came against Him with swords, but He did not.

He parted with His bow. Think of all the eternal pleasures He surrendered when He took upon Himself frail flesh to die!

He parted with His girdle. He suffered nothing, not even the smallest things of life, to come between His Father and Himself.

The one thing, however, Jonathan never gave to David was *himself*—his life! The vow, "I shall be next unto thee," was never fulfilled, for he gave his life in battle at Mount Gilboa. Thus, he never became David's subject, servant, or love-slave. He willingly gave his possessions, but never gave his life. In the last issue God wants, not what we have, but what we are, first of all. It is possible to surrender our possessions but not our *person*—our luxuries but not our lives—our substance but not ourselves. Christ, however, gave *Himself*. Therefore, the first note in the song of surrender should be—

> Take my life, and let it be
> Consecrated, Lord, to Thee

for if He has the full control of our heart and life, then grace will be ours to strip ourselves of all He desires or demands.

7

Asa
The King Who Became a Revivalist

The kings of Israel and of Judah were a mixed bag. Some were very good, others were good; some were bad, others, in between the good and the bad. The degree of morality among the people at a particular time depended on the character of the king on the throne. Asa, the son of Abijah and grandson of Rehoboam and of Maacah, the daughter of Absalom, can be placed in the category of the good kings (I Kings 15:1). He was the third king of Judah after the separation of Judah and Israel. The first ten years of his reign were prosperous and peaceful. On the whole, his kingship was commendable and successful, but as the years went by he became less and less faithful to God and His law. Towards the end of his reign he contracted disease in his feet and manifested lack of faith when "he sought not to God, but to the physicians" (II Chron. 16:12). After serving Judah for forty-one years, he died and was buried with great pomp in a tomb erected by himself in Jerusalem, the city of David. A zealous reformer, he sought to purge Judah of many evils, and it is in this capacity we wish to think of him.

The national revival under King Asa reads like a romance. It comes as an oasis in the history of the kings, as well as in the actual life and reign of Asa, king of Judah. "King Asa ... renewed the altar of the Lord" (II Chron. 15:8). What worldwide interest would be aroused if one of the kings or rulers of our time should become a flaming revivalist! Yet such a scene was witnessed two or three times in Old Testament days. King Hezekiah, for example, was another royal revivalist (II Chron. 30).

Chapters 14 and 15 of II Chronicles must be taken together in our evaluation of Asa's work. In chapter 14 we have the outward prosperity of the kingdom and Asa's superficial reformation. But in chapter 15 we come to a detailed account of the nation's inward and religious purification and rectification. And it is from this chapter that we can gather several striking features of the revival led by King Asa, applicable to the deep, spiritual needs of our own day and generation.

Power of a Spirit-Endued Messenger

The opening verse of chapter 15 tells us that the Spirit of God came upon Azariah. This prophet received a divine unction to proclaim the message that smote the consciences of King Asa and his people. Azariah went out to meet the king, as John the Baptist confronted Herod, with an authoritative word. "And he went out to meet Asa, and said unto him, Hear ye me, Asa, and all Judah and Benjamin: The Lord is with you, while ye be with him: and if ye seek him, he will be found of you; but if ye forsake him, he will forsake you" (v. 2).

The effect of such a Spirit-given word was tremendous. There came immediate restitution. Oh, the power of a Spirit-filled, Spirit-guided preacher! When preachers act under the Spirit's control, something is bound to happen. Do we pray as we ought that the Holy Spirit may come upon all pastors, teachers, and evangelists? All of us need this divine enduement if we would experience the joy of calling sinners to repentance.

We sadly need a heaven-sent prophet, another Azariah, who, filled with the Spirit, would arise to blister the conscience of the nation with a message of sin and repentance. The revival under John Wesley saved England from a bloody revolution. Well might we pray, "Lord, send us another Wesley!"

A Sad Condition of Barrenness

The warning of the prophet Azariah contains lamentable notes revealing the decadent condition of the nation.

No true God!

For a long season Israel had been without the true God (v. 3). Of course, God was still there, but the people had obscured Him with their idols. And because of intermittent idolatry God permitted surrounding nations to vex His people with adversity.

What truer description could we have of our own nation than this? For a long season now we have been without the true God. Paul's estimation of the multitudes is that they are "without God" and therefore "without hope." Coming to religious professors the apostle declares that many of them have a form of godliness but are destitute of its power. Today the nations are having a foretaste of hell, seeing they have forgotten God.

No teaching priest!

Being without a teaching priest also contributed to the plight of the nation. Priests there were in abundance, but none who had a deep spiritual understanding of the true character of God and, therefore, they were unable to teach the people. They were satisfied with the mere performance of altar duties. There was no heart concern for the soul of the people. And what is the curse of the church in our day? Is it not a dead orthodoxy? A cold professionalism has paralyzed

96

the church's efforts. She is not as terrible as an army with banners, because too many preachers who handle the law know not God.

No law!

Israel of Asa's time had known the law, but it had been forgotten or disobeyed. "For a long season Israel hath been . . . without law" (v. 3). When nations depart from God and drift into a barren religion it is not long before they begin to trample down the commandments of the Lord. Turning from the principles of the law, men come to do that which is right in their own eyes. Man's views on life and conduct, and not God's, are followed. So we have the sorry spectacle of nations drifting into tragic lawlessness all because of their godlessness. Surely it is time for God to work, seeing the people have made void His law!

No peace!

How God permitted Israel to suffer for her sins is declared by Azariah in no uncertain terms! "In those times there was no peace to him that went out, nor to him that came in, but great vexations were upon all the inhabitants of the countries . . . " (vv. 5-6). Religious apostasy resulted in social disturbances, political anarchy, and national disasters. Blood flowed freely because of Israel's departure from God. What of the times in which we find ourselves? With the constant threat of war upon us, is Azariah's word not applicable to a war-weary world, "There was no peace to him that went out, nor to him that came in"? Are there not religious causes for the present tensions? We lay all the blame upon economics or men who are drunk with the wine of power. But does not the Old Book affirm that when nations choose false gods, there is war in their gates?

Speedy Rectification of Apostasy

To all those who are out to bring men and nations to God, the Spirit-inspired message of Azariah has something to say. While what he proclaimed had a definite application to the desperate endeavor of King Asa to rectify national apostasy, the principles underlying the prophet's appeal are timeless.

The graciousness of God!

Azariah prefaced his warning by telling the king and his people that the Lord waited to be gracious. Promises of restoration and blessing can be found in the words, "The Lord is with you, while you are with him; and if you seek him, he will be found of you: but if you forsake him, he will forsake you" (v. 2). Thus, though the people had sinned, mercy and pardon awaited them if only they would turn in true penitence to God. And is this not the message we must unceasingly proclaim? God has been ignored and His counsels despised, yet He waits to bless with His favor all those who, in humility, seek His face.

The reward of restitution!

Strength of purpose was necessary on the part of King Asa to bring about a much-needed revival. "Be ye strong, therefore, and let not your hands be weak: for your work shall be rewarded" (v. 7). And how bountifully the drastic rectification of Asa was rewarded! The thorough expulsion of all that was responsible for the loss of divine favor met with divine approval. If revival is to come in our time, the hands of rulers and church leaders must not be weak in tackling the sins of the nation. Courageous action is necessary if civilization is to be saved from suicide.

The baptism of courage!

King Asa, we read, was so overwhelmed by the words of

the prophet that "he took courage and put away the abominable idols . . . and renewed the altar" (v. 8). And it certainly took courage on the part of the king to rectify the wrongs of his nation! Asa was never more kingly than when he turned revivalist and led his people back to God. Let us mark the steps in this wonderful national revival:

1. The abolition of abominable idols

Everything alien to the will and word of God was exterminated. King Asa did not entertain half-measures. There was no reservation in his reforms. Idolatry deserves drastic treatment. Idols must be torn from off the throne. And so, whatever the cost of revival, Asa was determined to cut through all that had robbed God of His rightful place in the nation. The only defect in Asa's revival, so far as we can see, was his failure to abolish the high places, which, although originally used for the worship of God, came to be identified with idolatrous practices.

It certainly took courage on Asa's part to displace and depose Maachah, his grandmother, from being queen (v. 16; I Kings 15:13) because of her association with idols. This queen mother was removed from the dignity she had enjoyed and the influence she had exerted. It must have cost Asa a great deal to dethrone such a near relative, but it had to be done. The court had to lead the way in the national revival.

Revival in our time and nation awaits the lead of those in places of trust and responsibility. If an idol is anything or anyone that takes God's place in our life, then some unpleasant work of removal must be faced. Revival means the unseating of all that has unseated God in national and personal life. And the narrative clearly shows that there are two kinds of idols to be dealt with, namely, those that must be destroyed and those that must be displaced.

Is there a thing beneath the sun
That strives with Thee my heart to share?
Ah, tear it thence, and reign alone,
The Lord of every notion there:
Then shall my heart from earth be free,
When it hath found repose in Thee.

2. The renewal of the altar

Asa's abolition of idols was negative; the renewal of the
altar was positive (v. 8). Polluted by unclean idolatrous practices, the altar had to be purified and then sanctified anew.
Its sacred purpose was restored. Offerings hitherto sacrificed
to idols were abolished and divinely ordained sacrifices were
restored (v. 11).

Coming to ourselves we realize that the tragic condition of
the church, world, and nation is attributable to desecrated
altars. Oh, for a land of renewed altars upon which worthy
sacrifices are placed! May grace be ours to renew the altar of
the heart and of the home!

3. The solemn covenant

The sacred historian tells us that "they entered into a covenant to seek the Lord God of their fathers with all their heart
and with all their soul: That whosoever would not seek the
Lord God of Israel should be put to death, whether small or
great, whether man or woman" (vv. 12-13). This high trans-
action of Asa and his subjects is parallel with the National
Covenant of the Scottish people to be found in Old Grey-
friars, Edinburgh, Scotland. In 1638, high and low affixed
their names to the scroll, covenanting to be faithful to God in
the resistance of all popish practices.

Have we need to enter into a personal covenant to put the
Lord first in everything? If we are conscious of any departure
from God, let us get alone with Him and write out our cove-

nant of fuller allegiance. It will help us to mortify the deeds of the body to have before us in black and white our decision to live only, always, for our King. Having given our word, it is only by the grace and power of the Spirit that we do not go back on it. An eminent saint had as his covenant: "May the appropriation of Christ as Saviour and Lord be the unvarying, initial act of each new day!" Is this not a covenant we could copy with profit to the soul?

4. The rededication of old vessels

What a day it must have been when King Asa "brought into the house of God the things that his father had dedicated, and that he himself had dedicated, silver and gold, and vessels" (v. 18). Sons who get on in the world are apt to throw off the restraints of a religious upbringing. The godliness of parents belongs to a past generation. Success in worldly matters is not compatible with ways that are too straitlaced. Such is the philosophy of many who have left homes in which God was honored. But Isaac redigged the wells of his father. And Asa had to bring back into the house of God the things his father had dedicated. All of this is a fruit of revival.

Are these not days when we have need to get back to our first love? Have we not lost our early glow and joy? We have need to return to faith and fervency. "Thus saith the Lord, stand ye in the ways and see, and ask for the old paths, where is the good way, and walk therein, and ye shall find rest for your souls" (Jer. 6:16).

Divine Blessing and Reward

True to Azariah's declaration, God was found of them that sought Him. "If ye seek him, he will be found of you" (v. 2). Turning to verse 15 we have two key phrases indicating how the people responded to the prophet's appeal. "They had sworn with all their heart, and sought him with their whole desire." Consequently, "he was found of them."

The employment of trumpets, cornets, and voices (v. 14), declared the united and joyful determination of the people to abide by their covenant. Thus there came streams of blessing and prosperity from the rectified life of king and nation. Although Asa lapsed from faith, as chapter 16 shows, he remained free from idolatry to the end of his days. As the result of the revival he brought about "his heart was perfect all his days," and therefore, through the years he enjoyed divine favor. Here is the double reward of adjustment to the will of God:

A harvest of souls!

With idols abolished and the altar renewed there "fell to Asa out of Israel in abundance, when they saw that the Lord his God was with him" (v. 9). Both Jews and strangers felt the impact of the revived and quickened life of Asa and his court. And thus is it with ourselves. If multitudes are not in the valley of decision, is it not partly because we have little evidence of being God-possessed and God-inspired?

When God is in the midst of His people, exalted, ungrieved, and unhindered, souls come to Christ in abundance. As the glory of the Lord is revealed, all flesh sees it together. Revival, which represents the quickening of God's people, always results in the ingathering of the lost round about. Blessed ourselves, we are made a blessing to others.

A season of rest!

King Asa experienced material blessings as well as spiritual ones as he swung his nation back to God. "The Lord gave them rest round about." "There was no more war" (vv. 15, 19).

Actual wars will only cease as nations learn how to please

God. A world, war-weary and blood-drenched as ours is, can only experience rest and peace as responsible rulers follow King Asa in his thorough extermination of all that is alien to God's holy will. A Holy Ghost revival is the only force that can calm the restlessness of our age.

Coming to the narrower world of our own life, we can only enjoy rest round about and live without strife and conflict as we live in harmony with God's purposes. The question is, "Are we willing and ready to pay the price of personal revival?" Victory and blessing can only be ours as we fully surrender all that hinders. "Up, sanctify yourselves" is the divine charge we must obey if the Lord is to do wonders in our midst. Irrespective of who or what led us away from complete abandonment to the divine will, we must take courage and put away our idols and then renew our altar.

8

Herod
The Roman Ruler Who Murdered a Godly Prophet

Because of the variety and value of its contents, the Bible is the most remarkable Book in the world. It contains some of the darkest and most fearful tragedies ever enacted, the cruelest of all being the murder of the holy, innocent Jesus in cold blood at Calvary. The tragedy we are to consider here is perhaps the most outstanding one other than the grim cross in New Testament history. The chief actors in this terrible drama can symbolize those bound together in a tragedy enacted on the stage of every soul.

Herod—He was the weak and wicked and licentious king. His name means "Son of a hero." "Son of Hell," would have been more appropriate.

Herodias—She was the adulteress, a passionate and lustful woman—a cruel-hearted she-devil, if ever there was one.

Salome—The beautiful yet debased, immoral daughter of Herodias, and the willing tool of her wicked, conniving mother.

John the Baptist—The stern, fearless, and faithful witness and messenger who, being in the road of the godless trio, had to be silenced.

Thus we have the mixture in the hellish scene of light and darkness, sensuality and sanctity; the fragrance of heaven, and the foulness of hell. Solomon, who could speak from experience, wrote, "He that ruleth over his own spirit, is better than he that taketh a city" (Prov. 16:22). But Herod could not reign over his lust and thus devoid of victory in the moral realm was, therefore, insensible to and incapable of responding to higher things. This member of the famous—or infamous—Herod family, was Herod Antipas, the son of Herod the Great and Malthace, a Samaritan woman. Thus he had a drop of Jewish blood in his veins. Galilee of the Gentiles was a fitting dominion for a prince who was far from princely. Let us try to trace the steps in his wicked career.

Unlawful Possessions

John the Baptist, troubler of Herod's conscience, told him bluntly that he was living in sin. "It is not lawful for thee to have her" (Mark 6:18; see Lev. 18:16; 20:21). He was, of course, referring to Herodias, his brother Philip's wife, whom Herod had seduced while in Rome. His marriage to this evil woman was doubly incestuous in that her first marriage was with her uncle, and her second marriage with Herod was entered into while her first husband, from whom she was not divorced, was still living. Furthermore, Herod's lawful wife, whom he had banished to her father's home at Petra, was also still living. Thus it was doubly unlawful for him to take Herodias as a wife. What an immoral tangle!

But the Baptist, who came upon the scene in the spirit and power of Elijah, whose New Testament counterpart he was, courageously condemned Herod's unlawful possession. The Old Testament provides a similar combination of characters: King Ahab resembles Herod; Jezebel, Herodias; and Elijah, John the Baptist. In both cases we have the king drawn in opposite directions—a strong-willed temptress on the one hand; a stern, ascetic, godly prophet on the other. The application of all this to our heart is clear. Conscience is our John the Baptist; our corrupt, old nature is our Herodias.

We read in Mark 6:18, "John . . . said," but the original implies "kept on saying." His stern voice constantly rebuked

105

Herod. Conscience, controlled by the Holy Spirit, never ceases to remind us of that which is unlawful in our lives. May we not be guilty of living in ways God's Word condemns! If we are conscious of harboring some dark, hidden thing in our heart or life, let us listen to the divine voice, "It is not lawful for thee to have [it]," and by the power God can impart, abandon it, no matter the cost.

Conflicting Desires

The comparisons and contrasts the Bible provides, form a most profitable line of study for those who love the Word. "Herod feared John." "Salome pleased Herod" (Mark 6:20, 22). There were times when Herod turned his better self to the light. His deep respect for John created a heart that yearned to climb out of the pit of corruption in which he found himself. Observing how just and holy the Baptist was, Herod feared him, heard him gladly, and was exceedingly sorry when he had to kill him. What a stricken conscience Herod must have had when he looked on the blood-spattered head of John!

But although one hour he feared John, the next he was half-drunk, and, pleased with the licentious dancing of a half-clad young woman, with passions aroused he promised her anything she cared to ask for. Thus, within the king were contradictory voices, and the evil voice prevailed. A John the Baptist and a Herod coexist within each of us. The angel and beast, antagonists as they are, strive for the mastery of the soul. The angel, or the new nature, longs to triumph over the beast, the old nature, delights to hear the truth, and determines to live victoriously; but Salome appears, and the lusts of the flesh sometimes win the day. When we would do good, evil is present with us, yet the evil cannot prevail if Christ occupies the throne of the heart.

Easy Persuasion

The record of Herod reveals how the appeal of lust gains a victory over conscience and God, for in one act he appears to have quenched the light shining in his soul. "He laid hold upon John and bound him in prison for Herodias' sake" (Mark 6:17). An inner voice told Herod to preserve the holy prophet but he was easily persuaded to yield to the demand of the temptress as she called for the blood of John. How useless it was to admire John, yet keep Herodias! He was confronted with purity and passion, and the latter triumphed. Too often we imprison the noblest and best for the sake of Herodias, or for unlawful desires and worldly company. There are more siren voices saying, "Come and sin" than there are prophets thundering out the warning, "It is not lawful to have the pleasures of sin."

The weak will of Herod was cleft in twain. There were the stern warnings of the prophet in the dungeon, and the foul kisses of a she-devil at his side. It was hard for the king to have the courage of his convictions and pack up Herodias and send her back to her lawful husband. If only he had manifested such a noble trait, what a different portrait his could have been. But no, Herod allowed the clamorous voice of a lustful woman to silence the voice of God through John. We read that the loud voices crying out for the blood of Jesus prevailed over the appeal of Pilate as to His innocence (Luke 23:23).

May we always be firm enough to dismiss Herodias and retain John, and never guilty of sacrificing John for Herodias's sake! What folly it is to be a slave, yielding to sin, because of someone else! It may be that Herod thought that the delight he manifested in hearing John would atone, in some measure, for his refusal to part with the woman he had no right to. There are those who respect the truth, love to hear it preached, but who yet condone sin. Being unwilling to part with the unlawful only aggravates their guilt. Failing to re-

107

member that their eternal welfare is at stake, they do not act courageously and independently in the hour of challenge.

Surrendered Possessions

Herod was guilty of the folly that he could have the best of both worlds: "He heard John gladly"—"the daughter of Herodias pleased him." But ere long John had to die, for it is impossible to have both—one destroys the other. If Christ and conscience are refused, then something must fill the void. Does this not remind us of the principle Christ laid down that "no man can serve two masters"?

What a thoughtless, foolish vow Herod made when he was half-drunk and roused to passion by the dancing of a low, debased princess in her seductive garment—"Whatsoever thou shalt ask of me, I will give it thee, unto half of my kingdom!" (Mark 6:23). Herod is called a *tetrarch,* meaning that he was a prince or ruler of "a fourth part," yet he was unable to rule his passions but heedlessly offered to sacrifice one-half of the one-fourth of a kingdom he governed. Perhaps he thought the temptress would ask for a gold bracelet, or costly jewels. Alas! he was forced to shed the blood of the man whose godly conversation he was glad to listen to (see Esther 5:6). Any swine's trough is good enough if a man turns from the rivers of salvation.

The tipsy monarch made a rash promise, a wild oath. He was willing to reward sin with his valued possessions. When men turn their back on Christ, sin makes a full claim, even to half of the kingdom. They were meant to rule, but their surrender to fascinating sins resulted in their losing their sovereignty and becoming slaves. The Monarch of Love can enable them to be more than conquerors over the Salomes who would captivate their heart and deafen their ears to His voice.

It would seem as if Salome was the only female in a stag-party hell-bent on drink and lust, for we read that "she went forth [from Herod's birthday orgy] and said unto her mother, what shall I ask?" (Mark 6:24). Does this not suggest a reckless disregard of all maiden honor and purity? There are bewitching forces at work around us, and we have to beware because sin, when it is finished, brings forth death. There is a legend to the effect that sometime after Salome received the head of John on a platter, that one day she fell on the ice, and in falling her head was severed from her body. Whether saints or sinners, we reap what we sow. Sin spells retribution. "Chickens," we say, "come home to roost." If men yield to their baser instincts and persist in serving sin, the time will come when it claims not a half, but the whole of their kingdom, or a soul eternally lost.

Useless Penitence

The heartless murder of John brought the drunken king to his senses, and he was sorrowful over such a foul deed. His tears, however, were unavailing, for conscience had lost the power to struggle for the liberation of the angel being crucified in his heart. "The king was exceeding [intensely] sorry" (Mark 6:26). The forces around and within fastened upon him, and he became too weak and powerless to save John's noble head, and that in spite of his tears. But as in the case of Judas, Herod's sorrow came too late. He had rejected John for the sake of a spiteful woman and for his oath made to her unbecoming daughter who asked for such a bloody gift.

The question arises, "Should Herod have kept his oath, once he heard what was demanded?" Our duty to fulfill an oath depends on the character of the oath we have made. No oath or bond is legitimate if it is unlawful. Shakespeare has the line, "Unheedful vows may heedfully be broken," and promises that should not have been made, should not be kept. Oaths, promises, bonds against your highest welfare and against God should be repented of, not fulfilled. All contracts with sin and the devil should be immediately broken. If they are not, conscience will be murdered.

109

Eternal Pangs

Mark goes on to recount that after the slaughter of John the Baptist, Jesus entered His public ministry and that His fame spread, reaching the palace and startling Herod so much as to make him confess, "It is John whom I have beheaded . . . he is risen" (Mark 6:16). The Greek is emphatic here implying, "I, I alone beheaded." Herod feels that he alone, and not Herodias or her daughter, was responsible for John's cruel death. It was *his* sin and he must face its consequences. A sinner can never blame another if his soul is lost. Although it was not a risen John Herod heard about, the deeds of those who die in their sin will rise again to condemn them.

What anguish there must have been in the voice of Herod when he said, mournfully, "It is John!" It calls to mind what the lost soul in hell heard, "Son, remember." Yet although Herod heard of the fame of Jesus, His message awakened no response in his dead heart. The day came when he actually faced Jesus and, acting in a childish way, treated Him as a conjurer; but Jesus kept silent. Lust, frivolity, and neglect had killed in Herod the desire for a better life. This called forth the silence of Christ. He uttered not a syllable before this incestuous adulterer and murderer of His remarkable forerunner.

The tradition is that Herod was afterwards stripped of his power, exiled from palace and kingdom to die in great misery in his banishment. If a man finally rejects Christ there comes eternal banishment for "nought that defileth can enter heaven." It is said that when Herodias received the severed head of John, that his dead tongue was moving as if speaking in rebuke and that she stilled it. But here that holy tongue seems to speak again to Herod's frozen heart—"It is John!" By procrastination and neglect men may stifle conscience and ignore the voice that pleads with them to repent, but the day is coming when it will be too late to respond. Their only hope is to flee to Jesus, even Him whom Herod saw but refused, and to bury themselves in His blood which can cleanse them from all sin.

9

Barnabas
The Christian Socialist Who Gave All to Christ

As we are discovering, there is no aspect of Bible meditation so adaptable to our personal lives as that of the biographies of its saints and heroes. How rich and abundant the
Scriptures are in their presentation of the character and service of so many of those whose hearts God touched! The Bible
is like one vast grand picture gallery with fascinating portraits
painted by the divine artist. Among those associated with the
Christian church in its infancy, no figure is so compelling and
charming as Barnabas, a Christian socialist who lived his
creed.

Think of his name

Originally it was "Joseph"—"Joses who by the apostles
was surnamed Barnabas" (Acts 4:36). His new name was a
mirror of his nature, for he was a man having a generous
heart and a warm spirit. His name has a twofold implication—

Son of consolation

The word used here is the same John uses of the Holy
Spirit when he speaks of Him as "Paraclete" or "Comforter."
Barnabas was an earthly reflection of the heavenly consoler.
What a need there is today for sons and daughters of consola-
tion!

Son of exhortation

The margin has "Son of Prophecy" or "Son of Counsel." All of these names fit Barnabas. Such a significance implies that he had received the special gift of persuasive utterance from the Holy Spirit. Later on we find him exhorting and rousing, encouraging and counseling the young converts (Acts 11:23). He belonged to the Society of Encouragers Isaiah mentions (41:7).

Think of His Lineage

Barnabas was a Levite and, belonging to the separated tribe, he had a slight connection with temple ministry (4:36). His conversion to the Christian faith proves how rapid and radical its spread was and how the New Evangel broke up the old system of Judaism. Barnabas was one of the priests who became obedient to the faith, and left the circumscribed service of the temple for the larger ministry of the gospel.

Think of His Home

He belonged to "the country of Cyprus," or as the Revised Version puts it, "A man of Cyprus by race." Cyprus was an island off the cost of Cilicia, and Barnabas was, therefore, a Hellenistic Jew. Very many were gathered into the church from this area.

Think of His Personality

What he looked like can be gathered from what the native of Lystra said of him—"They called Barnabas Jupiter" (14:12). This infers that he was a man who had a remarkable physique, seeing he was associated with a heathen deity who was supposed to have possessed remarkable powers. To those of Lystra there was no god like Jupiter before whose overwhelming grandeur and unsufferable awfulness other deities paled. So we can think of Barnabas as a strong, imposing, large man with a correspondingly large heart. Pertinent facts of his entrancing life can be gathered around the following features—

A Man with a Definite Spiritual Experience

All who would achieve great things for God must begin where Barnabas did, namely with an unreserved surrender to the claims of Christ. The impartation of a new life principle is always the starting point of the divine potter as He sets about the shaping of a character. If tradition can be trusted, Barnabas was one of the Seventy called and sent out by Christ to evangelize (Luke 10:1). Drawn to the Master by His life, works, and teaching, Barnabas became His avowed disciple.

Converted, Barnabas became fully consecrated, for he sacrificed not only his person but his possessions. But what, exactly, is behind the statement that "having land, he sold it, and brought the money, and laid it at the apostles' feet" (4:37)? Under the ancient Mosaic Law, a Levite was forbidden to own land, but Barnabas did, and as the result of his deep spiritual experience, he surrendered it. There is, however, a deeper significance connected with that sale of land and the donation of the price received to the apostolic treasury.

In the upper room, while prayerfully awaiting Pentecost, a sacred bond was forged between the disciples, a bond manifested in their being with one accord in one place, and in all of them being filled with the Holy Spirit. When they later formed into the church they had all things common—their possessions and goods were sold, and the money was deposited in a common fund for the relief of poorer brethren. This first burst of Christian generosity in the church was the first practice of Christian communism or socialism, in which each was for all, and all for each. Ellicott's *Commentary on the Whole Bible* says—

114

The description stands parallel with that of chap. 2:42-47, as though the historian delighted to dwell on the continuance, as long as it lasted, of that ideal of a common life of equality and fraternity after which philosophers had yearned, in which the rights of property, though not abolished, were, by the spontaneous action of its owners, made subservient to the law of love, and benevolence was full and free, without the "nicely calculated less or more" of a later and less happy time. The very form of expression implies that the community of goods was not compulsory. The goods still belonged to men, but they did not speak of them as their own. They had learned, as from our Lord's teaching, to think of themselves, not as possessors, but as stewards (Luke 16:10-14).

Barnabas placed all his sale money at the disposal of the communal fund. Ananias and Sapphira professed to have done the same, but they lied in that they secretly retained part of the price paid for what they sold. As the result of Pentecost there was the willing surrender of goods and money. When God gets a man, He gets his money. But the outburst of generosity the apostles experienced came from redeemed men and women filled with the Holy Spirit. Godless, hard, inhuman men such as present-day Communism produces can never reach the ideal displayed by the Early Church in distribution according to need. Barnabas and the rest practiced the purest form of socialism. Among other notable features of this admirable man, the following can be noted—

1. He was an apostle. "The apostles, Barnabas and Paul" (Acts 14:14)

This means that Barnabas was a member of the inner circle of those early believers. As an apostle had to be one called by

Christ, a witness of His resurrection, and endued by the Spirit with special gifts for ministry in the church, Barnabas qualified for inclusion within the apostolate.

2. He was a good man (Acts 11:24)

He must have been a man of deep spirituality to have earned the title Luke gives him. Dean Farrar wrote of "the dignity and sweetness of the character of Barnabas." As *good* is a contraction of *God,* the apostle was a Godlike man. We have differing conceptions of what a "good man" is. If one is just, conscientious, having a rigorous morality, we say how good he is. But a lot passes for goodness which is actually self-made and is all outward, not inward. Such superficial goodness is mere camouflage. Sometimes it is a deceptive covering for sin. But the goodness of Barnabas was the fruit of the "Good Spirit," and was the evidence of a man made gentle by the gentleness of Christ. Its source was a redeemed heart.

3. He was full of the Holy Spirit (Acts 11:24)

Nehemiah uses the phrase, "Thou gavest also thy good Spirit." It was from Him also that the goodness of Barnabas flowed. The word *full* here implies "an habitual condition." He was drenched with the Spirit's fullness, God-possessed, swallowed up of the divine. Is this description true of us? We were born anew by the Spirit, but are we full of Him? Too often, we are more full of self than the Spirit and thus fail to bear His fruit. No fullness—no goodness! It is the Pentecost birthright of every believer to live a life full of the Spirit. Are *you* claiming the birthright?

4. He was full of faith (11:24)

Faith has been called "a vision and an adventure." As with

116

Barnabas so both can be ours. This Son of Consolation had no doubt as to God's ability to do everything, or of the efficaciousness of the finished work of the cross, or of the Spirit's power. In his service for the Master, such habitual faith was rewarded.

5. *He was used to add many unto the Lord (11:24)*

Barnabas was not a go-getter for members of a church. Rather he was one greatly used to bring large numbers into saving contact with Christ. The secret of his effective soul-winning was a life full of the Spirit. It is not possible for one fully possessed by the Spirit to be fruitless or barren in service. Additions to the Lord, and even to church membership, are few today. What spiritual dearth we are experiencing! But a mighty spiritual upheaval in pulpit and pew alike would soon alter things.

A Man Who Believed in Encouragement

As his name suggests, Barnabas was a son of consolation, or exhortation, or encouragement. The tendency of modern life is to make us hard and indifferent to the need of others. Our frustrated society needs more sons and daughters of encouragement. Barnabas excelled in giving people fresh heart.

He encouraged Paul

After his remarkable conversion on that Damascus road, Saul of Tarsus, who became Paul the Apostle, desired to join the company of the disciples. But because of his previous persistent persecution of the saints, many in the church had doubts about the reality of the change in the persecutor's life. Barnabas, however, felt differently about the young convert, for he realized that he had gifts and graces the Lord would use. So although "the disciples believed not that Saul

117

was a disciple . . . Barnabas took him, and brought him to the apostles" (Acts 9:26-29). Many a young believer loses heart because of the lamentable lack of encouragement they ought to receive from those more mature in the faith.

It is affirmed by some writers that Barnabas was a fellow-pupil of Saul's in the school of Gamaliel. If this is so, then he knew his old fellow scholar well, and when he heard of his conversion he took it at its face value. How rewarded Barnabas was for his faith in Saul, and for his strong recommendation of him to the apostles! One wonders what would have happened to the one-time adversary of the church, if Barnabas had not consoled and encouraged him when others rejected him? There comes a moment in the experience of a young convert when he is either blessed or blighted by the action of elder brethren. We should never doubt the reality of change in one professing Christ but foster them all we can and encourage them to follow on to know the Lord in a fuller, richer way.

He encouraged converts

As a Hebrew Christian, Barnabas accepted the divine plan to make Jew and Gentile one in Christ. Through believers from Cyprus and Cyrene a great revival swept through Antioch, and a great number believed and turned to the Lord. The Church Council at Jerusalem heard of this unofficial religious upsurge, and sent Barnabas to inquire about it and to bring back the facts of the case. Being a man of Cyprus, he was the best man to send, seeing he would likely be known to these revivalists from his native city (Acts 11:19-26), and here is what he found on his arrival at the revival scene:

What He Saw—"The grace of God"

There was no church system or organization in the area. The Spirit of God is not confined to religious bodies and systems. Wherever the grace of God reigns there the true church can be found. Barnabas *saw* the grace of God in the mighty ingathering of transformed lives. Salvation is all of grace.

How He Felt—"Was glad"

Nothing can gladden the saints like a marvelous movement of the Spirit among saved and unsaved alike. The cry of the psalmist was, "Wilt thou not revive us again, that thy people may *rejoice* in thee?" (85:6). Barnabas had no criticism to offer for what he had witnessed. His heart was filled with unbounded joy. He poured no cold water upon the lively enthusiasm of those young converts. He was a true encourager of the many who had turned unto the Lord.

What He Did—"Exhorted them all, that with purpose of heart they would cleave unto the Lord."

Is it any wonder that the disciples were called Christians *first* in Antioch? As the result of the gracious ministry of Barnabas those converts in the city exhibited such Christlikeness that the inhabitants nicknamed them Christians, or Christ's ones. For a whole year Barnabas and Paul taught those new believers and formed them into a vigorous church (11:26). Does not such a stirring experience of revival blessing make us long for a repetition of God's grace and power in this sin-cursed, sex-ridden world of ours? Well might we pray, "O God, send a revival, and let it begin in me!"

A Man Entrusted with Great Service

Conscious that he had been saved to serve, Barnabas was an apostle who was always active for his Saviour. He served, as well as surrendered, to the limit. The great opportunity came when "The Holy Spirit said: Separate me Barnabas and

Saul for the work whereunto I have called them" (Acts 13:2). Reviewing the witness of Barnabas we note these features—

He was genuinely unselfish

This is always the mark of those who accomplish great things for God. They are not puffed up by their own importance. Although older in the faith than Saul, now Paul, Barnabas yet had grace to realize that his companion was meant to occupy a remarkable sphere of service. Knowing that Paul was a far abler teacher than himself, Barnabas sought him out to assist in the spiritual instruction of the converts at Antioch (Acts 11:25).

He was set apart by the Holy Spirit

Called to missionary work by the Spirit, Barnabas went everywhere preaching and teaching the Word. Separation unto service came as the result of having received the Holy Spirit. Many are trying to serve God in the church today who have never experienced His saving grace and power; consequently they are minus the indwelling Spirit to inspire them for service. Churches may *call* pastors, but only God the Spirit can *separate* those He desires to use. What folly it is for a man to choose the ministry as a profession, just as another may decide to be a lawyer! They are not called of God. The Spirit had separated Barnabas and he started at home. Sailing to Cyprus, he began there and was signally blessed. If we fail to witness for Christ at our Cyprus, we'll not be of much use to Him anywhere else.

He suffered for the cause of Christ

Along with vast numbers of the early saints, Barnabas found that true service and suffering are combined. It was from Antioch, the city in which he had had so many spiritual triumphs, that, along with Paul, he was expelled, forcing the two apostles to shake off the dust of their feet against those who rejected them. But even persecution could not crush their enthusiasm. "Filled with joy, and with the Holy Spirit," they went on to Iconium (Acts 13:50-52).

Evangelistic work in Iconium, however, was mixed with trials and tribulations, for Paul was cruelly stoned and left as dead at Lystra. When he revived he left the city with his companion and traveled on to serve and suffer still more. The church could speak of their "beloved Barnabas and Paul, men that have hazarded their lives for the name of the Lord Jesus Christ" (Acts 15:25-26). After Pentecost, Barnabas gave over his land, and then became willing to give over, or abandon, his life. Legend has it that he suffered martyrdom in his own country of Cyprus for Christ's sake.

A Man Who Brought a Successful Life to a Sad End

How saddened we are to find that our last glimpses of this most captivating man reveal him as being party to a most unfortunate quarrel over a relative! It is true, of course, that all great men make mistakes. Abraham Lincoln is credited with having said, "He who never makes a mistake, never makes anything." But sometimes mistakes can be very disastrous to God's work and to God's servants. The Bible never glosses over the faults of saints. It presents only one perfect, flawless life, namely the One "separate from sinners." Barnabas became faulty in two directions—

His amiability degenerated into weakness

It must have been with sadness of heart that Paul had to write of his one-time close associate in missionary labors, "Barnabas also was carried away [or "was too accommodating"] with their dissimulation" (Gal. 2:13). The narrative is taken up with Paul's censure at Antioch (Acts 15:37-39; Gal. 2:1-9). Peter, although a converted Jew, had no desire to carry out the distinctions enforced by the Jerusalem church between Jewish and Gentile converts to Christianity. When some of the Judaizing brethren approached Peter about this subject he swung round, and would not eat with the Gentiles. Barnabas, although he believed with Paul that there was no difference between Jew and Gentiles in Christ, was also swayed by the Jewish brethren and joined with Peter in his separation from the Gentile believers.

Paul, close companion of Barnabas as he was, condemned him for his lack of straightforwardness and firmness. The Son of Exhortation had had strong convictions about the abandonment of old laws for the new faith, yet now he turned against those convictions and earned, thereby, the apostle's condemnation. Too often principles are surrendered for the sake of obtaining favor. Paul never veered from his Spirit-inspired convictions. He kept every part of the faith.

His partiality for a relative

One of the saddest episodes in The Acts, is the painful and final parting of Paul and Barnabas. The latter wanted his own way, and the former thought it to be the wrong one. The sad severance of these two valiant warriors came as they faced their second missionary journey together. Barnabas wanted his nephew, John Mark, to accompany them, but Paul thought he was not suitable for the arduous task. The contention was sharp. A lot of unworthy words were exchanged. "Blood is thicker than water," and Barnabas held to his choice of his sister's son (Col. 4:10). This young missionary had left Paul and Barnabas during the first missionary tour, and had gone to Cyprus where he was known, and where there was less hardship and easier service. Lacking the daring spirit to evangelize strange lands, John Mark left his uncle, and Paul, both of whom were willing to throw away their lives for Christ's sake (Acts 13:13).

Paul was strong in his belief that Mark was not the man for this further sacrificial task. He evidently had the backing of the church (Acts 15:40-41). Barnabas, over generous, wanted Paul to overlook his faults, and try the young man again. But Paul was resolute in his refusal, feeling that Mark's absence from the party would assure greater success. Who was wrong? Perhaps there were faults on both sides, Barnabas being too soft and eager to urge the claims of his nephew, and Paul a little too hard and resentful. Throughout the Church Age there has been a repetition of the same regrettable separation of bosom friends over personal as well as doctrinal matters.

The first separation of Barnabas and Paul was when they were separated together by the Holy Spirit. How tragically different it was when they separated from each other, and went their separate ways! When the Canaanite and the Perizzite are in the land, let not Abraham and Lot disagree and part. It is both strange and significant that after his severance from Paul, Barnabas never appears in New Testament history again. The reference in I Corinthians 9:6 relates to their united apostleship before the tragic break came. He retired to Cyprus where he started to serve the Lord. Through one mistake he passes out of Scripture, and likely ended a life of great usefulness. Such a blessed yet broken fellowship serves as a beacon light to all who labor for the Master. There are signs that young Mark retrieved his position and afterwards became warmly attached to the apostle Paul (Col. 4:10). "Take Mark, and bring him with thee: for he is profitable to me for the ministry" (II Tim. 4:11; Philem. 24). Nothing would have pleased Paul more than that he could have written the same about the return of Barnabas as a companion in travel and tribulation. Knowing of Mark's return to Paul, as must have been the case because of the family relationship, Barnabas must have seen how the rigid discipline of his one-time companion had been beneficial to the work.

10

Timothy
The Evangelist Who Was Subject to Stomach Trouble

In our glimpse of the portrait of David and Jonathan we have already seen how two men were drawn together and made as "one soul." A deep, mutual affection resulted in an affinity of minds uncommon among males. It is most rare for the one to confess of his bosom friend, "Thy love to me was wonderful, passing the love of women." Until Jonathan's death, David and he were all in all to each other. Coming to the New Testament, Paul, the aged missionary and teacher, and Timothy, the young and ardent evangelist, provide us with a further illustration of how two men can be drawn together and "lock'd up in steel." In *Hamlet,* Shakespeare advises—

> The friends thou hast, and their adoption tried,
> Grapple them to thy soul with hoops of steel.

As we are to see, hoops of mutual love for Christ and for each other bound Paul and Timothy together in an indissoluble bond, with the one becoming increasingly dependent upon the other. Such a fellowship of kindred hearts is like to that in heaven. As a good deal of sentiment attaches to the last message of one we greatly revere, Second Timothy, the last letter Paul wrote before his martyrdom, must have been specially sacred to the heart of his much loved young companion. How Timothy must have treasured that warm final letter, coming as it did from a warm heart housed in a cold, damp dungeon.

For a full portrait of Timothy, we must string together all that the apostle recorded of the life and labors of his spiritual son, who was many years the junior of the two.

Timothy Was the Child of a Godly Heritage (II Tim. 1:5; 3:15)

He was the son of a Christian Jewess named Eunice, and the grandson of Lois. His unnamed father was a Greek and a non-Christian (Acts 16:1-3). It is said of his mother that she "believed"; but nothing is said of his father's faith. It may be that both were unbelievers when they married but that Eunice, along with her mother, came to embrace the Christian faith during Paul's first missionary tour to Lystra where the family lived and where Timothy was born.

It would seem as if the father had died when Timothy was quite young, seeing that his upbringing appears to have been in the hands of his mother and grandmother. The reference to the faith of these two godly women, and to the Scriptures in the home indicates the spiritual atmosphere in which the growing boy was lovingly nurtured (II Tim. 1:5; 3:15). Lystra was not far from Tarsus, Paul's birthplace, hence his intimacy with the family, and his knowledge of the faith of his kinsfolk, and his unbroken and devoted friendship for the son of the home, his dearest and best-loved partner in the Master's service. In the opening of his Second Letter to Timothy, Paul urges the young soldier never to forget those home influences responsible for the molding of his youth. Two precious phrases can be linked in this advice, "my prayers" and "thy tears" (1:3-4). Paul was unceasing in his intercession for his son in the faith, and Timothy's "tears" were shed over his friend's departure. This was the last sight Paul had had of him—*weeping*.

The Lycaonians among whom Timothy spent his childhood were heathen worshipers of Jupiter whose temple stood in the city. It was in this wild region, where Paul first worshiped and later was almost stoned to death, that the seeds of Timothy's education for his great future commenced. Aristotle spoke of the populace as "the inconstant Lycaonians." Yet Paul was to find a convert among them whose constancy he could lean upon. Even in those last days when forsaken by all those in Timothy's region (II Tim. 4:16), with no man standing by him at his trial, he could send for his young fellow-laborer knowing that if at all possible he would hasten to his side and be with him when he was taken out to die.

Timothy Was a Faithful Student of the Word (II Tim. 3:15)

From very early childhood he had been familiar with the sacred, saving Scriptures. The Revised Version has "babe" for *child* (II Tim. 3:15). The word Paul uses for "known" means more than a memory of Scripture which Timothy was taught to read and receive. It signifies to completely understand, or to have an inward perception as to the significance of Scripture. His early training in the Word was received from his mother and grandmother, and Paul urged his Bible-loving friend to continue in the things he had learned and had been assured of. Timothy *learned* the Scriptures from the lips of the two godly women in the home, and was *assured* of its reality and power by watching its effect in their lives. Thus lip and life gave the lad a love for Scripture, and his was an undying gratitude for the godly influence of his home. Too few parents these days make the Bible the child's book of letters.

How often from remotest quarters, from simplest homes, from lowliest parentage, God replenishes the exhausted treasuries of His church! How often a mother's unfeigned faith gives a David Livingstone or a Mary Slessor to the cause of Christ! The responsibilities of those who have known the Scriptures from earliest days are greater than those who have

126

been bereft of such a privilege. It is an inestimable boon to learn the Word from godly parents. To come to know Christ and His Word in later life and through other channels than those Timothy enjoyed is to start the Christian race somewhat handicapped, especially if the home background was positively unchristian. And yet a handicap can win the race!

Timothy Was Paul's Child in the Faith

Timothy was only a boy when the two preachers, Paul and Barnabas, came to town. He was greatly attracted to Paul and deeply impressed by his evangelical preaching, his stoning, and the miracles performed by the courageous evangelist (Acts 14:6-7; II Tim. 3:10-11). When Paul returned to Lystra, Timothy had developed into a fine young Christian, being a disciple well reported of by the brethren, and the apostle, observing his spiritual growth and worth, took him on his missionary tour, possibly filling the place of young John Mark who had proved a disappointment to Paul.

Although brought up in a Christian home, and familiar with Scripture from early childhood, there had not been a personal commitment to Christ by Timothy, and on Paul's visit to the community where he lived, the apostle led him to Christ. Thereafter he referred to him as "my dearly beloved son" (II Tim. 1:2); "my own son in the faith" (I Tim. 1:2); "as a son with the father he hath served with me in the gospel" (Phil. 2:22). It was from Paul that Timothy learned the first rudiments of faith in Christ, and he went on to receive from the gifted apostle his theological equipment as a Christian minister. What a tender relationship developed between Paul and Timothy.

In his most valuable commentary on The Acts, Dr. G. Campbell Morgan has this suggestive description of young Timothy's conversion to Christ—

> At last Paul came to Lystra, the place of stones,
> the scars of which were still on his body; the mem-

ories of the day when they beat fast and furiously upon him were still with him. At Lystra they found Timothy. How often God's servants return, after years of absence to some rough and rugged place of battle and of blood and of agony, only to find the fruitage.

When did Timothy become a disciple? The question cannot be answered dogmatically, but the probability is that he became a disciple in those days of Paul's previous visit. Paul had once been a young man, and had watched the stoning of a saint called Stephen, minding the clothes of such as stoned him. He had heard the dying prayer, and the vision of the face of Stephen had fastened like goads in his heart and life. At Lystra he had gone through Stephen's experience, and, perchance another man had seen the stones hurled. Now he went back to find Timothy in the place of stones, and from that moment that rare and beautiful friendship, the friendship of an old man for a young man.

The idea has been expressed that when Paul recovered consciousness after being mobbed and stoned, that on his reentry into the town it was in Timothy's home that he found shelter. If this is true, then we can imagine how easily young Timothy would be impressed with the reality of Christ when His servant Paul was willing to be battered and beaten for His sake. Timothy would be a lad somewhere about fifteen or sixteen years of age when, around A.D. 45, he came to know the Lord. As we have indicated, on his second visit to Lystra Paul adopted the earnest young believer as his missionary assistant. He circumcised Timothy out of deference to the Jews so that his usefulness might not be prejudiced by his semi-Greek extraction. Probably he was not circumcised in infancy owing to the objection of his heathen father.

Through Paul's act, it was possible for Timothy to obtain free admission to the synagogue.

Timothy Was Ordained a Minister of the Gospel

Paul refers to his son in the faith as "a minister of God" (I Thess. 3:2), and as "a good minister of Christ" (I Tim. 4:6). Having been led to Christ by Paul, it was quite natural that Timothy should be ordained as his spiritual father's fellow worker. The putting on of Paul's hands did not impart special gifts to be used in Christ's service; rather it was the recognition of qualifications already received. Timothy's entrance into the ministry stands out clearly. There was the laying on of the hands of the presbytery and of Paul's own hands (I Tim. 4:16; II Tim. 1:6). This indicated that Timothy had received the gift of God—the sealing with the Holy Spirit as the Spirit of power, of love, and of discipline (II Tim. 1:6). Admitted thus to a charge, a trust, Timothy could never surrender it in afterlife without being unfaithful. His call was to a sacred task, lifelong without reservation, arduous, devoted, even perilous; and, true to his name (for *Timothy* means "honor God"), he lived and labored for the honor and glory of his Lord until he finished his course.

Both of the Letters Paul sent to Timothy are loaded with practical exhortations as to how the young minister could make full proof of his ministry. Paul desired for him that he might have from God "grace, mercy, and peace," and he would need them all in the times of persecution ahead: *Grace,* for every service; *mercy,* for every failure; *peace,* for every circumstance. "Teachers," said Chrysostom, "stand more in need of mercy than others." Because Timothy was called to an office which carried high spiritual possibility and responsibility he was, on that very account, more liable to fall short of its ideals, hence the need for mercy.

Ordained thus for the particular work for which he was called, Timothy thereafter enjoyed the intimate companionship of the apostle. He left a loving mother and a pleasant home in which he had every comfort, to share Paul's sacrificial labors. Thus his entrance into a life of service became at once a life of true human fellowship, and from the moment of his ordination, "as a son with his father," he served Paul in the furtherance of the gospel. They became one in their journeyings, in their perils, and in their triumphs for Christ (Phil. 2:22). Such close fellowship of mutual trust and love between these two devoted souls was never severed. In times of separation between them Paul yearned for the presence of his child in the faith. "Do thy diligence to come quickly unto me." As a traveling companion he was indispensable to Paul (Acts 17:14-15; 18:5; 19:22; 20:4; etc.). Ever and anon he hastened to gladden the heart of the apostle in seasons of distress, solitude, and conflict. He was the one man nearest of all to the heart of Paul.

Timothy Was Subject to Physical Infirmities

Paul's advice to his young companion could be practical as well as spiritual. This is evidenced by the fact that Paul urged him "to take a little wine for thy stomach's sake, and thine oft infirmities" (I Tim. 5:23). What a human touch this was! How solicitous Paul was for Timothy's bodily health as well as for his spiritual welfare. It would seem as if Timothy was not constitutionally strong. Phillips translates the parenthetical passage to read— "By the way, I should advise you to drink wine in moderation, instead of water. It will do your stomach good and help you to get over your frequent spells of illness."

That Timothy was in the habit of abstaining wholly from the use of wine is seen in the injunction of Paul, "Drink not water *only,*" but for medicinal purposes mix a little wine with water. Paul favored the general habit of abstaining from strong drink and only asked Timothy to depart in some small degree from total abstinence in order to restore and preserve

130

his health. Too often this verse is taken to condone the use of wine by those who do not have Timothy's stomach troubles. Barnes' *Notes* give us a most satisfactory explanation of the apostolic advice—

> Paul was giving counsels in regard to an office which required a great amount of labour, care, and anxiety. The labours enjoined were such as to demand all the time; the care and anxiety incident to such a charge would be very likely to prostrate the frame, and to injure the health. Then he remembered that Timothy was yet but a youth; he recalled his feebleness of constitution and his frequent attacks of illness; he recollected the very abstemious habits which he had prescribed for himself; and, in this connection, he urges him to a careful regard for his health, and prescribes the use of a small quantity of wine, mingled with water, as a suitable medicine in his case. Thus considered, this direction is as worthy to be given by an inspired teacher, as it is to counsel a man to pay a proper regard to his health, and not needlessly throw away his life.

Timothy Did the Work of an Evangelist (II Tim. 4:5)

In his "swan song," as Paul's Second Letter to Timothy is called seeing it was the last Epistle to leave his mighty pen, the personal element is strongly marked, and thus contains the veteran preacher's final counsel to a much younger fellow laborer. In no Epistle does the true, loving, undaunted, and trustful heart of the great apostle speak in more consolatory and yet more moving accents. It is loving but strong and bracing, having the object of warning Timothy of heresies multiplying around him in the church, and of encouraging the young evangelist to prove himself courageous amid all the trials he would encounter as a preacher of the good news of salvation.

That Timothy made full proof of his ministry as an evangelist can be gathered from the way he broke up new ground as a pioneer, thereby emulating the example of his spiritual father (Acts 17:14). Enjoying in the highest degree the apostle's confidence and affection, Timothy had the benefit of Paul's constant instruction for his evangelistic labors (II Tim. 2:2; 3:14). At times the youthful evangelist was active on distant missions and at other times he remained behind to instruct and build up converts. Attention is drawn to his service in the crowded seaport of Achaia where a great spiritual awakening was experienced (Rom. 16:21). A glimpse is given of Timothy as an ambassador charged with a delicate and difficult mission to restore a backsliding church—a most responsible task for which gift and grace were required. He also knew how to comfort and establish Christians in the midst of tribulation (I Thess. 3:2). Thus as an evangelist his ministry had a positive and a negative aspect. He was called to win souls for Christ and to establish converts in the faith, building up the church thereby. He was also commissioned to repudiate error wherever he found it by emphasizing revealed truth. Timothy, then, must function as a faithful minister of the word, a protestor against false teachers, a prophet in perilous times, and a sufferer in Christ's cause.

It may be that Timothy did not have the commanding skill or overwhelming eloquence and literary ability of Paul and, therefore, was not fitted for a position of first consequence in the church, that is, if we judge from the repeated and urgent exhortation to courage and vigilance which the apostle sent him. He seems to have been of a gentler and even a somewhat irresolute disposition; yet he had qualities of piety and faithful affection and for full sixteen years he possessed the love, deserved the confidence, shared the labors, and alleviated the sorrows of his aged spiritual father. Bishop Handley Moule says of Timothy—

His face full of thought and feeling and devotion is

rather earnest than strong. But it has the strength of patience, of absolute sincerity, and of rest in Christ. Timothy repays the affection of Paul with unwavering ability. And he will be true to the end, to his Lord and Redeemer, through whatever tears and agonies of sensibility.

This, then, is the portrait of the young evangelist whom Paul loved who would be about thirty-seven years of age when his revered yoke-fellow, almost twice his age, laid down his life for the gospel. With the martyrdom of Paul, the curtain falls, and we have no further information about Timothy. We can be sure that he took up the torch and carried it on until death ended his evangelistic labors. Tradition has it that he, too, was martyred in the reign of Domitian or Nerva for his faithfulness as a bishop. While attempting to stop an indecent heathen procession during the Festival of Diana, this God-fearing evangelist sealed his testimony with his blood. He risked and lost his life preserving the "sobriety" he loved to proclaim, and thus became a "co-sufferer" with his spiritual father in the afflictions of the gospel (II Tim. 1:8).

In conclusion, the heart-relationship that existed between Paul and Timothy illustrates the goodness of God in pairing off those who complement each other. David had Jonathan, Elijah had Elisha, with each supplying the other's needs—contrasting characters, yet unified in a bond of mutual affection and allegiance. Thus it was with the veteran apostle and the youthful evangelist we have companied with for awhile. Theirs was a unity in spite of diversity of temperament: Paul was impulsive and enthusiastic; Timothy, reflective and reserved. Thus zeal and constraint were wedded together. Timothy met the intense craving for sympathy so characteristic of Paul's writings. He might have called himself, "The disciple whom Paul loved."

The way in which Timothy's life was wonderfully complementary to that of Paul's is touched on by Dr. A. Gurney, in his study, *The First Epistle to Timothy,* now out of print.

There is the deepest unity in its diversity. It is "not like to like, but like in difference." God needed a Timothy to place side by side with Paul. How weak he appears sometimes against the giant strength of "such a one as Paul the aged." Yet how confessed a source of strength he really was, how necessary, how helpful.

The one, "spiritual father"; the other, "beloved son."

The one, born leader of men, chosen pioneer of a new and untried faith, burning with intensity and zeal for Christ, as once he had breathed out threatenings and slaughter against the servants of the Lord.

The other, naturally wishful to be second, not fully sure of himself, dependent by natural characteristics, "fellow-laborer," not chief.

The one so strong, so fully persuaded, more than conqueror through his mighty faith, sure that, though deserted by men, he is helped by God, convinced that in authority he is "not one whit behind the chiefest of the apostles."

The other, so modest in his use of spiritual authority that he shrinks back from a self-assertion justified by the duties of his position, till he is in danger of being despised (I Cor. 16:10-11; I Tim. 4:12) and needs a stiffening up against too easy acquiescence: "Peace loving man of humble heart and true," the good second, the fervent and constant friend, the man in whom you see the mirror, not of the missionary so much as the pastor and overseer of God.

How perfectly these two contrasted characters are interwoven by a common faith and a common devotion to Christ: how much they each owe the other: how complete they are together—these two strings of one lyre which sounds forth the praise of their Saviour-God. For in undying love to the Crucified, in self-sacrifice to "make Jesus King" over the whole earth, in the unfailing optimism which knows that the Kingdom is sure, because His power and Word are sure, these two hearts and lives are absolutely one.

The Bible saints we have considered knew how to live in "eternity's sunrise," as William Blake expresses it. May ours be a similar endeavor! After cataloging the exploits of the heroes of the past and the martyrs of the then present, the writer to the Hebrews exhorts, "Whose faith follow!" May grace be given us to plant our feet in the footprints of holy men of old and follow them in the pathway of love and loyalty to God!

Part 2

Church History Biographies

Biographical reading and study is both fascinating and faithful, and Church History is replete with the lives and deeds of saints who were true knights who fought under the banner of the Lord they loved. Many of them were men and women of action as well as of vision. It mattered little to them where they pitched their tent as long as they could serve Him to whom they owed so much. Stirring deeds and extraordinary accomplishments embroidered their lives and kindle in our hearts the desire to emulate their faith, their sanctity, their courage. Their imperishable record reminds us that we, too, can "make our lives sublime." Meditating upon the character and magnificent labors of great lives crowding the roll of Church History we are impressed with the fact of Christ as a living and working power in the life of man; and that what He did for and with them He can still accomplish. Robert Browning, in "One Word More" reminds us—

> Other heights in other lives, God willing:
> All the gifts from all the heights, your own, Love!

The biographies we have selected are of men who were outstanding and strategic witnesses for Christ in their own times, and who not only molded the thought and directed the action of the age in which they lived but who today, though dead, still speak.

Shakespeare makes Cassius say at the burial of Caesar—

> The evil that men do lives after them,
> The good is oft interred with their bones.

While this sentiment is true of a great many who live without God, it is not applicable to the vast majority of church saints. Certainly they had their faults and made mistakes, for they were very human. But dominating their lives was the passion to serve God in a needy world and, although hardy adventurers on the sea of life, buffeted and beset by violent storms, they came safely to port with rich cargoes. Their good was not interred with their bones. Their stories still thrill our hearts and create within us a desire to follow them as they followed God.

11

Martin Luther
The Monk Who Shook the World

God had to shake the monk, before he could shake the religious world of his day—and shake him He did! Much can be said in favor of the contention that Martin Luther, German of the Germans, was the greatest spiritual force in the world since the days of the apostle Paul. Thomas Carlyle could say of him, "Luther, too, is one of our spiritual heroes; a prophet to his own country and time." In the dark Middle Ages a reformation was needed to throw off the tyranny of a powerful, ecclesiastical yoke, but the Reformer had to be a product of his own times, with qualities that made him a citizen of the world, and in the wide sense not for an age but for all time. Such a Reformer, as we shall see, was Martin Luther.

That all Christians who value their spiritual liberty should know of the life and labors of Luther is evident from the fact that we owe our enjoyment of gospel privileges to the freedom he gained for the church from Rome's yoke. It pleased God to lead him through a spiritual experience so deep and abiding, that there was awakened in him an intense craving to know the Word of Truth, which resulted in his emancipation from religious bondage. God chose Luther to be the bringer of life to the darkened peoples of Europe, and to blaze a trail of spiritual liberty for all time. But the conflict betwixt the two opposing forces had first to be fought out in his own soul. Paul Lindemann, the prominent Lutheran pastor says of Luther—

> It was the bold challenge of one man, flung out to the embattled forces of a despotic hierarchy, that four hundred years ago sounded the first note of human independence and broke the dread power that through the Dark Ages had kept the minds and the souls of men enthralled. . . . This year [1953] we are celebrating the four hundred and fiftieth anniversary of the man who set the wheels of Reformation progress going.

His Birth and Boyhood

The whole world was shrouded in spiritual darkness when on November 10, 1483, in the small town of Eisleben, Saxony, there was born to Hans and Margaret Luther, their first-born son. Hans was an ordinary poor mine laborer. One day, along with his wife, he went to the Winter Fair at Eisleben, and it was during the tumult of one of the scenes that Frau Luther was taken with pains of travail and sought refuge in a house nearby where she bore her child and called him Martin. Although the parents had very little of this world's goods, they were God-fearing in their way. Thomas Carlyle wrote of the importance of that lowly birth thus—

> In the whole world that day there was not a more entirely unimportant looking pair of people than this miner and his wife. And yet what were all the emperors, popes, and potentates in comparison? There was born, once more, a mighty man whose light was to flame as a beacon over long centuries and epochs of the world, the whole world and its history were waiting for this man.

Then Carlyle goes on to say that Luther's lowly birth leads us back to another birth-hour when One was born in the still meaner environment of a stable, and who was the One Luther was to live and fight for.

Born into a poor home, and brought up poor, this child of poverty "had to beg for bread, as the school-children in those times did, singing for alms and bread from door to door. Hardship, vigorous necessity was the poor boy's companion; no man nor no thing would put on a false face to flatter Martin Luther. A boy of rude figure, yet with weak health, with his large greedy soul full of all faculty and sensibility, he suffered greatly."

Hans gave his child the best education he could. Young Martin had a good intellect and was eager to learn and set himself to study law, but God had other plans for the son of poverty whose name was to become imperishable. It soon became evident that he had great natural advantages, all of which were to be harnessed to the chariot of the Lord. Luther was nineteen years of age when his companion, Alexis, was struck by lightning and fell dead at Luther's feet. Such a sudden blow smote his young heart, and he determined then and there to devote himself to God and to His service only. There developed within him a hunger for God and he cried out with Job, "Oh, that I knew where I might find him!"

His Spiritual Experiences

In spite of his father's adverse wishes, Martin entered an Augustine convent at Erfurt to train as a monk. Although, to his parents, this seemed the wrong step for their son to take, yet we can count it the first step in his spiritual development. To quote Carlyle again—

> This was probably the first light-joint of the history of Luther, his purer will now first decisively uttering itself; but, for the moment it was still as one light-

141

joint in an element of darkness. He says he was a pious monk: faithfully, painfully struggling to work out the truth of this high act of his: but it was to little purpose. His misery had not lessened: had rather, as it were, increased into infinitude.

Religious drudgeries, penances and prayers, could not relieve the burden of his soul. He lived in misery, but yet traveled far in his religious order, becoming a Professor of Philosophy at Wittenburg University and likewise its preacher. Strange to say, however, it was here that deliverance from darkness and despair and a burdensome life of fasts, prayers, and masses first came. At the time the young monk was twenty-four years old, but he had never seen a Bible. The Word of God was precious in those days of no open vision. One day in the convent library his eyes lighted upon an old copy of the Bible chained to the wall and, poring over Paul's letter to the Romans, he read, "The just shall live by faith," and a new world opened to this searcher for truth. He came to love the Bible and determined to hold by it, as he did to the end. Perhaps the Scriptures have become too common. The world is now flooded with Bibles. If they were as scarce as in Luther's day, we might value them more.

The next event in Luther's pursuit of God came at Bologna. Crossing the Alps on a mission for the Roman Church, he was entertained in a Benedictine convent, and while there fell ill and was forced to remain there some time. Despair and darkness possessed him, and his soul was filled with remorse. The sense of his sinfulness troubled him, and the prospect of judgment filled him with dread. He had no inner peace. But when his terrors reached their highest pitch, the Pauline message he had discovered at Wittenburg forced itself upon him, and his spirit revived. Thus restored and comforted he soon regained his health and he resumed his journey.

Reaching Rome, he felt mastered by the truth repeated thrice in the New Testament—"The just shall live by faith"

(Rom. 1:17; Gal. 3:11; Heb. 10:38; see also Hab. 2:4). This young German monk was twenty-seven years old when, in 1511, he saw Rome for the first time. Little did he know that his search for God would end here, and that his soul would find peace and the true church would find a mighty Reformer. Because of the fierce conflict within, he came to the pope to obtain the indulgences he gave. All pilgrims had to climb the staircase known as *Scala Santa,* made up of twenty-eight marble steps in the Lateran Church, which ranked as the first Roman church in Christendom. The so-called Holy Staircase was said to have been brought from the palace of Pontius Pilate at Jerusalem to Rome in A.D. 326, by Empress Helena, mother of Constantine the Great. It received its name because it was said to be the stair ascended by Jesus when He went up into the judgment hall, and that coming down again, wearing His mock crown, His blood fell and stained the marble slabs.

This was an object of great veneration and for centuries its marble was worn down by the constant pilgrimages of the devout as they kissed the supposed blood-spots of Christ. Martin Luther started to ascend this stair to receive an indulgence for a thousand-year deliverance from the fire of purgatory once he reached the top of the staircase. He was shocked, however, by what he saw in Rome, and as he crawled up those stairs, suddenly, halfway up, he stood on his feet and he heard a voice like thunder, thrilling his soul, saying, "The just shall live by faith." Overwhelmed, Luther said to himself, "This staircase can never be the ladder of salvation." At once he became ashamed that he had become a victim of such a horrid superstition. The miracle happened. The pursuit was ended. He had found God; or should we say, God had found him. Fleeing from Rome, he shook the dust of the city off his feet. He had left Wittenburg believing in justification by works; he returned believing in justification by faith.

Liberated from his religious shackles, Luther became the

father of all true Protestants by protesting against the blasphemous abuses of the system of papal indulgences. When he nailed his Ninety-five Theses on the door of the Castel Church at Wittenburg he little realized that "the blows of his hammer were to sound the death knell of an era of darkness and ring in an age of light." The miracle of what happened to Luther at Rome is testified to by his son, Paul, named after the apostle through whose writings his father found salvation. In a glass case in the Library of Rudolstadt there is a manuscript in the handwriting of Dr. Paul Luther, part of which reads—

In the year 1544 my late dearest father, in the presence of us all, narrated the whole story of his journey to Rome. He acknowledged with great joy that, in that city, through the Spirit of Jesus Christ, he had come to the knowledge of the truth of the everlasting Gospel. It happened in this way. As he repeated his prayers on the Lateran staircase the words of the Prophet Habbakuk came suddenly to his mind—"The just shall live by faith." Thereafter, he ceased his prayers, returned to Wittenburg and took this as the chief foundation of all his doctrine.

His break with Rome and Romish practices was radical. Evidence of his complete renunciation came when he cast over the vow of celibacy and married a nun, Catherine von Bora. He had always longed for domestic happiness and, when no longer young, he took unto himself a wife as a practical testimony to his transformed life. Luther believed in burning his bridges behind him. His became a happy home, rich in love, even though it was simple. Sometimes his humor played with her little failings, but his Kate was inexpressibly dear to him. "Kate," he said to her one day, "you have a good husband who loves you. You are an empress. You are dearer than the kingdom of France and the dukedom of Venice."

Affectionate, Luther was yet strict at home. Once he

would not suffer his son to appear before him because of some misdemeanor. Three days this separation lasted and ended only when the lad wrote an apology and entreated forgiveness. When his wife and others pleaded for leniency, Luther replied, "I would rather have a dead than an unworthy son." Perhaps the death of his little daughter Magdalene was the heaviest sorrow of his life. "My dear little daughter," he said as death parted them, "the spirit is willing but the flesh is weak." Loving music as he did, the home was often filled with song. Luther said of music that it was "the grandest and sweetest gift of God." At Wittenburg, in the university garden, the seat where Luther and his beloved wife would sit and give to the winds their fears with lute and song is pointed out to visitors. "Except theology," he would say, "there is no art which can be placed in comparison with music."

The home garden was a perpetual joy to this courageous man whose devout frame of mind enabled him to see God in flowers, birds, and animals. Like Francis of Assisi, he would talk winsomely to the birds. Speaking of flowers, he said, "If a man could make a single rose, we should give him an empire; yet roses and flowers no less beautiful are scattered in profusion over the world, and no one regards them." One day, watching the cattle in the field, he exclaimed, "There go the preachers, the bearers of milk, of butter, of cheese, and of wool, who daily preach faith in God and tell us to put our trust in Him, as our Father who cares for us and nourishes us." Such was the man who was to turn the religious world upside down and inside out.

His Marvelous Accomplishments

Popular power became Luther's because of his love for humanity. Said Dōllinger of him, "His greatness of soul and his marvelous many-sidedness, made him the man of his time and the man of his people. There were no conflicting impulses in his nature. He was a whole man, 'an absolute man; in him soul and body were not divided', and thus the man through whom Europe was saved from Romish dominion, and the darkness of the Middle Ages scattered. Luther's salvation gave birth to Protestantism." His fight against the papacy was long and bitter, but he faced the conflict and challenge with heaven-given courage, and he emerged triumphant.

A Reformer

Luther's first challenge in the great task of Reformation came in October 1517, when Monk Tetzel falsely accused him of selling indulgences. Antagonism between these two monks deepened as Luther gave the lie to Tetzel's untrue statements by writing so strongly against Romish practices. On December 10, 1520, the then pope issued a bull forbidding Luther to continue in his protestations; but, amid a large crowd of people gathered at the Elster Gate at Wittenburg, he burned the bull. When he went out to meet the pope's legate at Augsburg his fellow citizens who loved him watched him as, in his monk's brown frock, he walked out to the gates. They cried, "Luther forever!" He replied, "Nay, Christ forever! All the wisdom of the world is childish foolishness compared with an acknowledgement of Christ."

At the Diet of Worms on April 17, 1521, came a further test when, before the assembled powers of the Roman Catholic world, he declared, "My conscience is bound by the Word of God. I cannot and will not recant. . . . Were there as many devils in Worms as there are roof-tiles I would go on." Later on he backed up this fearless declaration of independence by the public burning of man-made dicta of the Roman Church. Luther, realizing the importance of his appearance at Worms, spent the previous night in prayer that he might be guided aright. He knew that he would be facing the young Emperor, Charles V, and many German princes, as well as papal authorites, when called upon to recant.

146

Many of his friends advised him with solemn entreaties not to appear before the diet, reminding him of the burning of another Reformer, John Huss; but no one and nothing could move him to desist, and forth he went to meet his foes and as Carlyle says, "The world's pomp and power sits there on this hand; on that, stands up for God's truth, one man, the poor miner Hans Luther's son." When commanded to recant, Luther replied, "Confute me by proofs of Scripture, or else by plain just arguments: I cannot recant otherwise. For it is neither safe nor prudent to do aught against conscience. Here I stand: I can do no other: May God help me, Amen!"

The emperor dismissed the gathering, and deemed Luther a madman, one possessed by devils. Effective measures were taken to check the influence of his growing popularity and protestations. "Luther's appearance at that diet may be considered as the greatest scene in modern European history." In 1526 and 1529 there were two further diets at Speier when Rome tried again to curb this brave and defiant Reformer who was becoming a growing menace to Catholic domination. But at each diet he defied threats and, obeying his God-possessed conscience, he declares, "We are resolved, with the grace of God, to maintain the pure and exclusive preaching of His only Word, such as it is contained in the Biblical books of the Old and New Testaments, without adding anything thereto that may be contrary to it."

Thus, through the extraordinary intensity of his convictions, Luther saw the fires of Reformation spreading. In him there were no extravagances of fanaticism. Determined, he was yet sane. "For the great works of the Protestant Reformation which was to be served with voice and pen, a man of this caliber rather than a scholarly recluse was needed." Referring to the reforming principles of a previous Reformation preacher who never tired of inveighing against the intellectual density of the monks, a current saying had it, "Erasmus laid the egg but Luther hatched it"—and what a brood that hatching produced! All Protestant denominations owe their religious liberty to serve and worship God as His Word dictates to Luther's gallant defense of the saving truths of the gospel. What he taught about justification by faith and of the universal priesthood of all believers might be called the Cornerstone of Protestantism.

That the Reformer's influence still lives is seen in the fact that the several branches of the Lutheran Church total up many millions of members. In America alone there are well over three million adherents. "Lutheran" was a nickname given to the followers of Martin Luther by their enemies in the days of the Reformation. But as Abdel R. Wenta expresses it, *"Lutheran* is a very inadequate name to give to a movement that is not limited to a person or an era but is as ecumenical and abiding as Christianity itself."

In his various protests, this fearless champion of truth revealed his love for picturesque and symbolic language. When he faced the king of England and the Roman hierarchy, his defense manifested how different he was from many other Reformers, in that he was essentially human and full of common sense and likewise humorous. Hear him, as he answers his foes, "Swine that you are! burn me if you can and dare. Here I am, do your worst upon me. Scatter my ashes to all the winds—spread them through all the seas. My spirit shall pursue you still. . . . Luther shall leave you neither peace nor rest till he has crushed in your brows of brass and dashed out your iron brains."

Well, Luther was not burnt at the stake nor his ashes scattered, but his spirit lives on, and pursues us still, calling us to stand up and be counted in these days of apostasy within the professed church in which the courage to protect against everything alien to the Word of God is a scarce quality.

An Expositor

Natural gifts and spiritual power, coupled with a love for the Scriptures, made Luther the great Biblical preacher and expositor his sermons and expositions reveal him to have been. Taught of God, he received a clear insight into fundamental truths. He believed in studying the sacred Word itself. "Through so many commentaries and books the dear Bible is buried, so that people do not look at the text itself. It is far better to see with our own eyes than with other people's eyes." Another saying of Luther's was, "A layman who has the Scriptures is more to be trusted than pope or council without it." It was while he was a young professor at Wittenburg that he commenced to expound the Word by lecturing on the Psalms. He had a hunger for the Scriptures as one who had been long deprived of necessary food. In his *History of Christian Preaching,* Professor Harwood Pattison says—

> Luther's choice of words was fresh and natural; he had at his command fancy, imagination, irony, sarcasm. The anecdote was always ready, the allegory revealed its hidden meaning as he used it, and he was a master of the plain speech needed for popular exposition.

The people who heard him preach and teach said that his words were "half battles." Philip Melanchthon, his close friend in his trials and triumphs, said that the secret of Luther's effectiveness was that "his words were born not on his lips but in his soul." From the heart he spoke to the heart, and thus moved audiences. Fearless plainness characterizes many of his utterances. Heinrich Heine, drawing attention to this feature of Luther's preaching, said, "The fine discernment of Erasmus, and the gentleness of Melanchthon had never done so much for us as the divine brutality of Brother Martin." Robert Browning wrote of him as "Grand rough old Martin Luther."

As an expositor and translator of Scripture, he stands without a peer in his familiarity with the spiritual meaning of the Word of God. After three months of incessant and enthusiastic labor, he completed his marvelous translation of the New

Testament. When he had finished translating the whole Bible from the Latin into the language of his own nation, he wrote, "You have now the Bible in German. Now I will cease from my labors. You have now what you want. Only see to it and use it after my death. It has cost me labor enough. What an unspeakable grace it is that God speaks to us." Today, multitudes have the Bible in the clearest and purest English possible. The question is, "Do they read it as passionately as Luther did?"

As an author, Luther left the church some masterly works. His Longer and Shorter Catechisms written in 1529, contains many of his pungent sayings. His *Commentary on Romans* remains to this day. Godet called it "The Cathedral of Christian Faith." It was the reading of the preface of Luther's *Romans* that led to John Wesley's heart being "strangely warmed," and to his mighty revival ministry. His *Commentary on Galatians* is a masterpiece. This was Luther's favorite book of the Bible because it unfolds the Protestant doctrine he thrust upon the world, namely, justification by faith. He regarded Galatians as his spouse among Bible books and named it after his beloved wife—"My own Epistle," he called it, "to what I have plighted my troth. It is my Katie von Bora." He found in Paul's Galatians a source of strength for his own faith and life, and an armory of weapons for his reforming work.

Among the evangelical themes and doctrines Luther loved to preach and write about, outstanding ones can be mentioned:

First and foremost was justification by faith that he so expertly expounds in his work on Galatians. Of such a doctrinal truth he wrote, "In my heart this article reigns alone, and shall reign, namely, faith in my dear Lord Christ, who is the only Beginning, Middle, and End of all my spiritual and divine thoughts. In His death He is a Sacrifice, satisfying for our sins. In His resurrection, the Conqueror. In His ascension, the King. In His intercession, the High Priest."

150

Secondly, there was the forgiveness of sins, which he preached and taught with great power and effect. To one concerned about God's direct forgiveness Luther wrote, "It is God's command that we should believe our own sins are forgiven. Hear what Saint Bernard says, 'The testimony of the Holy Spirit in thy heart is this—Thy sins are forgiven thee.' " There can be no question about what he meant when he used this descriptive illustration: "A man's heart is like some foul stable; wheelbarrows and shovels are of little use except to remove some of the surface filth, and to litter all the passages in the process. What is to be done with it? Turn the Elbe into it. The flood will sweep away the pollution."

There is the well-known story about Luther's encounter with the devil who confronted him with a list of his sins. Luther threw the ink-bottle at the devil, telling him to write over the sins, "The blood of Jesus Christ cleanseth from all sins." This story bristles with the Reformer's personal assurance of sins forgiven. We sadly need in the pulpits of today a revival of Martin Luther's sturdy straightforwardness in the preaching of the saving truths of the gospel.

His Closing Days

Samuel Johnson reminds us that "it matters not how a man dies, but how he lives." Yet how a man lives often determines how he dies. Does not the Bible say, "Mark the perfect man—his end is peace." Martin Luther had an old body before he was sixty years of age. Because of his diseased frame, he became irritable and a trial to his friends. Writing to Zwingli, a fellow Reformer, he described himself as "a worn-out, lazy, tired, old, and now one-eyed man." But he remained active to the end. It was on Wednesday, February 17, 1546, that those around him noticed how feeble and ailing he was. During the afternoon and evening he complained about a pain in his chest, yet he was cheerful. His two sons, Paul and Hans, thirteen and fourteen years old respectively, sat up all night with their father. Early in the morning he awoke with sweat on his brow, and said to his boys, "It is the cold sweat of death. I must yield up my spirit, for my sickness increaseth." Medicine was given him, then he repeated three times—"Father, into Thy hands I commend my spirit. Thou hast redeemed me, Thou faithful God. Truly God has so loved the world."

His sorrowful young sons said to him, "Venerable father, do you die trusting in Christ, and in the doctrine you have constantly preached?" Luther answered a joyous Yes—his last word on earth—as he folded his hands on his breast, and at 4 A.M., February 18, 1546, he was not, for God took the warrior home to his rest and reward. What better tribute can we pay to such a mighty Reformer than the one expressed by Carlyle in *Heroes and Hero Worship*—

> I will call this Luther a true great man: great in intellect: in courage, affection and integrity: one of our most lovable and precious men. . . . A right spiritual Hero and Prophet: once more, a true Son of Nature, a fact for whom these centuries and many that are to come yet, will be thankful to Heaven.

In his most valuable work, *Laws for Common Life,* Dr. R. W. Dale has this most appealing summary of Martin Luther's wonderful life and labors.

> He had a fiery and passionate hatred of falsehood and of sin; a dauntless courage in the assertion of the claims of truth and righteousness. He had a boundless faith and a boundless joy in God. His joy was of a masculine kind, and made him stronger for his work. His faith was of a masculine kind, and relieved him from worrying doubts and fears about his soul's affairs. He had his gloomy times, his conflicts with principalities and powers in dismal and solitary places; but he had no morbid dreams about

the sanctity of misery, nor did he suppose that the ever-blessed God finds any satisfaction in the self-inflicted sufferings of his children. His massive face and robust form were the outward and visible signs of the vigour and massiveness of his moral and religious character. He was a man, and did not try to be anything else. God made him a man; what was he that he should quarrel with God's work? He had flesh and blood; he could not help it. He did not desire to help it. He ate heartily, and enjoyed seeing his friends at dinner. He married a wife and loved her; and he loved God none the less. He liked music and songs as well as preaching and sermons. He could laugh as well as preach. He had a genial humour as well as deep devoutness. He was a brave man, strong and resolute, with abounding life of all kinds; a saint of a type with which for many evil centuries Christendom had been unfamiliar.

Around the time of Martin Luther's birth in 1483, many Protestant churches commemorate his great work by a Reformation Day when from pulpit and platform his courageous challenge of the embattled forces of a despotic religious hierarchy are reemphasized. American churches in particular recognize such a day, and rightly so, seeing the righteous principles for which he so nobly fought are woven into the very Constitution of the United States. The religious freedom so characteristic of the New World is the fruit of the Reformation. As Paul Lindemann states it—

> The spirit of Luther influenced the framers of that historic document in Philadelphia. Without him the statement never could have been written that all men are created equal. Never could the principle have been adopted among a whole nation that there must be freedom of the individual, of speech, of press, of conscience. Luther's principle is echoed in

the words of the first amendment to the Constitution—*Congress shall make no law respecting an establishment of religion or prohibiting the free exercise thereof.* We owe the blessed institutions of this land of the free to Martin Luther. . . . As the result of the Reformation we have today a marvellous system of education of which we may truthfully call Luther the founder.

Reformation Day gives preachers the opportunity to declare the truths that delivered the German monk from the shackles of sin and of religious oppression. The verse that gripped his heart and led him from a religion of fear to one of faith was the four-time-repeated one—"The just shall live by faith." This oft-quoted verse had a mysterious influence on the life of Luther. It was a creative sentence both for the Reformer and the reformed. Whenever this evangelical verse is preached on, Luther's own tribute to its revolutionary power in his own life should be quoted—

> Before those words broke upon my mind I hated God and was angry with Him because, not content with frightening us sinners by the Law, and the miseries of life, He still further increased our torture by the Gospel. But when, by the Spirit of God, I understood these words—*The just shall live by faith* —then I felt born again like a new man: I entered through the open door into the very Paradise of God. . . . In very truth, this text was to me the true gate of Paradise.

Salvation and justification by faith thereafter became Luther's predominant theme and the foundation of his undying work of Reformation. Here are some of his gems as to the substance and efficacy of saving faith.

Faith and human understanding are one against another. Faith dependeth upon the Word.

Faith is a Christian's treasure.
Faith in Christ destroyeth sin.
Faith maketh us Christ's heritage.
Faith is to build certainly on God's mercy.
To doubt is sin and everlasting death.

All of us are familiar with Luther's famous, stirring Reformation Hymn with its ringing confidence in God—

> Did we in our own strength confide,
> Our striving would be losing,
> Were not the right Man on our side,
> The Man of God's own choosing.
> Dost ask who that may be?
> Christ Jesus, it is He;
> Lord Sabaoth His name,
> From age to age the same,
> And He must win the battle.

12

George Wishart
The Noble and Illustrious Scottish Martyr

There can be no better approach to a study of Scottish martyrology than through the gateway of the Protestant Reformation Martin Luther was so conspicuously identified with. For the great principles that actuated the Reformation leaders in Europe became the central contendings and abiding heritage of Scottish Covenanters and martyrs, who, like many earlier Reformers sealed their testimony with their blood. Scotland is preeminently the land of those who were willing to die for the faith. The writing on an old stone in Kirkintilloch, erected in 1685 to commemorate two Scots worthies who died for Christ, reads—

'Twas Martyrs' Blood Brought Scotland's Liberty.

The thousands who stained the moors and glens with their blood are numbered among those slain for the Word of God whose souls are under the altar waiting for the Judge to avenge their blood (Rev. 6:9).

The standard biography and classic on the subject of the Scottish Covenant is the astonishing work of a lowly, self-taught peasant who lived on the moors far from the haunts of man, namely, John Howie, author of *The Scots Worthies*. This historic volume, appearing in 1775, is made up of stories the author received from those who had passed through the fire. Howie is all aglow with the glory of covenanting days in

Scotland, and expresses concern over Scotland selling its dearly bought religious freedom for a mess of pottage. The author exclaims—

> What would be the conception of these courses of defection of our Reformers and later Martyrs, if they were given a short furlough from their scenes of glory, to take a short view of their apostacizing children: for if innocent Hamilton, godly and patient Wishart, apostolic Knox, eloquent Rollock, worthy Davidson, courageous Melville, prophetic Welsh, majestic Bruce, great Henderson, renowned Gillespie, learned Binning, pious Gray, laborious Durham, heavenly-minded Rutherford, the faithful Guthries, diligent Blair, heart-melting Livingstone, religious Wellwood, orthodox and practical Brown, zealous and stedfast Cameron, honest-hearted Cargill, sympathising McWard, persevering Blackader, the evangelical Traills, constant and pious Renwick, etc. were filed off from the Assembly of the First-Born, and but as Commissioners to haste down from the ascent of God to behold how quickly their offspring are gone out of the way, piping and dancing after a golden calf, ah! with what vehemency would their spirits be affected, to see their labourious structure almost razed to the foundations, by those to whom they committed the custody of their great Lord's patience.

Howie ends this roll call of heroes, and their reaction to defection from the faith they died to preserve by quoting old Samuel Rutherford's letter to the Earl of Cassillis:

> Your honourable ancestors, with the hazard of their lives, brought Christ into our lands, and it shall be cruelty to posterity if ye lose Him to them.

If that was the religious condition in Scotland in Howie's

157

time, where are we now over two hundred years later? We say that "the blood of the martyrs is the seed of the church," but the impotent, divided church of today knows little of the martyr spirit and faith. Scottish martyrs, over eighteen thousand of them, have their names engraven in stone in Edinburgh, which is called by way of preeminence, *The Martyrs' Memorial.* The history of many of those and others can be traced in Foxe's *Book of Martyrs,* which, although it makes pathetic reading, is a tonic for faith. But what better Book of Martyrs is there than the Bible itself, as Hebrews 11 proves?

> They climbed the steep ascent to heaven
>   Through peril, toil, and pain.
> O God, to us may grace be given,
>   To follow in their train!

Some wag has suggested that we no longer "follow in their train," or emulate their sacrificial spirit, but prefer to follow more comfortably in a *train.* Well, let us think of one who did climb the steep ascent to heaven, "the godly and patient" George Wishart, as John Howie described him, and who was among the first in Scotland to be martyred. A memorial to him stands in Fordum Churchyard, about two miles from where he was born, and bears the inscription—

> *This Monument is erected to the Memory*
> *of Scotland's First and Most Illustrious Martyr,*
> *George Wishart.*

We do not have as much rich biographical material for study as is the case of John Knox, for Wishart's full life-story was not written. Yet he fills a niche all his own in the great annals of Scottish history, and is portrayed in a fivefold way.

A Gentleman

It is Foxe who calls this renowned Dundee preacher, "George Wishart—Gentleman." He was believed to be the only son of James Wishart, of Pitarrow, Kincardinshire. The date of his birth is uncertain, but is said to be between 1513 and 1514, in Mansion House, Pitarrow, long ago destroyed. The Wisharts were an ancient and honorable family, aristocratic and well-connected. George's father was of French extraction, but his mother came from Fife, Scotland. A writer of the time described him as: "A son of Pitarrow, the worthiest person of all who supported the new doctrines in the Kingdom." James Melville, another renowned Covenanter wrote in his diary: "The maist godlie, learned, and noble Scots Martyr, George Wishart." Sir Walter Scott said of him, "This martyr to the cause of the Reformation was a man of honourable birth, great wisdom and eloquence, and of primitive piety."

The Bible reminds us that "not many wise, not many noble are called," but thank God some are; and among them is George Wishart, God's gentleman who will ever remain a witness to those in the ranks of nobility who, because of their culture, education, and possessions, could be a great asset to the cause of Christ if only the Scottish martyr's faith and surrender were theirs.

A Scholar

In respect to his early days, little is known of his history and education. Such facts as we have are related to Wishart's afteryears. We have reliable information that he was employed as a teacher in a school at Montrose, the first town in Scotland to teach Greek. George Wishart taught German, which was counted heresy by the Roman Catholic Church. In 1538, he was summoned by Bishop Hepburn on a charge of heresy for teaching German and, threatened with a prosecution for teaching without authority the German New Testament, he was compelled to retreat to England. He was excommunicated by the bishop of Brechin with the accusation, "Thou false heretic, renegade, traitor, thief, and deceiver of the people, thou despisest the Holy Church, and in like case contemmest my Lord Governor's authority. Therefore curse thee, deliver thee into the devil's hands and give thee, in commandment, that thou preach no more."

In 1540 Wishart left England for Germany where he remained for two or three years associated with the Swiss Reformation. Being impressed with the Swiss Confession he translated it out of the Latin into his own tongue. Returning to England, he took up residence at Cambridge, where the nucleus of the English Reformation was to be found. He enrolled as a member of Corpus Christi College, intending to study and teach, and remained there about two years. Little is known, however, about this period. We can assume that with his thirst for knowledge, his stay in such a collegiate town proved to be a great spiritual and mental stimulus.

A Preacher

Having embraced the principles of the Protestant faith, these formed the absorbing themes of his preaching, and he became eloquent in their declaration. He labored for awhile at the Church of Saint Nicolas, Bristol. Wishart's messages were clear and decisive. "God's way of life for sinners is through faith in the work of Jesus Christ," was the key message in his preaching. To the delight of John Knox he preached Luther's doctrine wherever he went. "None but Christ—Christ as Mediator, Lawgiver, Example, Friend—such was the gospel which George Wishart preached."

He returned to Montrose, not to teach but to preach the everlasting gospel. Having commenced his work there, he was happy to go back. Hiring a house a few doors away from the Roman Catholic Church he exercised a most effective ministry. Preaching was a lost art in Scotland in those days, so many gathered to hear him proclaim the gospel. From Montrose, Wishart went to Dundee, which had the honor of being the first burgh in Scotland to openly declare for the Reformation. This is why it became known as "The Scotch or Second Geneva," because of its ardent zeal for the Reformed cause. One day Dr. Alexander Whyte, of Edinburgh asked his Bible class, "Why was Dundee after Wishart's day called 'The Scotch Geneva' "? Two things were cited in answer as to why the city had been raised to such a primary position.

First, the early labors of Wishart himself because it was one of his chief resorts and spheres of ministry. Here he preached publicly with great profit, lecturing at one time on Romans "to the great admiration of all who heard him."

Second, because of the influence of those who imbibed his spirit and followed up his labors. For many years a Wishart Memorial Church has flourished there. The ever-increasing spread of Reformation truth had to be stopped and Cardinal Beaton ordered Wishart to leave the city. Sorrowfully, he obeyed and, driven out by priestly devices, he said, "I have offered unto you the word of salvation and with hazard of my life. I have remained among you. Now ye yourselves refuse me and, therefore, I must leave my innocence to be declared by my God."

This noble defender of the faith went eastward and, following the way of his royal Master, was persecuted as he fled from one city to another. Ultimately he came to Ayrshire where he was welcomed by those hailing the dawn of the Reformation. In Ayr, where he began his labor, he preached with great power and freedom to the faithful. Rome, however, was determined to silence this fearless preacher of the gospel. The Archbishop of Glasgow came to Ayr to compel Wishart to desist, but to no avail. Forced to leave Ayr, Wishart went on to Galston to preach, but was forbidden to do so by the sheriff. Out into the fields he went saying, "Christ Jesus is as mighty in the fields as in the church. And I find that He Himself preached oftener in the desert, at the seaside, and other places judged profane than in the temple at Jerusalem." The people came in great numbers to hear him in the open air. One day he preached for three hours, with far-reaching results. Lawrence Rankine, Laird of Schaw, one of the most wicked men in the countryside, was melted to tears and converted to God.

After a month in Ayrshire, hearing of the desolation in Dundee because of famine and pestilence, he returned to the historic city and was joyfully welcomed by a faithful band. The spot where he chose to preach became known as Wishart's Arch, Cowgate. Here he stood or sat, inspecting and helping the sick, and preaching a message of comfort to the needy. He took as his text, "He sent His word and healed them," which verse was embodied in the inscription on the arch—

> During the plague of 1544, George Wishart, preached from the parapet of this port, the people standing within the gate, and the plague-stricken lying without in booths. "He sent His word and healed them" (Ps. 117:20).

During this terrible period, Wishart was diligent in visiting and comforting those in extremity, not only in preaching to them, but feeding them with necessary food. "The preacher pointed all the sick and dying, not to shrine or image of St. Rogue, the patron saint of plague-stricken folk, but to Jesus Christ, the Great Physician and Healer of both soul and body and thus raised all the hearts of those who heard him."

Laboring, as I did, in Dundee for many years it was always an inspiration to visit Wishart's Arch and bless God for his battle for spiritual liberty.

But while Wishart was doing good, the devil sought to do him harm. Cardinal Beaton attempted to assassinate the friend of the disconsolate by bribing a corrupted priest, a most desperate character, to slay him. One day, as he ended his sermon, the priest stood at the foot of the pulpit with a drawn dagger beneath his loose gown. But Wishart's sharp eye detected danger and said to the priest, "My friend, what would you do?" He reached for the dagger to slay Wishart, but he was not quick enough, for Wishart grabbed it. The priest fell down and confessed his sin. The congregation cried, "Deliver the traitor to us or else we will take him by force." Christlike, Wishart protected the repentant priest and saved his life.

Once the plague abated, Wishart left Dundee saying, "The battle here is over and God calls me to another." Invitations reached him to preach in many places, but he went to Montrose for a time of rest and meditation. The malice of Cardinal Beaton, however, followed him, and another snare was set to destroy him, but God delivered him. When refreshed he went on to Leith where he met many saints who desired to hear him preach. Wishart said to them, "Dare ye and others hear, then let my God provide for me as best pleaseth Him." The next Sabbath he preached to a large, responsive audience. Going on to East Lothian he visited several churches in which gentry and common people alike gathered to hear his outspoken messages against the papacy. In his messages he foretold of the shortness of his time, for he instinctively felt that he was approaching the day of his death—Rome's pressure was increasing: "What differ I from a dead man, except that I eat and drink? So this time God hath used my labours to the instruction of others, and to the disclosing of darkness: now, I lurk as a man that was ashamed, and dursn't show myself before men."

It was at Haddington where he went from East Lothian that he met John Knox, who became one of Wishart's most attentive hearers, and waited upon him. Knox's experience of saving grace can be traced to Wishart's influence. But Wishart received a letter that troubled him. It was in the form of a refusal to preach in the town. Rebuking those who barred him from preaching, he said, "O Lord, how long shall it be that Thy Holy Word shall be despised, and men shall not regard their salvation? Fearful shall be the plagues that shall ensue for this contempt. With fire and sword shalt thou be plagued, even thou, Haddington, especially." For an hour-

and-a-half he delivered his soul after this fashion. He had become disheartened over the decline of the Reformed cause, and spoke to John Knox about his weariness, and of the shadow of approaching doom.

A Martyr

Wishart was forced to leave Haddington, and John Knox was eager to accompany and defend him, but he forbade him saying, "One is sufficient for our sacrifice." Affectionately the two likeminded hearts embraced and Wishart departed. He came to Ormistion House to stay the night, and after worship retired to rest. But at midnight the house was surrounded and he sensed what would happen. The demand came for Earl Bothwell to open the gate. George Wishart said to him, "Open the gates, the blessed will of my God be done."

He was taken prisoner, brought to Edinburgh, then to the Sea Tower, Saint Andrews where he was imprisoned in the "Bottle Dungeon" in which he remained from January until March 1546. He suffered greatly during these months, yet he wrote much, all of which his foes suppressed. Word came that he was to appear to answer a charge of sedition and heresy. He came before Cardinal Beaton and made a bold defense. As he entered the church for his trial he passed a poor man begging for alms, and Wishart gave him his purse. The accusation was read by John Lauder, a priest, who then asked, "What answereth thou to these things, thou renegade, traitor, thief, which we have proved against thee?"

George Wishart bowed his knees and looked to God for an answer, and gave three reasons why he should not be condemned. The verdict, however, was "Guilty," and he was sentenced to die the next day. It is said that he prayed, "O immortal God! How long shalt Thou suffer the great cruelty of the ungodly to exercise their fury upon Thy servants which do further Thy Word in this world?" On the morning of the execution he breakfasted with the captain of the castle and a few others, and discussed with them the Lord's suffering and death, and then dispensed the Lord's Supper for the first time according to the Protestant form in Scotland.

The fire was made ready and gunners stood by, ready to shoot if any escape was planned. Wishart's hands were bound behind his back with an iron chain to the middle of his waist. As he was being led to the stake he met beggars pleading for money but the doomed saint said, "I want my hands wherewith I was wont to give you, but the merciful Lord vouchsafe you necessaries for your bodies and souls." Reaching the stake he kneeled and prayed three times, "O Thou Saviour of the world have mercy upon me. Father of heaven, I commend my spirit into Thy hands!" Then he addressed the sympathetic people gathered to see him burned, "I beseech you Christian brethren and sisters be not offended at the Word of God, for the torments and afflictions which ye see prepared for me. . . . For this cause was I sent that I should suffer fire for Christ's sake. Consider and behold my visage. Ye shall not see me change my colour. This grim fire I fear not, and so I pray you to do, if persecution come unto you. . . . I know surely that my soul shall sup with my Saviour, this night ere it be six hours, for whom I suffer this."

Then he prayed for his accusers, "I forgive them with all my heart: I beseech Christ to forgive them," thereby emulating the example of the Master. He forgave his executioner who asked, "Sir, I pray you, forgive me, for I am not guilty of your death." Wishart replied, "Come hither to me," and kissing him said, "Lo! here is a token that I forgive thee. My heart, do thine office." Believing that persecution turns its votaries into victims Wishart said of Cardinal Beaton, who never rested until he saw the Reformer die, "He who from yonder place beholdeth me with such pride, shall within a few days lie in the same, as ignominiously as he is now seen proudly to rest in himself."

The trumpet sounded and Wishart was hanged on a gibbet

and then burnt, and as the historian describes the scene, "The pile was fired, the powder exploded, the flames arose and Wishart was dismissed by a painful death to blessed immortality in the next world." He was only thirty-one years of age when on March 1, 1546, George Wishart was slain for "the Word of God and the testimony of Jesus," and the trumpets sounded for him on the other side. "Many cruelties were exercised," says Historian Scott, "but that which excited public feeling to the highest degree was the barbarous death of George Wishart, whose burning dates the new birth of the Scottish Church and of the Scottish Nation." His cruel death caused great mourning. The people were indignant, feeling that an innocent lamb had been slain.

But although God buries His workmen, He carries on His work, and the effect of Wishart's martyrdom was to give impetus to the Reformation cause and doctrines. As we shall see, John Knox, the spiritual son of Wishart, proved to be a most worthy successor. For ourselves, the lessons to be learned from the labors of the renowned Covenanters are obvious—

First, we should value our spiritual heritage, and make the most of our religious liberty. There are three kinds of liberty to preserve. *Civil* liberty, such as Bruce, Wallace, and Cromwell fought for. *Religious* liberty, procured by Knox, Wishart, the Covenanters, the Pilgrim Fathers. *Spiritual* liberty, the Saviour secured for us by the shedding of His blood. In the law of recurrence, history repeats itself, and religious liberty is becoming scarcer through the spread of atheistic Communism and the continuing domination of Catholicism.

Second, ours must be the courage of God in the face of opposition. George Wishart never flinched, nor changed the color of his countenance as he was burned at the stake. Threats, dungeons, and fires could not frighten this valiant soul. Alas! there are multitudes today who are cowards. They do not have the courage of conviction. They are afraid to commit themselves to Christ and confess Him before the world, and too often they fill a coward's grave. God is calling today for spiritual heroes. May we be found among the number willing to be faithful even unto death!

Third, we see the victory of grace in that Wishart never retaliated, as his attitude at the stake reveals. He died, as his Saviour did, forgiving his enemies, and praying for their salvation. If Wishart's death meant Scotland's new birth, the outcome of Christ's martyrdom is our regeneration. The executioner said to Wishart that he "was not guilty of his death," but we were guilty of the crucifixion of the Lord of Glory, for it was our sins that nailed Him to the cross. The martyr kissed the man putting him to death, and for us there is also the kiss of forgiveness and reconciliation, "Kiss the Son!"

> The Son of God goes forth to war,
>   A kingly crown to gain;
> His blood-red banner streams afar:
>   Who follows in His train?
> Who now can drink His cup of woe,
>   Triumphant over pain,
> Who patient bears His cross below,
>   He follows in His train.

13

John Knox
The Fearless Preacher Who Rebuked a Queen

It is but fitting that the compelling portrait of the indomitable and fearless John Knox should hang next to the picture of the sweetest and saintliest Reformer, George Wishart, in God's portrait gallery of saints. With the latter's martyrdom, his mantle fell upon Knox, and he became a prominent figure in the troubled life of Scotland. He would have gladly shared the fate of his teacher and friend, but although he was not to die a martyr, the iron went into his soul also, and for many years his was the life of an exile and wanderer for conscience's sake.

Carlyle tells us, "One comfort is that great men, taken up in any way, are profitable company. We cannot look, however imperfectly, upon a great man without gaining something by him. He is the living light-fountain which it is good and pleasant to be near." This is especially true of John Knox, who is always profitable company to be in. Much can be gained from learning about his life and labors. In the best sense it is always "good and pleasant to be near" him. Recognizing Knox as the most conspicuous figure on the pages of Scottish history, Carlyle in *Hero a Priest,* says, "In the history of Scotland I can find but one epoch: we may say it contains nothing of world-interest but this Reformation by Knox."

A Man of Culture

There is a division of opinion about the time and place of his birth. The general opinion is that he was born around 1505, in Haddington, Scotland, the son of a small landowner, and that he was educated at the grammar school, Haddington, proceeding to Glasgow University when he was about seventeen years of age. There is no mention of him taking any degrees, nor does he appear to have made a mark as a scholar during the years of his education. He was ordained to the priesthood when he was twenty-five, and became Professor of Logic, and tutor in the family of Hugh Douglas of East Lothian. Facts as to his early years are scanty, for he lived for many years almost in obscurity. Apparently he adhered to the Romish doctrines in which he had been educated, and was thus well qualified to combat them, as he fearlessly did after he embraced the doctrines of the Reformation on hearing Reformers like Patrick Hamilton and George Wishart preach them.

About 1544 Knox openly declared himself to be a Protestant, and in 1547 he was called to officiate as the Protestant minister of Saint Andrews, Scotland, whither he had fled from the persecution against Reformers which was raging at the time. But his ministry there lasted only a few months. Saint Andrews was attacked by the French fleet—the city capitulated, and Knox, with other refugees, was condemned for nineteen months to work at the galleys—hard and cruel labor which injured Knox's health for life. After his release in 1549, he returned to Scotland, but finding little to do there he took refuge in Berwick, and afterwards in Newcastle. It was during his stay in England that he met and married the daughter of a landed gentleman of Northumberland. In 1555, his wife and he went to Dieppe, and then to Geneva where he visited John Calvin and was greatly influenced by his teachings. On his return to Scotland he became the most representative preacher of Calvinism. "Scotland is the triumph of

Calvinism, and to John Knox in its first victorious stages that triumph is mainly due."

Possessed of a high mental caliber and wonderful eloquence, his fame as a preacher spread far and wide. He was made chaplain to King Edward VI in 1551, and was afterwards offered the bishopric of Rochester, which he refused, as being contrary to his principles. In 1559 he returned to Scotland, where the fires of persecution were abating but not quenched. It was a critical time, for several Protestant preachers were on the point of being tried for their lives, and Knox, who had been condemned in early days of the persecution, was again proclaimed a heretic.

The queen-regent at the time was alarmed over the sympathy felt by the common people for these ministers who were to be tried, and their trial was abandoned. Knox was appointed minister of the historic Church of Saint Giles, Edinburgh, in 1560, and remained there during the remaining twelve years of his life, delivering messages week by week that brought salvation to many. In addition to his potent pulpit labors, he furthered the cause of Christ by his numerous trenchant writings. He published works against the worship of Mary and the Roman Church. Perhaps his greatest work, published after his death, is *The History of Reformation in Scotland,* which gives us a mirror of the writer himself and of his times.

Knox's influence became far-reaching, even to being recognized as the great ecclesiastical power of his country. Intelligent, moral, and spiritual power enabled him to sway the common and cultured classes alike. Religiously a giant of a man, he was yet intensely patriotic. Devotion to Christ ennobled his character and made him God's battle-axe and weapon of war. To quote Carlyle's appreciation of his noble life—

> That he could rebuke Queens, and had such weight
> among those proud turbulent Nobles, proud enough
> whatever else they were: and could maintain to the

end a kind of virtual Presidency and Sovereignty in that wild realm he who was only "a subject born with the same"—this of itself will prove to me that he was found close at hand to be no mean-arid man, but at heart a healthful, strong, sagacious man.

A Man of Christ

Just when he gained an interest in the Saviour's blood and his chains of Romanism fell off, just when his heart was freed to rise, go forth, and follow the Saviour is not easy to determine. It would seem as if several factors contributed to his surrender to divine claims, making him God's hero of the Scottish Reformation.

First of all, there was his association with George Wishart. Possibly the time he spent with this godly martyr was the greatest formative influence in Knox's life. We do not meet him in Scottish history until after the death of Wishart. Yet he was his close companion standing by him, carrying a sword ready to defend Wishart while preaching, which powerful preaching deepened Knox's religious impression, and hatred for the Roman Church. Ever eager to assist Wishart, one night Knox saw him taken prisoner and committed to the dungeon. How eager he was to accompany him, but Wishart forbade his zealous disciple and, taking his sword from him, said, "Nay return to your bairns and God bless you! One is sufficient for sacrifice." If he witnessed Wishart's calm and courageous death at the stake, this must have had a profound effect upon his life.

Secondly, the words Knox uttered as he came to die indicate the probable means of his conversion. To his wife, he expressed a dying wish, "Go and read where I cast my first anchor," and she read the seventeenth chapter of John, and a part of Calvin's *Commentary on the Ephesians*. It may be that after witnessing the cruel martyrdom of Wishart, Knox

171

went home and read the high priestly prayer of Jesus, which he found so applicable, and the miracle happened, and he became one of those given to Christ by His Father. As Stephen's heroic martyrdom doubtless had a share in the transformation of Saul of Tarsus, so the blood of Wishart the martyr became a seed in Knox the Reformer.

Thirdly, the confession of his faith in Christ as Saviour. God gave John Knox a deep insight into truth. His understanding of the inner meaning of the redemptive work of Christ is borne out by the paragraph from one of his sermons—

> There is no other name by which men can be saved but that of Jesus, and that all reliance on the merits of others is vain and delusive: that the Saviour having by his own sacrifice sanctified and reconciled to God those who should inherit the promised kingdom, all other sacrifices which men pretend to offer for sin are blasphemous—all ought to hate sin which is so odious before God that no sacrifice but the death of His Son could satisfy it.

It was such evangelical preaching that raised the ire of the papal authorities to the extent of their passing the sentence of death upon Knox, but he went into hiding and the papists made an effigy of him and burnt it.

Fourthly, there was his prevailing intercession. Knox could not have been the mighty man of prayer he was had there not been the foundation of salvation. The spiritual emancipation from Rome of his beloved native land was always on his heart and in his prayers. One day, burdened about the very many still in darkness, he cried, "O God, give me Scotland or I die!" God gave him Scotland, and the land has never lost the impact of the heart-cries of Knox. The queen of the country at that time said that she feared the prayers of John Knox more than an army of soldiers. Does Satan tremble when he sees us on our knees?

A Man of Chastisement

From the time of his association with George Wishart, Knox was a marked man and had good reason to fear that he would be the next to be taken and sacrificed as a martyr. He took a bold step and made himself more conspicuous when he accepted with reluctance the call to minister to a small body of Reformers at Saint Andrews. Then the city fell to the French and Knox was taken captive and made to toil wearily at the oars. As the ship passed the Scottish coast on the way to France, one of the prisoners pointed out to him the steeple of the church he had ministered in. "Ah, I see the steeple of that place where God first in public opened my mouth to His glory," said the emaciated prisoner, "and I am fully persuaded how weak soever I now appear that I shall not depart this life till that my tongue shall glorify His godly name in the same place."

Those nineteen months as a galley slave took their toll of his health, and he was never the same afterwards. Returning after such hard and sore labor, he was offered but refused the bishopric of Rochester. Difficult times ensued, but courageously he bared his breast to the battle. He was censured, shot at through the window, and suffered as he strove to make the government of Scotland a theocracy during the reign of Mary. We have touched upon his exile in Geneva where he was greatly influenced by John Calvin, the Genevan Reformer. It was while there that he published his works against Mary and the tyranny of her court. He returned to Scotland for a while, but found it difficult to accomplish much. Receiving a call to a Genevan church, he accepted and, going back, spent the happiest three years of his life. He, his wife, and family were greatly honored and loved by all.

Hearing that the fires of Reformation were beginning to burn fiercely in Scotland, and being urged to return, in 1559, at the age of fifty-four, he came back to the Scotland he loved so dearly, and gave the remaining thirteen years of his life to the battle of bringing her religious liberty. A great and effectual door was opened to Knox, and with it many adversaries.

A Man of Combat

With the apostle Paul, with whose teachings Knox was saturated, he determined to fight a good fight. Queen Mary, his avowed antagonist, sought to make Scotland entirely Roman Catholic, but the converted priest would have none of it, and so thundered out against idolatry. He broke images, denounced the mass and false gods, and fought sternly against all Romish practices.

He testified against a prostituted royalty

Mary, the young Queen of Scots, was both clever and beautiful, and so fascinated the nobles of her court that they were ready to do anything she willed. She was cruel and devilish, had had several husbands, and was called *Bloody Mary* because of her dark and treacherous deeds against the people. John Knox stood his ground against her, and rebuked her sternly. "Who are you?" she once said to him, "that presume to school the nobles and sovereign of this realm?" Knox's reply was, "Madam, a subject born within same." In bold terms he denounced the queen on the subject of her marriage to young Darnley, and he was commanded to appear before her at Holyrood Palace to answer for his conduct.

The queen desired that in the future Knox should tell her privately of anything that he saw to be wrong, and on his refusal, finding him indifferent to her threats, tried to conciliate him. Knox was brought to trial for treason but was acquitted. He was, however, forbidden to preach because of the offense given by his sermon on the queen's marriage. This prohibition lasted until the queen's fall in 1567, and the accession of King James.

When Lord Darnley stretched a point, Catholic though he was, and went to hear Knox preach before his trial, the preacher took as his text "Other lords than thou have had dominion over us," and discoursed on God's way of sometimes permitting such lords to be "boys and women," and dwelt on the weakness of Ahab in not controlling his strong-minded queen, Jezebel. The service lasted an hour longer than Darnley had expected, and he flung himself out of the church. Queen Mary and her mother, Mary of Lorraine, feared no other person in all the land as they feared John Knox. "Yon man," the fair Mary cried, after one interview with him, "gart me greet, but grat never tear himself." *Greet* is Scotch for "weep," and what she meant was "He makes me weep, but never weeps himself."

He testified against papal religion

Having been reared in Roman Catholicism and ordained as a priest, Knox knew all about its inner workings and practices. But once his eyes were opened and he came, like Martin Luther, to experience justification by faith, he set about purging the land of a debased priesthood, and lived to see victory. It was through his steadfast spirit that in 1567, Protestantism was confirmed by an act of parliament for Scotland; and ever since the country has remained a stronghold of Presbyterianism. Throughout Christendom John Knox still lives wherever a Protestant church stands. In fact, an untold number of them bear the honored name of *Knox*.

A Man of Courage

Seneca, the ancient Roman philosopher wrote—

> He is a king who fears nothing;
> He is a king who will desire nothing.

Knox was a true king in that he feared no one but God,

175

and desired nothing save His glory. Familiar, as he was with Scripture, it may be that the Reformer was inspired by the command to the prophet Jeremiah, "Be not afraid of their faces: for I am with thee to deliver thee, saith the Lord" (1:8). Knox neither flattered nor feared anyone. At his burial, Earl Morton, present at the graveside, said of him after the coffin had been lowered, "He lies there who never feared the face of man." The fear of man was a snare Knox avoided. In the darkest hours as a galley slave, he would cheer his fellow prisoners by saying, "Be of good courage. The cause we have is a true one and must and will prosper."

Courageous in life, he was the same in death. After the accession of James he spent three years in fruitful service, and lived to see better times and to thank God that "the gospel of Jesus Christ is truly and simply preached throughout Scotland." It would seem as if his own preaching became stronger and more tender in his closing years. Toward the end he was so weak that he had to be lifted into the pulpit "where," says the chronicler, "he had to lean at his first entry; but before he had done with his sermon he was so active and vigorous that he was like to ding the pulpit in blads and fly out of it." The reporter went on to say, "When he entered into the application of his text he made me so to thrill and tremble that I could not hold a pen to write."

In 1570 he was seized with a fit of apoplexy, and although he recovered sufficiently to preach occasionally, he gradually deteriorated, and on November 24, 1572, his task was finished. In his last hours his mind wandered and he was heard to say that he wanted to go to church and preach on the resurrection of Christ. In one of his conscious moments, he was asked, "Have you hope?" and, no longer able to speak, he lifted a finger upwards, and so died. Among his final words was a request to his wife, "Go read where I first cast my anchor," and she read John 17. Before speech finally left him he softly said, "I praise God for that heavenly sound," then with a sigh of relief added under his breath,

"Now it is come." Thus the stalwart Reformer who never feared an earthly sovereign went home to the ivory palace to see the King he had honored in all His beauty. He was buried on November 26 in the churchyard of Saint Giles, now the courtyard of Parliament House, and only the two initials *J. K.* mark the grave of the man who gave Scotland her religious liberty.

The question remains, Are we continuing to reap the fruit of Knox's wonderful labors? Are we standing fast in the religious freedom he gallantly fought for and secured? One wonders what his attitude would be if he could come back to earth and witness the efforts of men to unite into one universal church all denominations and religions, whether Christian or non-Christian. With his uncompromising exposure of the practices of Roman Catholicism, we cannot imagine him having any sympathy with the plans to unify religious bodies accepting the fundamental truths of the gospel with those who reject them, or the merging of the so-called Protestant Church with the Roman Church. We sadly need a man of the caliber of John Knox to foster a spiritual Reformation.

As he died, he asked for the portion of the Word to be read to him in which he first cast his anchor. Today, the church is drifting, she has failed to cast her anchor in the infallible, unbreakable Word of God, in His infinite love and mercy, in the redeeming grace of Christ, in the everlasting gospel. If only all the energy spent on ecumenicism could be directed into a robust evangelicalism, what a mighty force the church would be in a world of sin and sorrow! After all, the supreme task of Christ's church is soul-winning, for He conceived and commissioned her to go into all the world making disciples—and such an anchor always holds.

14

Robert Murray McCheyne
The Young Minister Who Burned Out for God

In the economy of God it would seem as if He has honored certain places above others, causing them, because of events and experiences within them, to be sanctified. To mention Bethlehem is to remember the miracle of God becoming flesh. To think of Mount Olivet is to visualize Christ's ministry at such a sacred spot and of His return to it when He comes to reign. To speak of the place called Calvary, is to call to mind the perfect salvation secured there for a sinning race. That this is also true of cities and towns of later times is proven by the historic Scottish city of Dundee.

What has made this city, renowned for its jam and jute, so world famous? Certainly not its industries and its position on the silvery River Tee, but its roll of honor of saintly souls who lived and labored in it. As we have already seen, it was in Dundee that George Wishart preached reformation sermons and made it the "Scotch Geneva." It was in this same city that the great revivalist, William Burns, was mightily used of God, and went to China to accomplish great things for Him. Dundee was the home of Robert Annan, a remarkable saint whose life's story has been greatly used. Then, it was in Dundee that Mary Slessor lived and labored in a jute mill, and from which she went to West Africa to become the uncrowned queen of Calabar.

A host of others, less conspicuous, whose lives were fragrant and fruitful for the Master, served Him most faithfully in their day and generation. Our present portrait is of one of Dundee's most holy sons, Robert Murray McCheyne, whose appealing story has been told by many biographers, the greatest spiritual classic being *Memoirs of Robert Murray McCheyne* by his dear friend, Andrew Bonar. From various sources, then, let us try to picture him.

From His Youth Up

Godly home influences—a most valuable asset—helped to shape his life during his early years. In one sense he was never much more than a youth, for he died at an early age. The youngest of five, McCheyne was born in 14 Dublin Street, Edinburgh on May 21, 1813. His father was Adam McCheyne, a man of considerable means and good position. He was also known for his excellent Christian character. As a father, he was firm, yet approachable. His mother was Lockhart Murray McCheyne, a very sweet and charming lady, who sought to make her home Christ-centered and controlled. After Robert's death his father, who greatly loved his son and kept all his letters, wrote to a friend, "Robert was from infancy blessed with a sweet, docile, and affectionate temper—a mother's legacy to her child."

It is said that Robert's consuming passion and earnestness when he became a minister influenced his parents to leave their church where modernism prevailed and join a more evangelistic one. From infancy McCheyne was wonderfully endowed both temperamentally and mentally.

His natural endowments

As a lad he was good looking, attractive, and winsome, very quick in mind, quiet in manner, and the possessor of a fine melodious voice. The description given of David, son of Jesse, can be applied to Robert M. McCheyne. "He was ruddy

179

and withal of a beautiful countenance and goodly to look to." There came the day when the latter part of the verse was also applicable to this wonderful youth from a godly home—"The Lord said, arise and anoint him: for this is he."

His scholastic attainments

That McCheyne had a thirst and capacity for knowledge can be gleaned from the fact that when he was recovering from measles his father taught him the letters of the Greek alphabet. At five he went to a private school, and made great progress. Possessing a quick ear and an ability to recite, his instructor said of him, "The child's voice was like a sound from a better life and a better land, so simple and pure." So successful was he that after only a few sessions at his first school he carried off the second prize.

At the age of eight, he enrolled in the high school in Edinburgh, during October 1821, and continued his literary studies there for six years, distinguishing himself in geography and recitation. That this gifted scholar was loved by all his companions can be gathered from this tribute of one of them—"My recollections are of a tall slender lad with a sweet pleasant face, bright yet grave, fond to play, and of a blameless life."

Andrew Bonar says of McCheyne during this period of his life:

> His mind at that time had no relish for any higher joy than the refined gaieties of society, and for such pleasures as the song and the dance could yield. He himself regarded these as days of ungodliness, days wherein he cherished a pure morality, but lived in heart a Pharisee.

Reaching fourteen years of age, he entered the Edinburgh University, and for almost six years gave himself assiduously to his studies. Although not overly brilliant, he studied languages and gained a few academical honors. The holidays he always enjoyed were spent amid natural scenery. Being good with a pencil, he would make sketches of what he saw. He was also an accomplished musician, had considerable knowledge of music, and could sing beautifully. He became a hymnist of no mean order. A few of his hymns were written while in Palestine. His best-known hymn is "I Once Was a Stranger to Grace and to God." Others in his collection are, "When This Passing World Is Done"; "Beneath Moriah's Rocky Side"; "When I Stand Before the Throne"; "Chosen Not for Good in Me"; and "Oft I Walk Beneath the Cloud."

One who often observed young McCheyne said of him when he was seventeen years old, "A handsome and elegant lad and everything he did seemed to bear the stamp of early culture and native refinement." At twenty, he entered the Divinity Hall, Edinburgh, during the winter of 1831. As yet, he had experienced no spiritual awakening. While at the university he had had occasional religious impressions but none of great depth. During his theological studies, desiring to be useful, he visited the poorer districts of the city on mission work, and unconsciously laid the foundation for the great task he was to accomplish in the densely populated parts of Dundee.

His spiritual preparation

To his natural qualities, and acquired secular and theological knowledge, something deeper was necessary to fashion McCheyne into the saint he became. The first prompting Godward came when he was eighteen. His brother David, the eldest son of the family died suddenly when he was twenty-six after contracting a severe chill. Like his father Adam, he was a W. S. (Writer of Signet, or lawyer). Before young David died, he had a great spiritual struggle, but peace came at the end. That God used this break in the family to bring Robert to his need of Christ can be seen in a letter to a friend on

181

July 8, 1842, "This day eleven years ago I lost my loved and loving brother, and began to seek a Brother who cannot die." And, seeking, he soon found Him.

Spiritual progress was slow. Light dawned gradually. Occasionally, he would plunge into the gaiety of the world. His conversion was not an instantaneous one such as Saul of Tarsus experienced, as McCheyne himself wrote, "I was led to Christ through deep and ever abiding, but not awful or distracting conviction." It was the little book *The Sum of Saving Knowledge* that brought him to a clear understanding and acceptance of the way of salvation. Thus in his diary, March 11, 1834, he wrote, "Read in *The Sum of Saving Knowledge,* the work which I think first of all wrought a change in me. How gladly would I renew the reading of it, if that change might be carried to perfection."

At last he set himself the task of preparing his life's work as "a messenger of grace to guilty men." He started to keep his priceless *Memoirs,* and register his studies and incidents of his life and work. For instance, we read—

> Sept. 2. Sabbath Evening. Reading. Too much engrossed, and too little devotional. Preparation for a fall. Warning—we may be too engrossed with the shell even of heavenly things.
> March 12. Oh, for activity, activity, activity!
> Oct. 17. Private meditation exchanged for conversation. Here is the root of the evil—forsake God and He forsakes us.

Among devotional reading for the heart these *Memoirs,* edited by Dr. Andrew Bonar, are incomparable, and should be in every Christian's library.

A Good Minister of Jesus Christ

Paul's wish and prayer for young Timothy, his son in the faith, can certainly be ascribed to Robert Murray McCheyne who set out to equip himself in every way for the work of the ministry. After finishing his theological studies he was licensed to preach on July 1, 1835. He went to Annan, where his relatives were known, and preached before the Presbytery there and so became as he himself expressed it, "A preacher of the gospel, an honor to which I cannot name an equal." That he had a most solemn sense of his calling can be gathered from his statement that "the pulpit is a wonderful place. . . . God comes nigh you there when you cast yourself upon Him and His help." Is this not the secret of spiritual power in preaching the Word? McCheyne scorned any ambition to star as a popular pulpiteer. His burning passion was to be a pastor according to God's heart, feeding the saints with knowledge and understanding (see Jer. 3:15).

At Duniface

McCheyne's first charge was in the village of Duniface, about three miles from Larbet. He went to assist the Rev. John Bonar, minister of the Parish of Larbet, and brother of the renowned Andrew Bonar. Here the young preacher remained for almost a year. As his duties were light, he gave himself to much prayer and to the study of the Bible in its original languages, and to the reading of the works of Jonathan Edwards, Samuel Rutherford, and other saintly men. His preaching at this time was of an experimental nature, dealing with the inner life of the believer. There also came a passion to convert sinners. "Enlarge my heart and I shall preach," he prayed, and God enlarged his heart. He grasped every opportunity to spread the glorious evangel. He once passed a band of gypsies sitting around a camp fire, and he sat down with them and spoke to them on the parable of "The Lost Sheep." Recording this incident in his diary he said, "The children were attentive and the old people touched a little."

Much time was also consumed visiting the sinful and the

sick. When weary and disappointed, he would plead with God for "gales of spiritual life," and when refreshed he would continue to perform his manifold labors. His short ministry came to a close in August 1836, and he left behind in Duniface many who blessed God for the influence of his life and labors.

At Dundee

McCheyne's second and last charge was in this important Scottish city. A new church, Saint Peter's, was seeking a minister. McCheyne was asked to preach as a candidate, and on August 14, 1836, he preached three times. In the morning his message was on "The Sower." In the afternoon he preached on "The Voice of the Beloved." In the evening he spoke on "Ruth the Moabitess."

Borne along by the Spirit, the young minister preached with all his heart, and souls were blessed that day through his witness. By a large majority he was called, and on November 24, 1836, he was ordained as minister of the new church. His first sermon was on the words of Isaiah, "The Spirit of the Lord is upon me, because the Lord hath anointed me to preach good tidings" (61:1). Said the preacher, "May this be prophetic of the object of my coming here," and it was, for he never failed to function as God's messenger in God's message.

His first description of Dundee was somewhat severe, "A city given to idolatry and hardness of heart. I fear there is much of what Isaiah speaks of—'The prophets prophesy lies, and the people love to have it so.'" Interceding for the city, he prayed that "this city of chimney pots might be changed into the garden of the Lord."

The first months in this new charge were arduous and trying. The membership numbered eleven hundred, a task by no means easy as our glimpse of his six-year ministry there will prove. A fatal attack of influenza struck the city, and

McCheyne found it hard to cope with the visitation of the sick and dying.

A Preacher

McCheyne loved to preach—and he could preach! From the outset the church was full at all services, people attracted from the city and countryside to hear his heart-searching messages. Well over a thousand regularly attended, crowding the aisles and pulpit stairs. Because of his growing fame, calls to larger and wealthier charges reached him but, believing that Dundee was the will of God for him, he remained there. One day he wrote to his beloved mother, "Dear Mamma, you must just make up your mind to let me be murdered among the lanes of Dundee, instead of seeing me fattening on the green glebe of Skirling"—one of the places that desired him. His preaching was never commonplace. He studied earnestly, and refused to be interrupted when preparing his sermons. Often he would ride out "to the ruined church of Invergowrie to enjoy an hour's perfect solitude." There were two conspicuous aspects of his powerful and fruitful preaching:

His preaching was analytical

His messages were simple and lucid, clear and plain. Prominent as a textual preacher, as his printed sermons show, he kept close to Scripture. He was once asked if he had any fear that he would run dry and his reply was, "When the Bible runs dry, then I shall."

His preaching was passionate

McCheyne not only knew all about the *art* of preaching, he felt the *heart* of it as well: "He was often in an agony till he should see Christ formed in the hearts of his people," and this gave his pulpit discourses a love and compassion that compelled results. He spent much time pleading with God for men before he went forth to plead with men for God. One who knew him well wrote—

> He was one of the most complete ministers I ever met. He was a great preacher, an excellent visitor, a full-orbed saint. He visited the dying on Saturdays that his heart might be thrilled by what he saw, and that he might be put into an arrested and serious frame for Sabbath work.

An Evangelist

Ever faithful to his own church, he became practically the evangelist of Forfarshire. He found it hard to refuse an invitation to preach. He believed in scattering the light while the candle of his life burned on. At one time he embarked on an evangelistic tour of the north of Scotland, and for three weeks preached incessantly. Some came to stone him, and ended up entreating him to stay. One who had cast mud at him wept when, later on, he heard of his death. McCheyne's passionate preaching made sinners afraid. He often preached in Ireland, and during the last months of his life was often away spreading the flame. Once he preached in Ruthwell to a vast crowd in the marketplace on the topic, "The Great White Throne." He closed his message saying that they would never meet again on earth—and they never did.

A Missionary

Like the Master he dearly loved and so faithfully served, McCheyne believed that there were "other sheep" that must be brought into the fold; his was a missionary heart. From the time his soul was awakened he was eager to visit the regions beyond. He had a great love for the Jews. When his medical friends advised a change when he was suffering from ill-health, he went to Palestine in 1838 to undertake as a mission of inquiry among the Jews both in Palestine and on the Continent. To a Christ-loving soul like his, the Holy Land was full of the sweetest, tenderest interest. His descriptions and poetry of this sacred spot are without parallel. Wherever he met Jews he would repeat texts in Hebrew, and pray for their salvation. His report on what he saw greatly increased general interest in the work among God's ancient people.

While he was absent, William Burns, a powerful evangelist who later went to China where God mightily used him, substituted for him, and under his preaching at Saint Peter's a remarkable revival broke out. When McCheyne returned he was overwhelmed with joy and entered into the stirring work which continued until the close of his life.

A Revivalist

All through his ministry in Dundee, McCheyne was one of the chief instruments in Scotland in promoting evangelical revival. He strongly felt that modernism, worldliness, and carnal policy in the church were foes of the gospel. It was while he was in Hamburg that he heard of the revival under Burns, and he could not return to his church quickly enough, for this was what his heart hungered for. Doubtless this divine visitation was the fruit of his perpetual intercession and ceaseless toil. He found his church "a Bochim, a place of tears," for whole families were affected, with people falling to the ground groaning and crying for mercy. The Word of God grew and multiplied, and the fire kindled in Dundee spread throughout Scotland. Both Burns and McCheyne went here and there as two flaming revivalists. "The battle is beginning," they said. "The enemy will not give way without a struggle." McCheyne's *Diary* is full of what God wrought during this time. Here is one item—

April 5. Sabbath. Spoke to 24 young persons, one by one; almost all affected about their souls.

Alas! spiritual dearth prevails today, and our churches need another Holy Ghost revival such as swept Scotland over 130 years ago.

A Saint

Writing to a young student, McCheyne gave him this counsel, "Above all keep much in the presence of God. Never see the face of man till you have seen His face who is our life and all." And he practiced what he preached, for he desired above all things a holy walk and manner, and always cultivated his own spiritual life. He longed for "a deeper peace and holier walk." His prime concern was the nurture of his own soul, and so he wrote, "I ought to pray before seeing any one. . . . I feel it is better to rise early and begin with God . . . to see His face first, to get my soul near Him before it is near another." McCheyne learned the secret of perfecting holiness in the Lord. Is it any wonder, then, that he left such an impact on the lives of multitudes? The most effective instrument in the hand of God is a holy life, as the record of this famous Presbyterian minister proves.

> The cause of God is holy,
> And useth holy things.

Finishing the Race

The later years of McCheyne's life were marked by growth in holiness and likeness to the Lord. As he neared heaven, he became more heavenly in spirit and demeanor. His health had always been delicate and fragile, for he had contracted tuberculosis. Yet in spite of his fragility he labored on, never acknowledging defeat. One day he wrote his mother, "My cough is turned into a loose kind of grumble, like the falling down of a shower of stones in a quarry." He never married. During his swift and strenuous days in Dundee he was lovingly cared for by his sister Eliza whom he addressed thus, "How art thou thyself, my own Deaconness and Helpmeet of thy poor brother?"

Even though the valiant warrior felt his lamp was burning low and that the end of the battle was near, he did not relax. On October 5, a Sabbath, he preached three times. The following Sabbath he spoke to his own people morning and afternoon, then at night he preached in nearby Broughty Ferry, on "Arise, shine, for thy light is come!" How prophetic this was to be for him. Although typhus fever was prevalent in the district this tireless evangelist did not screen himself, but visited the afflicted. Because of his poor physical condition and lack of resistance he caught the infection and succumbed. On Wednesday, October 22, his parents and Andrew Bonar were sent for. A friend who visited him lamented that he was not in the pulpit and McCheyne answered, "I am preaching the sermon God would have me do." This was his last conscious message. His sister quoted Cowper's hymn, "Sometimes the light surprises the Christian as he sings."

In his delirium at times he prayed, "This parish, Lord, this people, this whole place." Then he would break out pleading with sinners to repent. This delirious condition continued until Saturday morning, March 25, 1843, when he lifted up his hands in benediction, and without a sigh or pang went home to the bosom of God. He was under thirty years of age when he finished his race, and people spoke of his premature end. Yet in the will of God, his death was not untimely. God never makes a mistake when a young saint is removed.

> Oh sir! the good die first,
> And they whose hearts are dry as summer's dust
> Burn to the socket.

McCheyne had finished his course, even although a short one, and so God took him. The following Lord's Day was a dark one at St. Peter's. Thronged congregations mourned the passing of their beloved pastor. Says the historian, "All Dundee was moved, and the day of his funeral was one of the greatest and most subduing in the annals of the city." Robert's father yielded to the request that his body should rest alongside the church in which he had been so signally used of God, and was so dearly loved.

But dead, Robert Murray McCheyne still speaks. Although he was in the ministry for only some six years and died at twenty-nine, his is an abiding influence. We are apt to forget that it is not the *length* of life that counts, but the *quality* of it—

> We live in deeds, not years; in thoughts, not breaths;
> In feelings, not in figures on a dial.
> We should count time by heart-throbs. He most lives
> Who thinks most—feels the noblest—acts the best.

While some of his sermons and poems are in print, he published no books, and took little part in public movements. He died young, yet his story has traveled the world over. One item in his precious diary reads, "O God for grace to live that when dead, I shall be missed!" How deeply he was missed! Age after age has risen to call him blessed. Dr. Bonar's *Memoirs and Diary of Robert Murray McCheyne* has been used for the conversion of many. Although he has been in the ivory palaces now for some 130 years, his garments still have the fragrance of myrrh, cassia, and aloes. As one writer has expressed it, "McCheyne's beautiful Christian life is an example to aspiring believers and a rebuke to desponding sluggards."

Jesus said to His disciples, "Learn of me." What are some of the outstanding traits of McCheyne's life we can learn much from? In what ways has he left an example to follow?

His sense of sin

In his most moving hymn, H. Twells bids us remember that—

None, O Lord, have perfect rest,
For none are wholly free from sin;
And they who fain would serve Thee best
Are conscious most of wrong within.

That this was true of McCheyne can be gathered from many entries in his diary. One day he wrote, "The lust of praise has ever been my besetting sin." Vastly popular, with physical beauty that satisfied the eye and a personality that commanded attention, it must have been hard for him to resist admiration. After his death, his father said that he could understand why his son's life was cut short. It was to prevent the townsfolk making an idol of him. A tenth part of the popularity accorded McCheyne has puffed up and ruined many a minister. But, conscious of his failing, young Robert tried to mortify self and lay in dust life's glory dead. Under the date July 7, Sabbath, we read in his diary—

> Two things that defile this day in looking back are love of praise running through all, and consenting to listen to worldly talk at all.

On another day we find an entry revealing his deep sense of sin—

> None but God knows what an abyss of corruption is in my heart.

Would that we could always be aware that in us, apart from grace, there dwelleth no good thing!

His walk with God

In spite of his constant care of over a thousand members, he made time to feed his inner fires. His diary abounds with references to the hours he spent in secret prayer. A friend of McCheyne's wrote, "During the last years of his short life he walked calmly in almost unbroken fellowship with the Father and the Son." His constant incentive to a holy walk was the truth of the return of Christ. How he loved the thought of His appearing! Scotland never had a saintlier man than Robert Murray McCheyne. His was a God-centered life. He had no other interest in life save the glory of God. To his soul God was the center and circumference of all things.

His passion for souls

Living so near the Saviour, he caught something of His passion and compassion for the lost and, therefore, was extremely active in plucking brands from the burning. One day, while standing by a fireman fighting the flames, he said to the man, "Does that fire remind you of anything?" Like Livingstone of Shotts, he often preached "as out of the very heart of the Weeper of Olivet." Another diary entry reads, "O, when will I plead with my tears and inward yearnings over sinners?" The church's tragedy today is her possession of far too many passionless pastors whose eyes never run down with rivers of water for the destruction of God's people (Lam. 3:48-49). They know so little of what it is—

> To weep o'er the erring one,
> And lift up the fallen.

One Monday, McCheyne met his dear friend Andrew Bonar, and said to him, "What did you preach on yesterday?" Bonar replied in all solemnity, "Hell!" McCheyne replied, "Were you able to preach it with tears?"

His loyalty to Scripture

While the modernistic approach to the Bible was not as prominent in McCheyne's day as it is today, yet there was a movement in the direction of doubt as to its divine inspiration and veracity. It was because of his reverence for the Word as a divine revelation that he was so mightily used of God. How can a preacher achieve victories with a blunt sword? Dundee's renowned saint always read Scripture, first of all for his own edification, then for the spiritual benefit of others. He took his stand upon Scripture, authoritative, all through, and found any part of it he preached on as being "quick, powerful, and sharper than any two-edged sword." As a result his church was crowded with eager listeners and continued to be that way.

Such, then, is the portrait of the short life of one who burned out serving the Lord whom he loved with an intense passion. He lived and labored so as to be missed when his eyelids closed in death. We read of Jehoram who departed this life "without being desired." Because of the pernicious influence of his character, it was better for his contemporaries that he was dead. How different it was with McCheyne, and with all who serve the Lord as faithfully as he did!

> I would be missed when gone
> I would not—my life done—
> Have no eyes wet for me,
> No hearts touched tenderly,
> No good of me confessed:
> Dead—yet not missed.

15

David Livingstone
The Scot Who Lighted a Dark Continent

It is to be questioned whether any nationality has contributed more outstanding missionaries, theologians, preachers, and writers to the cause of Christ than the Scotch. As the result of the Reformation under John Knox, there emerged a host of men of culture and sturdy caliber, each of whom left footprints behind them on the sands of time. The picture gallery of Scottish church history is crowded with magnificent portraits. For instance, when we read *Bible Characters* we think of Alexander Whyte; and when we sing "O Love That Wilt Not Let Me Go" the image of the famous blind preacher, George Matheson comes before us.

In the missionary room of the Scottish picture gallery, no portrait is so prominent as that of David Livingstone, who carried the light of Christian civilization to the world's most backward area, and who remains one of the world's most intrepid missionaries. He joined Barnabas and Paul in hazarding his life for the name of the Lord Jesus Christ. Youth of today should be persuaded to read the record of Scotland's noble son. His life and labors reveal what God is able to accomplish through one wholly committed to Him. Livingstone certainly knew what it was to climb the steep ascent to heaven through peril, toil, and pain.

The Blantyre Youth

The early years of Livingstone have never ceased to fascinate the hearts and grip the attention of the young with a desire to serve the Lord. It was his thrilling story that nerved the factory girl, Mary Slessor, and helped to stir within her a longing to work in heathen lands. The facts of his young days have been told a thousand times or more. This Clydesdale lad was brought up in a tenement house in Blantyre. The home was a Bible-loving one, a factor that wielded a formative influence over his life and laid the foundation of his monumental work.

His father was Neil Livingstone who was described by a friend who knew him as "a man of great spiritual earnestness and his whole life was consecrated to duty and the fear of God." Would that the world had more fathers with the same reputation! He was a deacon in the Independent Church, Hamilton, a member of the local missionary society, an earnest Temperance worker. He was also a great reader, and acted as an unpaid colporteur. For a living he traveled the countryside selling tea. His income was meager, and the family had to live sparingly.

His mother, was Agnes Hunter Livingstone, who was remembered as "active, orderly, and of thorough cleanliness." She trained her family in the same virtues. She was a delicate little woman, with a wonderful flow of good spirits. She was remarkable for the beauty of the eyes, to which those of her son, David, bore a strong resemblance. Neil and Agnes were married in 1810, and resided first in Glasgow, removing later to Blantyre. Five sons, two of whom died in infancy, and two daughters were born to this commendable pair. David often recalled his mother's love, care, and thrift. She died June 18, 1865, but lived long enough to share the triumphs of her illustrious, much-loved son. In his *Journal,* Monday, June 19, Livingstone wrote,

When going away in 1858 she said to me that she

would have liked one of her laddies to lay her head in the grave. It so happened that I was there to pay the last tribute to a dear good mother.

What a tremendous asset a godly home is! If in the goodness of God you have one, respect and value it.

It was on March 19, 1813, that David was born in that poor, humble, yet lovely home in Blantyre, Lanarkshire, Scotland. As a young man, I served as an evangelist with the Lanarkshire Christian Union, and often preached in Blantyre. Whenever I was there I would visit the old Livingstone home which has been preserved as a memorial. The tenement building, so familiar in those days, and to this day existing in slum areas, were made of two-roomed flats—"But 'n a' Ben," as they were called. *But* is the Scotch for "kitchen," while *ben* means "within or inner," and was the description of a kind of a parlor off the kitchen. In the *but,* or kitchen, there were usually two recesses built out from the wall which served as beds. These recesses were sometimes called "hole in the wall," for that is what they looked like. It was in one of the *buts* that Livingstone saw the light of day. When my wife and I were married in Motherwell, near to Blantyre, over sixty years ago we set up house in a "But 'n a' Ben," and our son was born in one of these kitchen *buts.*

Livingstone was named David after David Hunter, his mother's father. The compelling name Livingstone has suggested several things to those who loved the missionary. Professor George Wilson, acknowledging a book David Livingstone had sent him in 1857, wrote expressively, "May your name be propitious: in all your long and weary journeys may the *Living* half of your name outweight the other: till after long and blessed labors the white *Stone* is given you in the happy land." After his death, a very sweet eulogy appeared, of all places, in *Punch,* the last verse of which ran—

He needs no epitaph to guard a name
Which men shall prize while worthy work is known.

He lived and died for good—be that his fame:
Let marble crumble: this is *LIVING - STONE.*

About his earliest days there is little to say. He helped his mother with household chores. He always insisted that his mother would lock the door so that no school chums could come in and make fun of him. As a child, he was calm and self-reliant. At the age of nine he received a present of a New Testament from his Sunday school teacher for repeating Psalm 119, with its 176 verses, on two successive evenings with only five errors—a proof that perseverance was bred in his bones. He was very fond of reading travel books, and would always go with his father to missionary meetings to hear missionaries relate their adventures.

Factory life

Because Livingstone's parents were poor, he began to work in a neighboring factory to help out with the home finances. All the children had to work, for the mother was not able to feed and clothe them all on her husband's meager earnings. So at ten years of age, David entered the Blantyre Mill and began as a "piecer," and when nineteen he became a "spinner." He had to work fourteen hours a day, from 6 A.M. to 8 P.M. To his mother's delight he put the first two shillings, six pence he earned in her lap. She gave him back a little of it and with it he bought a secondhand Latin grammar. From an early age he evinced a thirst for knowledge. Later on in his life he was to write of those hard days—

> The dictionary part of my labors was followed up till midnight or later, if my mother did not interfere by jumping up and snatching the books out of my hand. I had to be back to the factory by six in the morning and continue my work with intervals for breakfast and dinner till eight at night. I read in this way classical works, and knew Virgil and Horace better at sixteen than I do now.

His method was to place a book on his machine and read in spare moments. Livingstone never hid the fact of his hard, poor life. When, in after years, the highest in the land showered compliments upon him, he wrote to a friend about "my own order, the honest poor." On the gravestone of his parents were their names and the names of their children who had died, and the phrase "Children of Poor and Pious Parents." What a rebuke the perseverance of those factory days is to much of the indolent youth today! The prevailing spirit seems to be—work as little as you can for as much as you can get.

University life

It was during the winter of 1836-1837, that David Livingstone entered the Glasgow University. During the summer months he worked in the mill, and the wages earned supported him during the winter months at the university. He lived sparingly, and cut down spending to the lowest. He took his degree in medicine in 1840. Glasgow is some fifteen miles from Blantyre, and he would walk there and back. Theological studies were taken at the Edinburgh University. Dr. John Clifford, speaking at the centenary of Livingstone, said of him, "He had many teachers, and we remember how the teaching of his parents helped in molding him for after years. His home was poor, but it was the household of saints. Luxury was not there, but the Word of God was there. His toil was bitter, but no bitter word escaped his lips because his parents had sent him to these early labors."

Christian life

Livingstone had a consuming desire to be a medical missionary, hence his university studies, but as to any exact spiritual crisis whereby he became the Lord's he was not able to trace. Reared in a godly home, he had from earliest childhood a Christian consciousness, and knew that he was the Lord's. It would seem as if he owed his spiritual impetus to Dr. Thomas Dick, of Broughty Ferry, whose book on *The Philosophy of a Future State* pointed out some of his errors, and pointed out to him the way of salvation. When he was about twenty years old, he passed through a deep experience and wrote of it years later—

> I saw the duty and inestimable privilege immediately to accept salvation by Christ. Humbly believing that through sovereign grace and mercy I have been enabled to do so, and having felt in some measure its effects on my still depraved and deceitful heart, it is my desire to show my attachment to the cause of Him who died for me by devoting my life to His service.

Without such a solid, spiritual foundation, Livingstone would never have become the renowned missionary-explorer God made him. He believed he had been saved to serve. Far too many seek to serve who are not saved.

The African Missionary

When the young medical-missionary set out for darkest Africa, he had no idea of the trials and triumphs that would be his before he died on his knees in a lonely hut. Little did this handsome, well-built youth, shy and ill-at-ease in public, realize what fame would be his.

His first missionary impulse

At first, Livingstone had no direct thought of being a missionary, although he felt his responsibility in this direction. "Feeling that the salvation of men ought to be the chief desire and aim of every Christian," he made this resolution, "That he would give to the cause of missions all that he

199

might earn beyond what was required for his subsistence." Having such a missionary enthusiast as a father must have influenced young David in the direction of the regions beyond. It would seem, however, as if his first definite decision to be a missionary came through Dr. Karl Gatzlaff, the German Apostle to China of whose work Livingstone had read and heard so much. He decided to offer himself for work in China when he was but twenty-one. "The claims of so many millions of his fellow-creatures, and the complaints of the scarcity of qualified missionaries," made China his first love, and "his efforts were constantly directed toward that object without any fluctuation." But, owing to the Opium War raging at that time, the door into China was closed.

His definite call to Africa

While engaged in his theological studies at Edinburgh, he went out on his first preaching engagement and, rising to speak, words failed him. "Friends, I have forgotten all I had to say," he gasped, and in shame came down from the pulpit. Dr. Robert Moffat was in the city at the time after having establishing a mission in Kuraman, South Africa. Meeting David in the moment of his discouragement, he advised him not to give up, telling him that perhaps God wanted him to be a doctor instead of a preacher. But the young student was determined to be both, and a missionary besides. There is no doubt that Livingstone owed his entrance into Africa to Robert Moffat, who was to become his father-in-law. Moffat himself describes the interview with the young man so desirous of serving the Lord abroad.

> By and by he asked me whether I thought he would do for Africa. I said I believed he would, if he would go not to an old station, but advance to unoccupied ground, specifying the vast plain to the north, where I had sometimes seen, in the morning sun, the smoke of a 1,000 villages, where no missionary had

ever been. At last Livingstone said, "What is the use of my waiting for the end of this abominable opium war. I will go at once to Africa!" The Directors concurred, and Africa became his sphere.

Thus in 1838, the London Missionary Society accepted his application. That he had fully counted the cost of his decision to go to Africa can be gathered from his own statement. "The hardships and dangers of missionary life, so far as I have had the means of ascertaining their nature and extent, have been the subject of serious reflection, and in dependence on the promised assistance of the Holy Spirit, I have no hesitation in saying that I would willingly submit to them, considering my constitution capable of enduring any ordinary share of hardship and fatigue."

His departure for the field

The last night in the old Blantyre home that he dearly loved, was a sad one. Father and son sat up late discussing missions. The next morning, the seventeenth day of November 1840, the family rose at 5 A.M., and his mother prepared breakfast for all, after which David conducted family worship, reading Psalms 121 and 135. He then prayed, commending one and all to God. Sorrowful farewells over, father and son left the humble home and walked the fifteen miles to Glasgow, where David caught the Liverpool steamer at the Broomielaw. At the quay they looked into each other's faces for the last time on earth, for in the will of God they never met again. The noble old man walked back slowly to Blantyre with a lonely heart, no doubt, yet praising God for a son he could give to Africa. As for David, his face was now set in earnest toward the Dark Continent where he was to give his life accomplishing great things for God.

Livingstone was twenty-eight years of age when on December 8, 1840, he sailed on the *George* for distant shores. To an old companion he wrote, "I want my life to be spent as profitably as a pioneer as in any other way." Livingstone took as his motto, "I am ready to go anywhere, provided it be forward!" And forward he went into the darkness of the unknown as a messenger of Him who came to banish darkness in a world of sin.

It was when he reached Cairo while he was on his way home for his first furlough that he heard news of his father's death. He reached England December 9, 1856, and then learned of his father's great desire to see him again. "You wished so much to see David," said his daughter to him as his life was ebbing away. "Aye, very much, very much," he replied, "but the will of the Lord be done."

The first thing David did when he reached the home of sorrow was to sit in his father's empty chair. This experience moved him deeply. One of his sisters wrote later to a friend—

> The first evening he asked all about father's illness and death. One of us remarked that he knew he was dying and his spirits seemed to rise. David burst into tears. At family worship that evening he said with deep feeling—"We bless Thee, O Lord for our parents. We give Thee thanks for the dead who have died in the Lord."

His first sphere

Livingstone first spent time in the Bechuana Country, Central Africa, where he developed a burning compassion for the black people. Entering a tribe he would make friends with the chieftain, treat the sick, and preach to the natives about a God who became the heavenly Father of all who trusted Him. The traffic in slaves shocked and saddened his heart, and he vowed that he would dedicate his life to stamping out such an evil. Because of the way his healing medicines relieved people and because he taught about a better way of living, he earned the title of "The Good One." One who observed Livingstone in those initial years wrote of him, "His marvelous qualities became manifest even before he had mastered any of the native languages. The chiefs recognized in him a man of noble character, tender sympathy, and infinite helpfulness."

His marriage

For the first four years of his missionary career Livingstone was a bachelor, with no thought of marriage, feeling that it was best to be free. Then he came to realize that perhaps marriage would aid him in the tasks ahead. He had contact with the Kuruman Mission, where the Moffats labored, on their return from furlough. He visited their home, and one day beneath the fruit trees he proposed to Mary, the daughter of Dr. and Mrs. Robert Moffat. Having been born in Africa, Mary was used to the hardships and dangers of the jungle and desert and was a fit companion for the pioneer missionary-doctor. A few months later they married, and were very happy, although often separated because Mary was not strong enough for the hard life of trekking through trackless jungles. In the course of time there were three little children at her skirts, and she decided to stay at a mission center and care for her bairns and pray for her husband as he pressed tirelessly on. Both husband and wife were united in putting Christ first. Here is a heart-moving extract from a letter he wrote to Mary—

> And now, my dearest, farewell. May God bless you! Let your affections be towards Him much more than towards me: and kept by His mighty power and grace, I hope I shall never give you cause to regret that you have given me a part. Whatever friendship we feel towards each other, let us always look to Jesus as our Common Friend and Guide, and may He shield you with His everlasting arms from all evil.

Both of them returned to England to bring their three children to be educated in the country, and after a while journeyed back to Africa very lonely without their children. Little did those young children know they would not see their beloved mother again. On April 21, 1862, Mary became ill, and on Sunday, the twenty-seventh the end came. The heart-stricken husband "was sitting by the side of a rude bed formed of boxes; but covered with a soft mattress, on which lay his dying wife," and held her close as she breathed her last. "The man who had faced so many deaths, and braved so many dangers, was now utterly broken down and weeping like a child," over the passing of his Mary. He buried her beneath a large baobab tree at Shupanga there to await the resurrection morn.

What a touching scene that must have been as the bereaved husband found himself alone in vast Africa! Yet, "solitude is the mother country of the strong." That Livingstone deeply felt the loss of his wife can be gathered from his *Journal*, which contains many references to her, "It is the first heavy stroke I have suffered, and quite takes away my strength. I wept over her who well deserved many tears. I loved her when I married her, and the longer I lived with her I loved her the more. God pity the children, who were all tenderly attached to her, and I am left alone in the world by one whom I felt to be part of myself." On May 11, we read: "My dear, dear Mary has been this evening a fortnight in heaven—absent from the body, present with the Lord." On May 31, "The loss of my ever dear Mary lies like a heavy weight on my heart." A year later, April 27, 1863, this item appears in his *Journal*—"On this day twelve months ago my beloved Mary Moffat was removed from me by death."

Familiar, as he was with the poets, doubtless the words of Tennyson brought comfort to his empty heart—

If I can, I'll come again, mother, from out my
    resting place:

Though you'll not see me, mother, I shall look
   upon your face;
Though I cannot speak a word, I shall hearken
   what you say,
And be often, often with you when you think I'm
   far away.

The Intrepid Explorer

Although Livingstone became world renowned for his explorations, he retained his missionary zeal. Writing home to his brother Charles he said, "I am a missionary, heart and soul. God had an only Son, and He became a missionary and a physician. A poor, poor imitation of Him I am, or wish to be. In this service I hope to live, in it I wish to die."

Afterward he severed his connection with the London Missionary Society and spent the last part of his life exploring what was then the unknown parts of the dark continent of Africa. He became, as one put it, "Traveler, geographer, zoologist, astronomer, missionary, physician, and mercantile director; did ever man sustain so many characters at once? Or did ever man perform the duties of each with such painstaking accuracy and so great success?"

O. K. Armstrong in his article on Livingstone in *Reader's Digiest* wrote,

> His feats of exploration rank with the greatest. Exploring one third of a huge Continent—from the Cape almost to the Equator and from the Atlantic to the Indian Ocean—he opened up a vaster unknown area of the earth's surface than any other single man. He charted all the regions he visited and sent precise reports to the Royal Geographical Society, London. He was the first European to find the Great Lake Ngami. He came upon some magnificent falls, more than twice as high as Niagara, and named them Victoria Falls in honor of his Queen.

He traveled some twenty-nine thousand miles in Africa, and added to the then-known part of the globe about a million square miles. Said his friend, Maclear, the Astronomer Royal at the Cape to whom his observations were regularly forwarded for verification and correction, "Such a man deserves every encouragement in the power of his country to give. He has done that which few other travelers in Africa can boast of—he has fixed his geographical points with great accuracy, and yet he is only a poor missionary."

His sacrificial labors

What a striking parallel there is between the many sufferings of Livingstone as he pursued his missionary and exploration activities, and the numerous perils of another indomitable pioneer-missionary, the apostle Paul. The African explorer knew what it was to be "in journeyings often," and to experience the hardships of being "in weariness and painfulness, in watchings often, in hunger and thirst, in fastings often, in cold and nakedness" (II Cor. 11:26, 27). When we compare the "peril, toil, and pain" others have endured for Christ's sake with our easy life and lack of suffering, we feel somewhat ashamed.

> Must I be carried to the skies
> On flowery beds of ease,
> While others fought to win the prize
> And sailed through bloody seas?

Livingstone was in perils oft. All the world knows about the thrilling story of his encounter with a lion at Mabotsa. The animal seized him by the shoulder, tore his flesh and crushed his bone. He would have been killed had not his life been miraculously saved by a native teacher who was supported by a lady in England for twelve pounds a year. This native was one of his converts, and Livingstone had chosen him as his first native superintendent of schools. It was he who succeeded in drawing the lion away. Never again was the missionary able to lift that arm above his head without pain. Exposed at all times, not only against wild beasts but also savage men, Livingstone had no fear. The hardy preacher's endurance and scorn of danger became legendary.

In his toil and travel, he became subject to fevers and also apprehensive of them, seeing it was from a fever that his beloved Mary had died. His work as a doctor was vitally important to his preaching. In caring for the bodies of the sick, he was able to reach their hearts for Christ. Daily he demonstrated the use of quinine in treating malaria. For the first five years of his work in Africa he himself had thirty-one attacks of fever. Without quinine he would have died. With it he revived whole families and tribes. Writing to his sister about a new venture he had embarked on he said,

> Fever may cut us all off. I feel much when I think of the children dying. But who will go if we don't. Not one. I would venture everything for Christ. Pity I have so little to give. But He will accept me for He is a good Master. Never one like Him. He can sympathize. May He forgive, and purify and bless us.

One of the most trying experiences of a missionary's life is isolation. Cut off from home and dear ones and all the comforts and amenities of civilization is not an easy cross to carry. Livingstone had a full share of loneliness, as extracts from his *Journal* prove. Before his wife died, he felt deeply the separation from her and the children. Many of his letters to his much-loved Mary, at whose grave he lingered for several days, are too sacred to spread before the public. But here is a brief paragraph from one of them.

> How I miss you now, and the children! My heart yearns incessantly over you. . . . Take them all around you, and kiss them for me. Tell them I have left them for the love of Jesus, and they must love Him too, and avoid sin, for that displeases Jesus.

While his medical knowledge and supplies proved valuable to Livingstone amid his physical sufferings, yet there were times when pain and sickness was hard to bear. An item in his *Journal* reads, "Very ill from bleeding from the bowels and purging. Bled all night. Got up at 1 A.M. to take latitude." Attempting a new journey with his native helpers, he had to cut the way through trees and jungle thorns, and must have presented a pitiable sight. Writing of this experience in his *Journal* he said, "With our hands all raw and bloody, and knees through trousers, we at length emerged." Livingstone had to tear his handkerchief in two, to tie over his cut knees.

In 1869 he took desperately ill with pneumonia. He was on the memorable expedition to discover the sources of the Nile so that European trade might come from the north to the interior of Africa. He was ill much of the time. Unfriendly savages stole his supplies. Many of his helpers deserted him. Incessant rains and tsetse flies made travel almost impossible, and he succumbed. Faithful natives carried him on a rough litter for the two month trek to Lake Tanganyika for rest and treatment.

His *Journal* for 1867 ends with a statement about scarcity of food, and the consequent physical weakness that ensued. There was nothing to eat but the coarsest grain of the country. He began his *Journal* for 1868 with a prayer that if he should die that year, he might be prepared for it. Describing his difficulties in a letter to his daughter he humorously wrote, "I broke my teeth tearing at the maize and other hard food, and they are coming out. One front tooth is out, and I have such an awful mouth. If you expect a kiss from me, you may take it through a speaking trumpet."

His encounter with Stanley

For over two years he recuperated from his emaciated condition at Lake Tanganyika. During this time nothing was heard of him in Britain, and much concern was felt about his welfare. On every hand the question was being asked, "Where is Livingstone?" Two relief expeditions were organized and sent out to find him, but because of tropical diseases, the parties had to return. Then the enterprising manager of the *New York Herald* sensed the possibility of a great story of this missionary-doctor-explorer *lost* in the heart of Africa. The manager was James Gordon Bennett. He commissioned star reporter, Henry Morton Stanley, the twenty-nine-year-old foreign correspondent of the *Herald,* to go to Africa and find Livingstone no matter how long it took and how much money it cost. Reaching Zanzibar, Stanley assembled a party of almost two hundred carriers to transport the loads of goods and medicines the *Herald* supplied.

But Stanley was to experience some of the hardship of the man he had set out to seek. There were those who tried to kill him, and malaria and dysentery wore him down. Because of torrential rains progress was slow. "Yet for nine months, with courage worthy of the noble man he sought, Stanley pushed on into the interior." Then, 236 days after reaching what is now Tanzania, the most moving meeting in all missionary history took place. On November 3, 1871, four of the most famous words of the Victorian Era were uttered. Here is the wonderful scene as related by O. K. Armstrong,

> On November 10 the people of Ugigi rushed to Livingstone to tell him the exciting news: a white man had arrived! Livingstone, emaciated but erect, stood before his tent, peering in astonishment at the big caravan headed by a tall white man flanked by a porter carrying the Stars and Stripes. The people parted to form a living avenue, down which Stanley stalked to one of the most dramatic meetings of all time.
>
> *Dr. Livingstone I presume?*
>
> Stanley came just in time. For two years Livingstone had been without medicine of any kind. Gratefully

he accepted the new clothes and supplies, eagerly read letters and heard news of the outside world.

Stanley was never the same man after those days with Livingstone. His life was completely changed as he witnessed the faith, courage, and determination of this great man. He pleaded with Livingstone to return with him to England; but he refused saying, "I still have much work to do." Reluctantly Stanley left the lonely explorer, and returned with reports for his newspaper that made David Livingstone a hero, and the most-talked-of man of his day. But fame had little attraction to this courageous man who gave his life for Africa.

His prolific honors

When he returned to England for his first furlough and to write his missionary travels, he was astonished to find himself famous. He was received at the palace by the prince consort. Scientists were eager to hear him, and the government gave him civil authority to deal with African tribes. Manifold honors were heaped upon him for his work. Altogether some 507 medals, freedoms, degrees, and awards were received. Yet as one speaker said at a banquet in Livingstone's honor—"Notwithstanding eighteen months of laudation, so justly bestowed on him by all classes of his countrymen, and after receiving all the honors which the universities and cities of our country could shower upon him, he is still the same honest true-hearted David Livingstone, as when he issued from the wilds of Africa."

Amid all the adulation coming his way, however, there was a dark cloud that humbled him. To a friend he wrote—"My son, Robert, is in the Federal Army in America, and no comfort. The secret ballast is often applied by a kind hand above, when to outsiders we appear to be sailing gloriously with the wind."

The Slave Emancipator

Livingstone not only expanded the geographical knowledge of Central Africa through his explorations, and healed the sick and preached the gospel to the poor, but he also fought most relentlessly the Arab slave trade which destroyed potential village preaching centers, as means to promote missionary effort. This unholy, inhuman traffic was strongly denounced by this fearless emancipator who wrote fervent letters to the British government begging them to help in stopping such a terrible trade. Abraham Lincoln and David Livingstone were both freedom lovers, and they both hated slavery. Of the latter it is said— "For thirty years his life was spent in an unwearied effort to evangelize the native races, to explore the undiscovered secrets, and abolish the desolating trade of Central Africa." There are those to set themselves to evangelize—others to explore—and still others to emancipate. But as Frank Boreham expressed it, "David Livingstone, with a golden secret locked up in his heart, undertook all three. *Evangelization, exploration, emancipation,* these were his watchwords."

That he was haunted by the specter of the slave traffic can be gathered from the last words he wrote before his death, and which are inscribed on his grave in Westminster Abbey as his epitaph for thousands to read—

> All I can say in my solitude is, may Heaven's rich blessing come down on every one—American, English, Turk—who will help to heal this open sore of the World.

At another time he wrote, "Can the love of Christ not carry the missionary where the slave-trade carries the trader?" His testimony was clear and emphatic wherever slavery prevailed. Neither personal friendship nor any other consideration under the sun could repress his denunciations. He lived to

211

free unhappy souls. As J. D. Jones wrote of his master-passion,

> Better than all his discoveries would be the healing of this open sore. He tracked the traders to their hunting grounds. He laid bare their unspeakable cruelties. He stirred up the consciences of the people at home. He fought the fight almost single-handed. He surrendered home and comfort, he endured loneliness and suffering: he risked health and life in this holy war, and at last he died, and by dying won his triumph. Other travelers may have made greater discoveries than Livingstone but no one can rob him of this title to immortal fame—*He was the Liberator of Africa!*

The anchor of his soul amid all his toils, trials, and tribulations was his implicit and simple trust in God. He had a profound belief in prayer, and his prayers were direct and plain. Once, when surrounded by savages, he sensed danger in the air, but looked to Christ and rested upon His promise—"I read that Jesus said, 'All power is given unto me in heaven and in earth. Go ye therefore, and teach all nations, and lo, I am with you alway, even unto the end of the world.' It is the word of a Gentleman of the most sacred and strictest honor, and there is an end on't."

His Lonely Death

After Stanley left, Livingstone, provided with a new caravan and supplies, determined explorer that he was, went on in the search for the sources of the Nile. Strength was ebbing, yet stubbornly he continued, and when too weak to walk he was carried on a litter. As he entered further into the interior, he looked about him for a suitable grave. Although he underwent several physical agonies, he was reluctant to give up. Six weeks before he died he wrote, "Nothing will make me give up my work in despair. I encourage myself in the Lord my God and go forward." The loss of his much-valued medicine chest was the beginning of the end, for after January 1867, he had no remedy against African fevers and other grievous maladies. He described his poignant loss thus, "I felt as if I had now received the sentence of death: this loss of the medicine gnaws at the heart terribly." What a pitiable sight he must have presented far in the lonely interior of Africa, in pain and sickness with neither wife nor child nor brother to cheer him with sympathy, or lighten his dull, drab hut with a smile! Such was the heavy price he paid to make Christ known in a heathen land.

The solemn end of this warrior has been told over and over again, and it cannot be too often repeated for the inspiration of the young. April 29, 1873, was the last day of his missionary travels. He directed Susi, his faithful servant, to take him to Ilala and lay him on a rough bed in a hut. The next morning at 4, his servants saw the light of a candle burning but David Livingstone was not in his crude bed. He was kneeling beside his bed with his head resting on his clasped hands—*dead.* Somehow he had crawled out and, doubtless knowing that the end was at hand, died in the act of prayer, interceding for his loved ones, and his own dear Africa with all her sins and wrongs. Thus, on May 4, 1873, at sixty years of age, he entered the presence of the King to be reunited with his beloved Mary and his dear godly parents. For this gallant saint there was no moaning at the bar as he put out to sea to explore the heavenly land.

From hut to hut, and village to village the sad announcement was relayed. "The Good One is gone!" Crowds of his converts came to pay their last respects to the one who had brought them life, light, and hope. Those nearest him knew that those in England who loved and honored him wanted to bury the missionary-doctor, so with loving hearts they dried and embalmed his frail frame, and covered it with bark. But before doing so they removed his heart and buried it beneath a moula tree—a symbolic act, for his heart belonged to their soil. *Africa* was engraven on that heart, the life's blood of which was poured out for its salvation.

Then began the most perilous and longest funeral march in history. The native mourners set out on their nine-month trek to the coast, singing the gospel hymns "The Good One" had taught them. A British vessel at Zanzibar brought the body home to England, arriving on April 15, 1874. On April 18, the famous Scot was laid to rest in honor in Westminster Abbey, where a vast throng had gathered to pay their last respects. Perhaps one of the most intimate and inspiring biographies of this missionary-explorer is *The Personal Life of David Livingstone,* by W. G. Blaikie, whose very good summary of his worth and witness we quote,

> Amid all the vicissitudes of his career, Livingstone remained faithful to his missionary character. His warmth and purity of heart, his intense devotion to his Master, and the African people for his Master's sake, his patience, endurance, trustfulness, and prayerfulness, his love of science, his wide humanity, his intense charity, have given to his name and memory an undying fragrance. After his death, church after church hastened to send missionaries to Africa; and it would take a long space even to enumerate all the agencies that are at work there. His death, that seemed to give the death-blow to his plans, gave a new impulse to the cause of African evangelization and civilization, which bids fair, with God's help, to accomplish great results.

Although Livingstone did not live to see the cessation of the slavery he utterly abhorred and fought so hard to abolish, yet after his death Queen Victoria publicly acclaimed the missionary for his unceasing crusade against this horror, and in 1880 announced that treaties had been signed with the sultan of Zanzibar and other sovereigns prohibiting this terrible traffic by land and sea.

What are some of the lessons to be gleaned today from the noble life and magnificent labors of this renowned medical missionary who suffered and yet achieved so much for the Master he dearly loved and faithfully served?

Give the best to God

David Hogg, his old Sunday school teacher, from his death-bed gave young Livingstone the instruction, "Now, lad, make religion the everyday business of your life and not a thing of fits and starts; for if you do, temptation and other things will get the better of you." From first to last, David Livingstone made religion, or rather Christ and His cause, his everyday business. As his *Journal* records, on his last birthday he dedicated himself anew to Him to whom he had surrendered his life. If Christ is worthy of anything it is our best, seeing He shed His blood for our redemption. Calvary has a claim upon all that we are and have.

> Just as I am, young, strong, and free,
> To be the best that I can be,
> For truth, and righteousness, and Thee,
>   Lord of my life, I come.

Reliance upon divine companionship

With all his heart, Livingstone believed the promise of the Master to accompany without fail those He would send forth into all the world to extend His cause among men. When home on furlough after years of service in Africa, Livingstone went to his old university in Glasgow to receive the degree of Doctor of Laws. As he rose, he was not met with student banter. His gaunt haggard frame, the result of his long exposure to African sun, was received in reverential silence. Already he had on thirty occasions suffered fevers and severe illness. His crushed arm, the result of his encounter with the lion, was hanging at his side. Replying to the honor conferred upon him, he said, "I return to my work without misgiving and with great gladness. Would you like me to tell you what supported me through all the years of exile among people whose language I could not understand, and whose attitude towards me was always uncertain and often hostile? It was this, 'Lo, I am with you alway, even unto the end of the world!' On those words I staked everything, and they never failed."

Livingstone proved that with the *Go,* there was the *Lo;* that whoever God appoints for soul-saving service, He accompanies. Is it not said of the disciples after Jesus had ascended to heaven that as they went forth preaching everywhere, that the Lord worked *with them,* and confirmed their witness (Mark 16:20)? Facing the unknown, Moses received the divine promise, "My presence shall go with thee." Without divine companionship the leader of the people would not go forward: "If thy presence go not with me, carry us not up hence" (Exod. 33:14-15). Whether we are called to follow Livingstone into the regions beyond or tarry by the staff at home makes no difference. Every follower of the Master has the assurance that He will never leave nor forsake them.

> Wherever He may guide me,
> No want shall turn me back;
> My Shepherd is beside me,
> And nothing can I lack.
> His wisdom ever waketh,
> His sight is never dim;
> He knows the way He taketh,
> And I will walk with Him.

Live the life that counts

After visiting Cambridge to address the university students, Livingstone received a most encouraging letter from one of the tutors, part of which read, "That Cambridge visit of yours lighted a candle which will never, never go out." Such a sentiment is true of the renowned missionary's work in Africa. His light continued to shine until extinguished by his lonely death, and the influence of his wonderful labors continues. Florence Nightingale, writing to Livingstone's sister after hearing of his death in Africa, said, "He has opened those countries for God to enter in. He struck the first blow to abolish a hideous slave trade. He, like Stephen, was the first martyr."

Although his heart is buried under an African tree, and his body reposes in Westminster Abbey, his spirit goes marching on. The history of his life was not completed with the record of his death. Africa is a different continent today because of Livingstone's sacrifice on its behalf. Do you remember the appealing lines of Rudyard Kipling?—

> If you can talk with crowds and keep your virtue,
>   Or walk with Kings—nor lose the common touch,
> If neither foes nor loving friends can hurt you,
>   If all men count with you, but none too much;
> If you can fill the unforgiving minute
>   With sixty seconds' worth of distance run,
> Yours is the Earth and everything that's in it,
>   And—which is more—you'll be a Man, my son.

The thrilling biography of David Livingstone proves that he was such a man. For over thirty years he lived life to its limit, and gave until he could give no more for the soul of Africa. The story is told of a man in a Scottish prison who had been a fellow Sunday school scholar of Livingstone's young days, who was deeply moved when he heard of his burial in Westminster Abbey. What a contrast in the use of life! The one lad went forth to make his life count for Christ, but the other lad made his life count for crime. If we

> Live for Christ, we live again,
> Live for self, we live in vain.

16

John Bunyan
The Famous Tinker of Bedford

No book has been translated into so many languages, apart from the Bible, as *The Pilgrim's Progress* by John Bunyan; yet it is to be regretted that what used to be household names mean very little to many young people—and older people, too, for that matter—today. For centuries these were not only names but subjects and sources of great spiritual instruction and profit. To countless numbers now "high in bliss upon the hills of God," Bunyan's *Pilgrim's Progress,* first set "the joy-bells ringing in the City of Habitation."

There are those who argue that since this has always been such a popular book and Bunyan such a famous man in English history, that any explanatory word about the man and his works are quite superfluous. But while the majority of Christian people may possess a copy of Bunyan's masterpiece, yet the author and his works are practically unknown by young people of today. Perhaps they are neglected because, compared with the light, popular literature of today, books like *Pilgrim's Progress* and *The Holy War* make hard and dry reading to all save devout and diligent Bible students. Thus a shallow, superficial knowledge of the Bedford tinker satisfies the majority of young people, even in religious circles.

S. W. M'Gown in his *Ten Bunyan Talks,* speaks of a twenty-three-year-old-daughter of a minister's home who had been to both private and boarding schools who was asked if she knew who John Bunyan was. "O he wrote *Paradise Lost,* and he was born blind." The poor girl had him mixed with John Milton. Evidently she had not spent much time in Bunyan's company. Had she done so she would have found it yielding fruit an hundredfold for the strengthening and stimulating of her spiritual being.

When I preached in Bedford several years ago I remember how I stood in awe before Bunyan's magnificent monument reposing where four roads meet in the heart of the city. It was in 1874 that the then Duke of Bedford, a descendant of Lord William Russell the martyr to liberty, presented this most costly and beautiful statue of Bunyan to the city, in Bunyan's memory. The unveiling day on June 10, 1874, was one of the greatest days Bedford had ever known. Thousands of distinguished persons from all over the country assembled for the unveiling, which was performed by Lady Augusta Stanley, sister of the Earl of Elgin and wife of Dean Stanley of Westminster.

The statue itself is of bronze, cast of cannons and bells brought from China, weighing two-and-a-half tons. The figure of Bunyan, cast from a portrait of him painted by Sadler, is ten feet high. The sculptor was Boehm who tried to present the inscription on the pedestal of "a very grave person," and he admirably succeeded. There Bunyan in bronze has stood for one hundred years now, "as if he pleaded with men." The entire press of the time in laudatory articles on the Tinker of Bedford called him blessed among men.

The immense crowds assembled that historic day were addressed by several conspicuous persons, including Dean Stanley who concluded his eulogy by saying, "Let everyone of you who has not read *The Pilgrim's Progress*—if there be any such person—read it without delay. Let those who have read it a hundred times read it again for the hundred-and-first time; and then follow out in your lives the lessons it teaches.

219

You will then all be better monuments of John Bunyan than even this magnificent statue."

The England of Bunyan's period from 1628 to 1688 embraces one of the most stirring in English history. Dr. George Cheever, in his lectures on "Bunyan," tells us that "it was an age of great revolutions, great excitement, great genius, great talents, great extremes in both good and evil, great piety and great wickedness; great freedom and great tyranny and oppression. Under Cromwell there was great liberty and prosperity; under the Charleses there was great oppression and disgrace." Charles II, whose reign was one of tyranny, was one of the most dissolute, worthless, corrupt kings that ever sat on England's throne.

Yet in the midst of such darkness, God had those who were true to His cause. In spite of the passing of hard measures like the Corporation Act, concocted for the destruction of religious liberty, there were men willing to endure hardship and sacrifice for Christ's sake. In eminent saints like Baster, Owen, Howe, Goodwin, and others, who were contemporaries of Bunyan, we have a few pearls sunk in deep and troubled mire, out of which they were to be taken and placed in a more glorious setting.

Bunyan himself was born in the village of Elstow about a mile from Bedford in November 1628. His father was a brazier, that is, a mender of pots, pans, and kettles—as this writer's father was for over sixty years. In common with the majority of workers in tin who did not carry on their trades all the year round at the same bench, Bunyan, Senior, was dubbed a tinker, and was considered by some as being of gypsy descent. The records of his family are traceable to about A.D. 1200, and the name, then known as *Buignon*, indicates that the family was of Norman origin. As the great descendant of such an ancient house, Bunyan, by his life and work, brought much credit upon it. One of his time described him as being "tall of stature, strong-browed, with sparkling eyes, wearing hair on his lip after the old British fashion; his hair was reddish, but in his latter days sprinkled with gray; his nose well cut, his mouth moderately large, his forehead something high, and his habit [dress] always plain and modest."

In his matchless *Grace Abounding,* Bunyan's autobiography, he reveals his own lowly parentage and descent, of which he was unashamed.

> For my descent then, it was, as is well known by many, of a low and inconsiderable generation; my father's house being of that rank that is meanest, and most despised of all the families in the land.

It would seem as if Bunyan learned much about the work of a brazier, for after his marriage and conversion, he worked for five or six years at the trade in order to support his family. He wandered from village to village as a tinker, his swarthy face made swarthier yet by the smoke of his pitch kettle. The outstanding facts of Bunyan's early life prove how the Divine Potter was at work, shaping His honorable vessel.

As to his education, Bunyan was not a child of the university. He attended a Bedford school for the poor. There was no compulsory education in his day. Legal enforcement would have been laughed at then. While an apt pupil, he must have quickly lost all he learned—"I confess I did soon lose that little I learned, and that almost utterly," was his own confession. One of the expositors of *The Pilgrim's Progress* remarks that such a classic could not have had so much of its beauty or truth if Bunyan's soul had been steeped in scholastic discipline. He was divinely taught. Under the schooling of the Holy Spirit, unaided by acquired wisdom, he produced one of the greatest literary masterpieces in the world.

Bunyan's boyhood years were reckless and profane. He narrowly escaped death when he fell from a boat in the River Ouse. This experience had a good effect on him for the time being, but he soon lost his contrition and gratitude in further prodigality. In those years of his sinful youth he had dreams full of horror because of terrible judgments hanging over his guilty head. His mind was haunted by visions of merited punishment at the hands of a despised and insulted God.

He appears to have developed in early years a headstrong disposition that often led him into youthful excesses. But his youth was not peculiarly loose or disreputable. His own harsh self-accusations were the severe judgment of a heart and conscience keenly alive to a sense of sin. We may be inclined to feel that he was apt to overdo his expression of self-defamation. But as G. W. M'Gown expresses it, "Such strong denunciations must be taken as the exaggeration of a highly strung and sensitive moral nature in revolt against its former lawless and reckless self."

Yet even in those tender years, Bunyan was notorious for his command of language—of a lurid sort—and for his power of story-telling, especially when he wanted to get out of a difficult situation. What a master of the rich Anglo-Saxon tongue he became!

Something must be said about the military career of this young man who had few equals in swearing and who gathered fame as a ringleader in all manner of vice and ungodliness. Around 1645 Bunyan enlisted in the Parliamentary Army, and took part in the siege of Leicester. During his military career he had another providential escape from death, which made a deep impression on his wicked mind. He was drawn by lot to be one of the besiegers, but just as he was ready to go out on the perilous mission, another soldier desired to substitute for him. "To which," says Bunyan, "when I had consented, he took my place; and coming to the siege, as he stood sentinel, he was shot in the head with a musket bullet, and died." Unhappily the impression soon faded as Bunyan's own confession states, "Here were judgments and mercy, but neither of them did awaken my soul to righteousness; whereof I sinned still, and grew more and more rebellious against God, and careless of my own salvation."

Bunyan was converted through an experience which had its Slough of Despond and its Valley of the Shadow of Death that he was to write so vividly about. One day he overheard the talk or gossip of three godly women as they exchanged thoughts about holy things and the state of their souls "as if joy did make them speak." "This was indeed true gossip— God-sib—conversation that showed the relationship of God to human souls." Bunyan's heart tarried with them as the female trio spoke, and true conviction set itself firmly in his heart. Through the influence of these good women he was introduced to the Baptist minister of the town, John Gifford, a stalwart Christian whose godly life and teaching did much to set Bunyan up as a staunch and valiant soldier of the cross. He was baptized in 1653, and very soon after entered the Baptist ministry.

At twenty-eight years of age he ventured to preach, and began by telling others of his own strange journey from *The City of Destruction* to the *Cross,* where his burden fell off, and he was free. With a growing passion to preach he evangelized the countryside around his home. Crowds gathered to listen to the man they had learned to revere as "Bishop Bunyan." One of his contemporaries wrote, "I have seen about 1200; and I computed about 3,000 that came to hear him on a Lord's Day, so that a half of them were obliged to return for want of room. He had an intense love for souls, and an absolute faith in the power of the Gospel to save all who would believe."

As he progressed in his preaching he developed an incomparable style, and came to use the noblest and purest Saxon ever used in the pulpit. He had an imagination which places him beside Dante, the greatest poet of the dead, and the blind John Milton. He won the hearts of all by "his homely humor, charmed with his shrewd mother-wit, and touched with his wise and hospitable sympathy."

Another significant episode in his life was his marriage at the age of twenty. When the Parliamentary Army was disbanded, Bunyan returned to Elstow, and in 1649 set himself up as a tinker, trundling his machine from village to village. The sweet young girl he married brought him no dowry of worldly wealth. "She was virtuous, loving, born of good, honest and godly parents who had instructed her as well as they were able in the ways of truth and saving knowledge."

The only marriage dowry the young wife had consisted of two pious books brought from her home—*The Plain Man's Pathway to Heaven* by Bishop Baily, and *Practice of Piety* by Arthur Kent. Bunyan and she read these books together, and they greatly influenced him. His *Life and Death of Mr. Badman,* published in 1680, somewhat resembles the truth gathered from these two books, which God used to arouse desires for a new life in Bunyan. Now he started to attend church, and read religious books with more enthusiasm. He found delight in the Bible and no storm-tossed mariner upon an unknown sea could have poured over his chart with greater eagerness. These two small volumes served to deepen the conviction of spiritual need which already had brought the young tinker into great trouble and depression of mind. Through the reading of these books Bunyan gave up worldly amusements and set out to live a life of strict and austere conflict. Reformation had started, and finally led to peace of heart in believing on Christ.

After nine or ten years of wedded bliss, Bunyan's wife, who enlivened the home with six children, passed away. In 1659 Bunyan remarried, principally because he was often away preaching, and someone was needed to care for his home and children, especially his beloved blind daughter Mary. He was happy in his choice of a second wife, who was a noble woman, and earnestly but unsuccessfully pled Bunyan's cause before Judge Hales after her husband had been imprisoned for a year. Dr. Cheever says of this court case, "The scene is worthy of the pencil of some great painter when, without a creature to befriend or sustain her, this young and trembling woman, unaccustomed to and abashed at such presences, entered the court-room and stood before the judges, in the midst of the crowd of justices and gentry of the country assembled." Truly she was a partaker of her husband's own spirit, a heroine of no ordinary stamp. Her advocacy, however, was of no avail. Bunyan spent twelve full years in prison, all because he refused to discontinue public preaching. While in prison he was allowed to make boot laces which enabled him to contribute to the support of his family.

During the dark days of the persecution of the Nonconformists in England, Bunyan was thrown into prison. There he preached to all who could gain access to him. The story runs that his prison-keeper had such confidence in Bunyan's honesty that he would often let him out to meet his congregation in the half-hidden dells and retired woods, where he could minister to them disguised as a carter, while scouts on the outskirts of the crowds kept watch against intruders.

The magistrates offered him his liberty if he would refrain from preaching, but he scorned the offer saying, "If you let me out today, I should preach tomorrow." He could not be silent for he had a passion to preach what he himself had tasted and handled of the Word of Life. The visits of his wife and children make sorrowful reading. Parting with them was like "cutting the flesh from my bones," Bunyan would say. Under the Declaration of Indulgence granted by Charles II, Bunyan was released. His prison days, however, were overruled by God. Out of them came the first part of *The Pilgrim's Progress*.

As a writer of allegory, Bunyan has never been excelled. Our admiration for him increases as we remember that although he lived in an age of unparalleled literary profligacy, there is not a line in his writings, and not a word in his sermons, which can be charged with coarseness. English literature of his day had become thoroughly imbued with all the elements of poetry, fiction, and romance. Saxon English was "prepared to his hand; being full of image and awe, of wonder and grandeur, which he could express to the popular mind in a very racy style. Unconsciously he felt the force of his mother tongue; it stimulated his genius, became the groundwork of his thought and the model of his utterance; a choice which places him side by side with Shakespeare and the English Bible, as one of the great conservators of our powerful language."

Both as a writer and a preacher Macaulay's estimation of him is true, "No writer has said more exactly what he meant to say. For magnificence, for pathos, for vehement exhortation, for subtle disquisition, for every purpose of the poet and orator and the divine, the homely dialect is perfectly sufficient. No book shows so well as does *Pilgrim's Progress* how rich our language is in its own proper wealth, and how little it has improved by all it has borrowed." Matthew Arnold in his *Mixed Essays* wrote,—

> We have the Philistine of genius in Religion—Luther
> We have the Philistine of genius in Politics—Cromwell
> We have the Philistine of genius in Literature—Bunyan

Bunyan's pen was always busy. Altogether some sixty works flowed from it. His publisher added this quaint note to his literary productions. "Here are 60 pieces of his works, and he was 60 years of age." None of his many books, however, bear comparison with *Pilgrim's Progress*. Untold thousands of copies of this book have been published since he wrote it in prison. In Lennox Library, New York, can be found the most extensive collection in existence. Some three hundred editions of the work in English, and seventy-four in different foreign languages are housed there. It passed through eight editions in the first thirty years of its pilgrimage. In fact, no book has been rendered into so many editions and languages, except the Bible itself. *Pilgrim's Progress* has always been the delight of the lowly and it has exerted a fascinating power on the most cultured and gifted minds. It ranks among the masterpieces of English literature, and eternity alone will reveal the blessing it has been to multitudes in finding Christ as the Way, the Truth, and the Life. It has intrinsic worth as an inexhaustible mine of Christian stimulus and example.

That *Pilgrim's Progress* takes its place among the transcendently great works of our English literature is testified to by many outstanding writers. J. R. Green, for instance in his remarkable *Short History of the English People,* says of it—

> In its range, its directness, in its simple grace, in the ease with which it changes from lively dialogue to dramatic action, from simple pathos to passionate earnestness, in the subtle and delicate fancy which often suffuses its child-like words, in its playful humor, its bold character painting, in the even and balanced power which passes without effort from the Valley of the Shadow of Death to the land "where the Shining Ones commonly walked because the border of Heaven," in its sunny kindliness, unbroken by one bitter word, the *Pilgrim's Progress* is amongst the noblest of English poems. For if Puritanism had first discovered the poetry which contact with the spiritual world awakes in the meanest souls, Bunyan was the first of the Puritans who revealed this.

This is indeed high, yet worthy praise, and many others have joined in it. Dr. Samuel Johnson said that *Pilgrim's Progress* was one of two or three works which he wished were longer. "He praised John Bunyan highly," wrote Boswell in his *Life of Johnson,* "and said that his *Pilgrim's Progress* had great merit both for invention and imagination, and the conduct of the story, and it had the best evidence of its merit, the general and continued approbation of mankind."

Robert Louis Stevenson was another who lauded the worth of this great work of Bunyan's. Writing on books which had influenced him, he said, "Lastly, I must name

Pilgrim's Progress, a book that breathes of every beautiful and valuable emotion." Dr. John Kelmen, who himself wrote an appealing appraisal of Bunyan and his word, said of Stevenson that *"The Pilgrim's Progress* was the book in all English literature which he knew best, and to which he oftenest alluded."

While it ranks among the most original of English works of genius, actually there is no book so little original or so dependent throughout on a higher source. As to Bunyan's terse English, doubtless he learned it from Spenser and Chaucer; of human nature, he borrowed from himself and his circumstances; of history, he gathered much from Foxe's *Book of Martyrs;* of hallowed conviction, he caught from the Holy Spirit; and of uncrippled boldness, this was inspired by his love of soul-liberty. But his writings are full of truth because of his daily delight in Bible meditation. Bunyan was the man "with a Book in his hand"; and Scripture was the source of his unique, incomparable literary style. His entire dependence upon "the best of books," made him the creative genius he was. J. R. Green says:

> The images of *The Pilgrim's Progress* are the images
> of Prophet and Evangelist; it borrows for its ten-
> derer outbursts the very verse of the Song of Songs,
> and pictures the Heavenly City in the words of the
> Apocalypse. But so completely has the Bible be-
> come Bunyan's life, that one feels its phrases as the
> natural expression of his thoughts. He has lived in
> the Bible till its words have become his own. In no
> book do we see more clearly the new imaginative
> force which had been given to the common life of
> Englishmen by their study of the Bible. Its English is
> the simplest and homeliest English which has ever
> been used by any great English writer; but it is the
> English of the Bible.

Bunyan represents the Bible as having tremendous influence upon Pilgrim, the hero of his story, who "opened the Book and read therein," and broke out with a lamentable cry, "What shall I do?" Later on, we have the phrase, "He was, as he was wont, reading in his Book." Coleridge said of *The Pilgrim's Progress* that it was "incomparably the best compendium of Gospel truth ever produced by a writer not miraculously inspired." Macaulay said of another work of Bunyan's—*Grace Abounding*—that it "is indeed one of the most remarkable pieces of autobiography in the world." It is in this that we have the charming natural account of his own progress in Bible reading. From the time he "began to look into the Bible with new eyes," he found himself held captive by its revelation of what his own soul needed most.

Dr. Thomas Armitage in his monumental volume, *The History of Baptists,* in the section devoted to John Bunyan the Baptist preacher of Bedford, reminds us of Dean Stanley's witness to the influence of *The Pilgrim's Progress* on his own life:

> When in early life I lighted upon the passage where the Pilgrim is taken into the House Beautiful to see the pedigree of the *Ancient of Days,* and the varieties and histories of that place, both ancient and modern, I determined that if ever the time should arrive when I should become a Professor of Ecclesiastical History, these should become the opening words in which I would describe the treasures of that magnificent store-house. Accordingly, when, many years after, it so fell out, I could find no better mode of beginning my course at Oxford than by redeeming that early pledge; and when the course came to an end, and I wished to draw a picture of the prospects still reserved for the future of Christendom, I found again the best words I could supply were those in which, on leaving the *Beautiful House, Christian* was shown in the distance the view of the

Delectable Mountains, "which they said would add
to his comfort because they were nearer to the desired haven."

Then Dr. Armitage observes, "This was a worthy and heartfelt tribute from Westminster to the dreaming tinker whose
effigy now adorns the House of Commons, side by side with
those of orators, heroes and statesmen in honour of the man,
who though he 'devilishly' abstained from attending the
church, 'contrary to the laws of the king,' has preached in all
pulpits and palaces ever since."

What are some of the lessons to be gleaned from the sixty
years of this Bedford preacher and author who lived while a
long list of the most remarkable events occurred in England?
First of all, his experience magnifies the grace abounding he
wrote so wonderfully about. Too many present-day preachers
are either afraid or ashamed to preach the glorious evangelical
truths Bunyan clothed with such picturesque imagery. Men
are lost in sin and are on their way to The City of Destruction, and we fail in our vocation if we do not lead them to
the cross where the burden of sin rolls away. Sin and salvation, heaven and hell, were real to Bunyan and he was per-
petually valiant for these truths.

Then there was his deep and ever-deepening love for the
Bible, which to Bunyan was not one of the best, but *the* best
of books. The Word was part and parcel of his life. After he
had been in prison for three months, he was offered his freedom if he would go to some Bedford church to hear the
Prayer-Book which he detested, read. But Bunyan stoutly
refused, and said to the clerk of the court who came with the
message of proffered release, "I will stand by the truth to the
last drop of my blood." Perhaps the tragic decline of church
membership would be arrested if only we had more men of
this caliber. Bunyan never preached uncertainties, but always
positive truths.

Further, Bunyan was willing to suffer for the faith. At the

beginning of his imprisonment he expected to suffer martyrdom on the gallows. "This, therefore, lay with great trouble upon me, for methought I was ashamed to die with a false face and tottering knees for such a cause as this"—his hatred for the Prayer-book that "muzzles up prayer in a form," which he resisted to the end. Listen to this brave confession of his, "I have determined, the Almighty God being my helper and shield, yet to suffer if frail life may continue so long, even till the moss shall grow on mine eyebrows, rather than thus to violate my faith and principles."

Today, young men leave many schools of cultural and theological learning and are pitch-forked into the ministry Bunyan deemed so sacred, with little "faith and principles." We know those who in their training gained degrees but lost their convictions, and who made it evident in their effort to preach that they doubted their beliefs, and believed their doubts. Would that these messageless preachers would saturate their minds with the sixty volumes of John Bunyan, who stood at all times as if he pleaded with men!

At the early age of six C. H. Spurgeon, with a passion for books and pictures, delighted in reading *The Pilgrim's Progress* and Bunyan's other works. No wonder he became a prince among preachers!

After Bunyan's release from prison he became one of the most popular gospel preachers in all the land. People of all ranks listened to his impassioned appeals. Charles II asked Dr. John Owen how he, a man of profound learning, could listen to a tinker preach. Dr. Owen replied, "May it please your Majesty, had I the tinker's abilities for preaching, I would gladly relinguish all my learning."

Upon the death of John Gifford, pastor of Bedford Church, Bunyan was called to the oversight of the work and became a much-loved minister of the gospel. The year of the Revolution, 1688, saw the end of his earthly pilgrimage. He died at the age of sixty, on August 12, 1688. One of his last acts was the reconciliation of a father and son who had quarreled. Successful in this blessed act, he returned home in a drenching rain, caught a chill, and died ten days later. His last words were, "Take me, for I come to Thee." He was buried in Bunhill Fields, where his well-kept monument—bearing simply his name—gives inspiration to all visitors of every nationality.

Bunyan's much-loved little blind daughter, Mary, often visited her father in prison and brought him small gifts for his solace. She had great concern for him and often, when parting from him, put her delicate little fingers to his eyes and cheeks to feel if the tears flowed that she might kiss them away. This precious, sightless child died and left her father, who treasured her precious memory, in prison. She entered the Celestial Gate first to wait as a "shining one" to watch for the coming of her dear father. She did not have to wait long. When Bunyan entered into the Celestial City he saw not only the King in His beauty, but for the first time he saw his Mary's sweet eyes ablaze with light. She did not raise a hand to her valiant father's cheek as she did in prison, however, for God had wiped away all tears from his eyes, even as He had banished blindness from the young pilgrim's eyes. What a meeting that must have been!

On his dying bed, Bunyan acted the part of *Hopeful*, crossing the River of Death, "So he passed over, and all the trumpets sounded for him on the other side."

At last, as *Pilgrim* himself, Bunyan entered the *Celestial City*, whose towers glisten with a light fairer than day. Although dead for nearly three centuries, Bunyan still speaks in those monumental writings he left behind, which continue to enrich countless lives.

17

John Wesley
The Evangelist Who Prevented a Bloody Revolution

Lecky, the historian who affirmed that "the conversion of John Wesley formed one of the grand epochs of English history," is the one who tells us that the Methodist revival saved England a terrible revolution, which at that time had engulfed France, and seemed ready to sweep across the Channel to bring a blood bath to England. But the mighty spiritual revival under George Whitefield and the Wesleys caused the tide to turn through the remarkable outburst of practical Christianity. John Wesley, more than any other man since that sixteenth century, stands out as the most outstanding religious leader who influenced the masses for God and righteousness.

John Wesley was born in some of the darkest days of English history. Appalling conditions made the country ripe for a revolution. There was the iniquitous slave-traffic. Prisons were dens of cruelty and the foulest immorality, from which prisoners could escape only by starvation or by jail-fever that festered without ceasing in those haunts of human wretchedness. Purity and fidelity to the marriage vow were sneered out of fashion. Schools were scarce, crowds of children being denied moral or religious training of any sort. Mobs rioted, burned houses, flung open prisons, and robbed homes and ships at will. Ruthless laws, like the one which ruled that a person should be hanged for cutting down a tree or for thieving, only caused the criminal class to become more bold and prolific. In higher circles anyone who talked of religion was laughed at.

Hannah More, the English religious writer and reformer, reported, "We saw but one Bible in the parish of Cheddar and that was used to prop up a flower-pot." Drunkenness also prevailed, for people could get drunk for a penny. It was a time of open profanity. "The Blasters Club," so called of youths who professed to be servants of the devil, came together to offer prayers in his name. Such utter disregard for sacred things had never been known in England before. At one time Wesley visited the low quarter of Newcastle-upon-Tyne, and stood by the old pump and preached the gospel. His text was, "He was wounded for our transgressions, he was bruised for our iniquities." One who was present said afterwards that "Wesley's tenderness was such that these poor and wicked people clung to his hands and his clothes when he had finished." But Wesley himself said of the crowd, "Such blasphemy, such cursing, such swearing, even from the mouths of little children! Surely this place is ripe for the Master."

Such were the bad old days Wesley was born in, and God made him the channel of a spiritual revolution that helped to change society, the fruit of which abides in religious and philanthropical agencies. As Woodrow Wilson, the twenty-eighth President of the United States (1913-1921), wrote, "The 18th century cried out for deliverance and light and God prepared John Wesley to show the world the might and blessing of His salvation." As we think of the corrupt, violent forces at work today well might we pray for another mighty movement of the Spirit of God such as England experienced at the beginning of the eighteenth century. We thus come to look at the portrait of England's never-to-be-forgotten evangelist of the highways and byways.

His Godly Heritage

Behind John Wesley was a godly ancestry that helped to

mold him into the potent influence he became. His pedigree proves that God was preparing Wesley to come to the kingdom at the time he did.

His great-grandfather was Bartholomew Wesley, a Puritan of renown, and a great stalwart for the truth during the reign of Charles II.

His grandfather was John Wesley, Bartholomew's son, who for a time acted as a minister at Poole. (The John Wesley we are considering was named after him.) Thus as one historian expresses it, "As far as we can trace them back we find Wesley's ancestors respectable for learning, conspicuous for piety, and firmly attached to those new views of Christianity which they had learned from Scripture."

His father was Samuel Wesley, who was born in Dorset in November 1662, and died at Epworth in 1735. While his early life was spent among the Dissenters, he came to associate himself with the Church of England in 1685. After graduating from Oxford in 1688, he served several churches but ultimately settled down in Epworth, Lincolnshire. His salary was paid by Queen Mary in 1696 in recognition of his dedication of his *Life in Christ: An Heroic Poem*. A versatile writer, both in prose and verse, he was able to eke out his salary by his pen. He wrote several hymns, one of them being, "Behold the Saviour of Mankind." He also penned an exposition on the Book of Job. For some forty years he struggled against poverty, yet he toiled on in obscurity and penury and became the father of the great Apostle of Methodism.

His mother was Susannah, born in London, January 1669, and died there in July 1742. Her father was Samuel Annesley, LL.D., an eminent Nonconformist minister. At the age of thirteen, Susannah united with the Church of England. She was twenty when she married Samuel Wesley in 1689. She became the mother of nineteen children, nine of whom died in infancy. The story of her home life, the training of her children, and the beauty and devotion of her Christian character reveal her as a remarkable woman. Herself one of twenty-five children born to her parents, she knew all about the young. She educated her children herself, and although she subdued their wills she did not forfeit their affection. On her John Wesley based an idealized picture of woman that in later years frustrated his own dreams of happy marriage and family life. Adam Clarke, the renowned expositor, wrote of her, "Many daughters have done virtuously but Susannah Wesley has excelled them all." Although her family was so numerous, yet she had time for each one. Each night she would take one aside for instruction in divine things. John, the second son, born on June 17, 1703, was nurtured in this way, and in afterlife wrote of her he revered, "I cannot remember ever having kept back a doubt from my mother. She was the one heart to whom I went in absolute confidence from my babyhood until the day of her death."

In the day of his great power Napoleon said, "The greatest need of France is mothers." Our generation sadly needs godly mothers and homes in which spiritual giants like Charles and John Wesley can be reared. When he was only six years of age John nearly lost his life through the burning of the parsonage, set on fire, according to his own account, by some of the angry parishioners who resented his dear father's plain preaching. The fire always remained vivid in his memory, and he frequently mentioned it in his writings. He described himself as "a brand plucked out of the burning." His gifted, musical brother, Charles might have spiritualized this same incident when he wrote—

> Where shall my wond'ring soul begin?
> How shall I all to Heaven aspire?
> A slave redeem'd from death and sin,
> A brand pluck'd from eternal fire.

The Scholastic Career

At the early age of six, John Wesley was sent to the Charterhouse School, London, where he stayed for six years. There he cast off some of the home restraints. Commenting on his sojourn at this renowned school he said, "I entered it a saint and left it a sinner." Maintaining a semblance of outward goodness he hoped to be saved, as he expressed it, by—

Not being as bad as other people.
Having still a kindness for Religion.
Reading the Bible, saying my prayers, going to church.

During his first years at Charterhouse he had to endure a good deal of bullying from the older boys who used to eat his meat and leave him nothing but a piece of bread for a meal. But he was hardy, and he obeyed his father's strict command to run around the school grounds three times every morning. He remained affectionately attached to Charterhouse, and visited it yearly to the end of his life. While a resident there he became a diligent and clever scholar, and taught Greek before he left.

In 1720, Wesley went up to Christ Church, Oxford, where he distinguished himself. During his second year there he began to plan his studies more carefully with a view to the future. He wrote grammars in five languages and for years was a Fellow of Oxford. Graduating in 1724, and encouraged by his godly parents, he resolved to take Holy Orders, and for two years assisted his father as curate at Epworth. In 1725, he was made a deacon by the bishop of Oxford, and in 1726 was elected a Fellow of Lincoln College. In 1728, he was ordained a priest. In spite of his strong academic leanings and strong religious background, his religion was all of works. He seemed to be groping in darkness and yearning for the true light.

It was in 1729, when Wesley was recalled to Oxford to fulfill the residential conditions of his Fellowship, that another milestone was reached in his spiritual pilgrimage. Returning, he found his brother Charles, who was to become the Poet of Methodism and now an undergraduate, joined with Robert and William Morgan in regular studies and devotions. John Wesley immediately joined up with them, and his brother Charles handed over to John the leadership of this religious study circle. It grew in numbers and influence, and earned many nicknames from less religious students. George Whitefield, who became Orpheus of the pulpit and one of the greatest of revival orators, was also closely identified with the circle.

Because these young men undertook self-imposed strict religious ways they became known as "The Holy Club." They would read divinity on Sunday evenings, and the classics on other days, along with Greek Testament readings. When possible they would visit the prisons and also the sick poor of the town. Said John Wesley, "We were now about fifteen in number, all of one heart and of one mind." The nickname *Methodist* was coined because of the methodical way these students decided to live. They were unusually precise, strict and *methodical* in the observance of their religious duties, and in the regularity of their lives. They would rise at four every morning for prayer and devotion. So although this nickname was tauntingly given, it actually described their belief that "order is heaven's first law." As the club grew, social service became an important feature of its activities. They taught prisoners to read and write, and helped them to find work when they were released. They visited workhouses, and homes of the very poor, and distributed food, clothes, medicine, and books among the needy. Members of the club also ran a school.

His Church Affiliation

Although Wesley became the founder of one of the largest Nonconformist denominations in Christendom, he himself never ceased to be a Church of England minister. He once declared, "I affirm once more I live and die a member of the Church of England and that none who regard my advice will ever separate from it." It was his father's wish that he should succeed him as minister at Epworth, but he was so wedded to college life and to his chosen companions, that he could not be persuaded to consent, even though he loved the Anglican Church. To the last Wesley clung passionately to that church, and looked on the large body of followers he had gathered as but a lay society in full communion with the church he considered himself a part of.

The reason he broke with the Moravians, who were his earliest friends in the new movement he founded, was because of their contempt for the religious forms of the Church of England. When he became convinced that his life's work was the proclamation of the good news of salvation by faith, he felt that he was recalling his church to its spiritual minion and therefore had no thought of creating a new ecclesiastical organization. All he wanted to do was to make others sharers of his own new-found spiritual riches. The world he lived in was weary of apologies for Christianity. What it needed was the declaration of the love of God for sinners—and Wesley became such a herald.

Calm Wesley, the Arminian, parted with his friend, the impulsive Whitefield, because of his extravagant Calvinism. Yet this untiring evangelist was extremely tolerant. In fact it has been said of him that no other Reformer whom the world has ever seen "so united faithfulness to the essential doctrines of revelation with charity towards men of every church and creed." When rebuked by the bishop of Lincoln for his recognition of other church bodies, Wesley replied, "Alas! my lord, is this a time to persecute any man for conscience sake? I beseech you do as you would be done by. Think and let think." The increasing opposition of the Church of England towards his work, and its expressed hatred for it, compelled Wesley to act independently of it, and so on July 27, 1730, the first Methodist Society was formed with its own rules of government, with Wesley ordaining his own preachers. On June 25, 1744, the first Methodist Conference was held in

London with six ministers and four laymen present.

From then on, Wesley's powers were bent to the building up of a new religious society which might give to the ever-increasing enthusiasm of the people a lasting and practical form. While the whole body was placed under the absolute government of a conference of ministers, as long as he lived the direction of the new religious society remained in Wesley's hand. Replying with a charming simplicity to objectors to his autocratic control he said, "If by arbitrary power you mean a power which I exercise simply without any colleagues there in, this is certainly true, but I see no hurt in it." C. H. Spurgeon is credited with having said that he believed in a committee of one, the one being himself.

His Marital Problems

He had had such a happy, godly home life with so many other children around him in his childhood days, that he must have longed for a similar home of his own with children to rise up and call him blessed. His experience with women with a view to matrimony was not a very satisfactory one. Sally Kirkham, daughter of the Rector of Stanton, Gloucestershire, who encouraged him to become a Church of England minister was referred to as "a religious friend." What feelings they had towards each other we are not told. She faded, however, from the picture. Then there was Grace Murray who nursed Wesley during an illness and to whom he became attached. In fact they became engaged, but friends intervened and interfered and she married another. Grace was the housekeeper at the Newcastle headquarters, but his brother Charles, not knowing the full circumstances of his brother's engagement, and, afraid that Methodism would suffer, persuaded Grace Murray to marry one of Wesley's preachers, John Bennet. Pressed by his friends to make the matter a legal issue, Wesley refused. Writing to her Wesley said, "Grace Murray, you have broken my heart."

When he went on his mission to Georgia, which did not prove to be altogether successful, he formed an attachment to Sophy Hopkey, niece of the chief magistrate of Savannah; but she married someone else. Unwisely Wesley courted criticism by not allowing her to partake of Holy Communion. The misunderstandings and persecutions brought to a head by this Sophy Hopkey affair, was one reason why Wesley left Savannah for London in December 1737. Then Wesley wrote a tract recommending celibacy. But shortly after this he met Mrs. Mary Vageillo, a widow with four children. Brokenhearted over the loss of Grace Murray, on the rebound he married the widow in 1751, with disastrous results. Wesley stipulated that he was not to preach or to travel less, but his wife became dissatisfied at his continual absences.

Further, Mrs. Wesley became jealous and bitterly resented her husband's intimate pastoral oversight of hundreds of young women, and scolded him continually. Wesley, having a high opinion of marital authority, wrote to her to know him, and to know herself, "Suspect me no more, aspere me no more, provoke me no more. Do not any longer contend for the mastery: be content to be a private, insignificant person, known and loved by God and me."

Several times she left her husband, but he induced her to return to him. When she left him again, he besought her no more. He wrote, "I did not dismiss her, I will not recall her." She died in 1771, and Wesley lived on for another twenty years untroubled by marital problems. What hurt him most during this affair was perhaps the attitude of his brother Charles during the scandal caused by Mrs. Wesley's publication of stolen, interpolated, or forged letters. Charles was in a fever of excitement over the matter and felt John should do something about defending his character. But, master of the situation, he said to Charles, "Brother, when I devoted to God my ease, my time, my life, did I exempt my reputation?"

One wonders what would have happened if John Wesley

had married a godly woman in full sympathy with his glorious task and cheered his heart with children of his own. Seeing that the supreme task of evangelism overshadowed all else in Wesley's life enabling him to stem the rising tide of a bloody revolution in the land, perhaps his unfortunate marriage was a blessing in disguise.

His Spiritual Quest

Although reared in the godliest of homes and closely identified with religious activities at Oxford and after, Wesley did not have the assurance of a personal Saviour. He felt that he could not promote holiness in others until he had achieved it himself and that he could best do this at Oxford, but it was not to be so. The text that kept coming to his mind was, "Thou art not far from the kingdom of God." But in his inmost heart he knew he was not in that kingdom. Then something happened that was to result in a chain of events ending in his definite conversion. After his father's death, he took his father's monumental Latin work on Job to London to consult with publishers about its translation and publication. While in the city he met an old Oxford friend, John Burton, who had become the most influential trustee of the new British colony of Georgia, in North America. Burton introduced him to Col. James Oglethorpe, governor of the colony, and both of them persuaded Wesley to return with them and undertake the spiritual oversight of the colonists, and to evangelize the Indians as an agent for the "Society of the Propagation of the Gospel." Wesley accepted, and his brother Charles was ordained in order to accompany and serve with him. In giving his reason for accepting the invitation John said to the two friends, "My chief motive is the hope of saving my own soul. I hope to learn the true sense of the gospel by preaching it to the heathen. I cannot hope to attain to the same degree of holiness here which I may there."

Crossing the Atlantic John and Charles became acquainted with some emigrant Moravians who clearly possessed the spiritual peace John had hitherto sought in vain. On board was the notable Moravian preacher Spangenburg, who dealt with Wesley about his soul. The faith and calmness of the Moravians during stormy days at sea greatly impressed the Wesleys. The party landed in America on February 6, 1736.

Alas! however, after two years of hard labor, the mission to the Indians proved somewhat abortive. Both John and Charles had served them and the colonists faithfully, but the stiff high churchmanship they sought to impose antagonized the people, and their efforts at social changes and spiritual fellowship were rejected. Heart-sick, the Wesleys returned to England in 1738, with John a still greater seeker after truth. Sorrowfully he wrote, "No such faith in Christ as will prevent my heart being troubled—I went to America to convert the Indians, but oh! who shall convert me? I have a fair summer religion: I can talk well, but let death look me in the face and my spirit is troubled." Yet in spite of all the trials and failures of Georgia, Wesley looked upon the two years there as "the second rise of Methodism"—the first being the Holy Club at Oxford. The weekly fellowship meetings he organized in Savannah were, as he said, "the first rudiments of the Methodist societies."

On the sea voyage home Wesley was again brought into contact with the Moravians, people of tranquil faith. During a storm that threatened disaster, these saints were calm. "Why be disturbed by the waves and the winds," they said, "God will take care of us all." This was the inner peace the forlorn missionary craved but could not find. He arrived in England on February 1, 1738, only to find that his friend George Whitefield had sailed for America the day before to assist him in his work among the Indians in Georgia. Characteristically, on the way up from Deal to London Wesley preached and read prayers at several places. Inwardly, however, he was still troubled by a sense of sin and a lack of assurance of forgiveness. The great change that overtook his religious feelings is best told in his own words—

It is upward of two years since I left my native country, in order to teach the Georgian Indians the nature of Christianity, but what have I learned, myself, in the meantime? Why, what I least of all suspected, that I, who went to America to convert others, was never converted myself. . . . All this time that I was at Savannah I was beating the air. Being ignorant of the righteousness of Christ, which by a living faith in him, bringing salvation to every one that believeth, I sought to establish my own righteousness, and so labored in the fire all my days.

But on May 24, 1738, the miracle happened. In the morning, he opened his Bible haphazardly at Mark 12:34 and read again the verse he had often pondered, "Thou art not far from the kingdom of God," and he was deeply moved by the Master's word to the rich young ruler. In the afternoon he attended a service in Saint Paul's Cathedral and was further impressed by the singing of the anthem form of Psalm 130: "Out of the depths have I called unto thee, O Lord!" But at night, the despairing Church of England clergyman made his way to a small gathering of Moravians and other believers in Aldersgate Street, London. Someone was reading the Preface to Martin Luther's exposition of *The Epistle to the Romans,* and the phrase that gripped Wesley was, "By faith the heart is cheered, elevated, excited, and transported with sweet affections towards God."

Immediately it seems as if his chains fell off, and he thereafter spoke of this experience as his conversion—"I felt my heart strangely warmed. I felt I did trust in Christ, Christ alone for salvation and an assurance was given me that He had taken my sins, even mine, and saved me from the law of sin and death: and then I testified openly to all there what I now first felt in my heart." About ten that night he cried, "I believe!" Lecky the historian says that "the conversion of John Wesley formed one of the grand epochs of English history." Wesley had studied closely William Law's book, *Serious Call,* and after his conversion he wrote Law a strong letter reproving him for not showing him the way of salvation before.

Wesley had to stand a good deal of scorn for his professed change of life. One critic wrote, "If you have not been a Christian ever since I knew you, you have been a hypocrite; for you made us all believe that you were one."

Some three weeks after this conversion experience, Wesley retired to Germany to spend some time with the godly Moravians in their settlement, and on his return to England in 1739, he began his open-air preaching, and mighty things happened. He had been urged often by George Whitefield to share his "ministry of the open air," but Wesley shrank from preaching outdoors with "a pile of stones as pulpit." Now, however, Wesley took the plunge and became renowned as the Evangelist of the Highways and Byways of England. Although he was only five feet four in height, he commanded the attention of the crowds assembled to hear him. Something about his manner and voice gripped the audience, as, clear as a bell, his words flowed to the outer rim of the throng. Wesley was about thirty-five years of age, and had been a clergyman for ten years at the time he came to see that the rest of his life must be spent as a herald of salvation by faith.

His Manifold Gifts

From the dawn of his new life, Wesley dedicated all he was and had to the furtherance of the gospel. A quaint saying of one of the earliest Methodists was, "I do love those one-eyed Christians," referring to the Biblical phrase of "a single eye to the glory of God." This became Wesley's trait. He wore his hair long to save the money for the Lord's work and lived a life of austerity and activity. First of all, he dedicated his time to Him who was the length of his days—"Leisure and I have taken leave of one another. I propose to be busy as long as I live, if my health is so long indulged in me." On one occasion he spoke plainly to his preachers telling them that they should do one of three things. "Either spend time in chit-chat or learn Latin or Hebrew, or spend all your time and strength in saving souls. Which will you do?" The hearers replied, "The last by the grace of God." Wesley practiced what he preached, for he knew how to make the most of a day. Once, when he had to wait for a carriage he said, "I have lost ten minutes forever." Although he appeared to be always in haste, he declared himself to be never in a hurry. The amazing amount of work he got through could only be accomplished by the most rigid use of each minute. The strain would have broken most men down, but Wesley's resolution to redeem the time urged him forward and his health remained good until about three years before his death.

This tireless preacher would rise at four in the morning for prayer and meditation, preach his first sermon by five A.M., and be on the road by six, riding horseback often sixty to seventy miles a day and preaching at least three times. And he demanded the same strict regimen of his preachers. Any man who felt he could not gladly rise at four in the morning and be ready at five to preach to needy souls was no worker of his. Laziness he stoutly condemned.

Wesley practiced a strict economy of time, believing with the apostle Paul that he must redeem the time, seeing the days were evil. In a letter to Boswell, Samuel Johnson wrote, "John Wesley's conversation is good, but he is never at leisure. He is always obliged to go at a certain hour. This is very disagreeable to a man who loves to fold his legs and have out his talk, as I do."

In Wesley's day, the English clergy were the idlest and most lifeless in the world. By one observer they were branded as "the most remiss of their labors in private, and the least severe in their lives." No wonder these lazy clerics were aroused to strong opposition to Wesley's strict discipline and indefatigable industry! His full use of time for God shamed them. He knew how to give each flying minute something to keep in store.

Wesley also believed in the dedication of money to the Lord. Stoutly he condemned wasting money on drink, tobacco, and extravagant dress. One year, he spent five pounds nineteen shillings on himself, and six hundred pounds in charity for the needy. Throughout his wonderful career his asceticism was that of a monk. At times he lived on bread only, and often slept on bare boards. Yet it must be remembered that in spite of the rough-and-tumble world in which Wesley lived, he never restricted his devotion to learning. He mastered six languages and studied their best literature. In the saddle on his long rides he read the classics or made shorthand notes for his voluminous daily journal which became a spiritual classic. One of Wesley's biographers says—

> The inconveniences and dangers which he embraced that he might preach the Gospel and do good of every kind to all that would receive it at his hands; the exposing of himself to every change of season and inclemency of weather in the prosecution of his work, were conditions which few but himself could have submitted to. He frequently slept on the ground as he journeyed through woods, covered with the nightly dews, and with his clothes and his hair frozen, in the morning, to the earth. He would wade through swamps and swim through rivers, and then travel till his clothes were dry. His health, strange as it may seem, was uninterrupted.

As a preacher, evangelist, and teacher he was eminently used of God. His presentation of truth was both doctrinal and practical. Pattison says of Wesley as a preacher that "violent ranting was as offensive to him as was heartless reasoning." In preparing for the pulpit, he wrote much, but he did not read his sermons. He expanded or contracted his material as occasion demanded. The arrangement of his thought was admirable. To systematize was as natural with him as to breathe. He spoke, as he lived, by rule.

> On board ship, at the mouth of a coal pit, amid the distractions of a country fair, surrounded by thousands of rough miners in the natural amphitheatre of the Cornish hillside, Wesley never seems to have failed to make himself understood. His slight, compact figure, his flowing silver locks, his benignant countenance, his clear, resonant utterances, immediately impressed his hearers with a sense of authority, and needed not the clerical garb which he always wore to command respect. His voice and his gesture were not dramatic, his manner was that of a man of fearless spirit, of intense earnestness, and of rare spiritual fervor. Robert Hall said of him, "While he set all things in motion, he was himself perfectly calm; he was the quiescence of turbulence."

Wesley had a unique gift as an organizer and became identified with many causes. His genius for organization was recognized by Macaulay who described Wesley as one "whose genius for government was not inferior to that of Richelieu." Yet, as Dr. Dinsdale T. Young, the eminent Methodist preacher, points out in his admirable volume on *Popular Preaching,* it was—

> John Wesley's popular preaching, rather than his organizing genius, which, speaking after the manner of men, founded Methodism. . . . That John Wesley was a regally great popular preacher can never be successfully disputed. . . . Where he found the secret of popular preaching all preachers will discover. . . . It is at the Cross of Christ that this transcendent

248

worth is discovered. . . . If preachers live at Calvary, I do not shrink from saying, they possess the secret of popular preaching. Nowhere else is that inestimable secret to be learned.

As a writer, Wesley had a gifted pen that wielded a tremendous influence for God and righteousness. He was as versatile as he was intense. He published grammars in at least five languages, issued a library of religious literature, and even wrote a novel. His famous *Journal* is still the best history of the rise of Methodism, and his written sermons the best compendium of its theology. Wesley's incomparable *Journal* was described by Augustine Birrell as "the most amazing record of human experience ever penned or endured," and, "a book full of plots and plays and novels, which quiver with life and is full of character." In 1778, he founded a monthly magazine, a weapon in his theological warfare with the Calvinists. Then there is also his *Primitive Physic,* a book that reads quaintly today but which because of its plain practicability went through nearly a hundred editions in as many years.

There is a most interesting sequel: Wesley sent a copy of this family medicine book for the poor folks to Dr. Hawes, a well-known London physician. He bitterly attacked it as being full of magic and ignorance. His adverse review boosted the sales of the book so much that Wesley wrote to him—

> Dear Sir, My bookseller informs me that since you have published your remarks on the *Primitive Physic, or an Essay and Natural Method of Curing Most Diseases,* there has been a greater demand for it than ever. If, therefore, you would please publish a few further remarks, you would confer a further favour upon your humble servant, J. Wesley.

This medical work stressing plain food, fresh air, abundant exercise, and a contented spirit netted Wesley thousands of pounds which he ploughed back into publishing the book for free distribution. His four hundred publications, covering all sorts of topics, followed the broad conception of doing good to all men, to their bodies and minds as well as their souls. This Christian library summarized in fifty volumes "the choicest pieces of practical divinity in the English tongue, especially skimming the cream from the somewhat long-winded writings of the Puritans.

"No man in the eighteenth century did so much to create a good taste for good reading, and to supply it with books at the lowest prices than Wesley." He had a skill and learning in writing no other of the Methodists possessed, which is further seen in the quality of *Rules,* published in 1743 to avoid the scandal of unworthy members of his society. Possessing and reading this book was a condition of acceptance as a member. It listed evil practices to be avoided and inculcated positive forms of social service and regular use of the various means of grace. Members who habitually broke these rules were expelled from membership. Though slavery in his day was protected by law and considered highly respectable, Wesley did not hesitate to fight it. His volume, *Thoughts upon Slavery* did for England what *Uncle Tom's Cabin* did for America.

Then there was his work *Compendium of Natural Philosophy* in which he wrote on the habits of beasts, birds, and insects. Years before Charles Darwin, Wesley leaned toward evolution, concluding that "there is a prodigious number of continued links between the most perfect man and the ape."

Wesley gave away forty thousand pounds—a terrific sum in those days—in royalties from his books and pamphlets, and limited himself to thirty pounds a year for personal expenses. He once said that he would give people the privilege of calling him a robber if at the time of his death he owned more than ten pounds.

As a hymn writer, he was next to his musical brother Charles Wesley in output. Many of the hymns John composed will live as long as our language. He believed that Methodism was raised up "to spread Scriptural holiness over the land," and his hymns, and the three thousand or more Charles Wesley wrote, greatly helped in such an effort. In the revivals under the Wesleys we are apt to stress a division of labor between the two brothers, and speak of John as the preacher and Charles as the hymn-writer. "But this is not strictly accurate," says Julian in his mammoth *Dictionary of Hymnology*:

> On the one hand Charles was also a great preacher, second only to his brother and George Whitefield in the effects which he produced. On the other hand, John by no means relegated to Charles the exclusive task of supplying the people with their hymns. . . . When he speaks of the hymns, it is, "My brother and I." . . . He saw at once that hymns might be utilized, not only for raising the devotion, but also for instructing and establishing the faith of his disciples. . . . The part which John played in actually writing the hymns is not easy to ascertain, but it is certain that more than thirty translations from the German, French, and Spanish were exclusively his; and there are some original hymns, admittedly his composition, which are not unworthy to stand by the side of his brother's.

The hymns of the Wesleys expressed the fiery conviction of their converts in lines so chaste and beautiful that its more extravagant features disappeared. "The wild throes of hysteric enthusiasm passed into a passion for hymn-singing, and a new musical impulse was aroused in the people which gradually changed the face of public devotion through England."

As an organizer and administrator, Wesley was without peer. He controlled the various societies he had created as a statesman would. He labored on, unwearied, and the flame of revival spread and converts became so numerous that Wesley's powers were bent to the building up of a great religious society which might give to the new enthusiasm a lasting and practical form. Thus, his followers were "grouped into classes, gathered in love-feasts, and purified by the expulsion of unworthy members, and furnished with an alternation of settled ministers and wandering preachers." J. R. Green goes on to say that "the great body which he thus founded—a body which numbered a hundred thousand members at his death, and which now counts its members by millions—bears the stamp of Wesley in more than its name."

Wesley's spiritual and beneficial creations were most remarkable. Not only was he the founder and director of a great religious movement, but also the founder of England's first free medical dispensary—the forerunner of the national health system. To give employment to the poor, he organized various outlets like spinning and knitting shops. He actually established Wesley's Benevolent Loan Fund to help finance new business enterprises, and also The Strangers' Friend Society to give relief to "poor, sick, friendless strangers." As the result of his monumental activities, a wonderful philanthropic movement began after his death—Sunday schools by Raikes, Hannah More's fight against poverty and crime, Wilberforce's crusade against slavery, and Howard's far-reaching reform of prisons, which was an extension of Wesley's fight against a horrible prison system, with its filth, starvation, and degradation.

His Constant Persecution

Although a great and effectual door had opened to John Wesley, he came to experience that with it there were many adversaries. This forced him to write, "A Christian will be despised anywhere, and no one is a Christian till he is despised." At one place where he preached, he was mobbed, and the cry rose, "Knock out his brains! Kill him at once!" The leader of the gang intervened and rescued Wesley. "Tuberculosis threatened him, mobs stoned him, churchmen denounced him, and his own sensitive nature cringed from the roughness of the life he led. But with faith aflame he rode on to accomplish his purposes." His ruthless denunciation of drunkenness and immorality aroused fierce hostility. As crowds gathered to hear the Wesleys preach, antagonists would let loose vicious animals to stampede the people gathered for worship and ministry. Drunken mobs would attack the meeting houses of the Methodists with stones and clubs. Charles Wesley, John's brother, said that he could identify the homes of Methodists by the marks of missiles hurled against them.

There was an occasion when John Wesley was stoned by a mob, but although beaten to the ground, he prayed with such fervor that the mob was silenced. George Clifton, prize-fighter, and leader of the mob, put his hand on Wesley's head, and said, "Sir, I will spend my life for you. Not one soul shall harm a hair of your head." Completely reformed by grace, this man not only became Wesley's bodyguard, but an ardent Methodist preacher. "Mobs might pursue him with stones, but Wesley would retreat with a deliberateness which was in itself victorious, and, once there, would comb out his white locks, and find relief in the pages of his *Horace*."

Although Wesley was a clergyman of the Episcopal Church, and never failed to respect her in spite of the rejection she caused him to suffer, yet because of the nature of his deep, revival preaching, the church closed her pulpits against him, and he was forced to preach in barns and fields. Preaching that could move the hearts of grimy miners at the pithead and cause them to weep, "making white channels down their blackened cheeks," was more than an apathetic church could stand. Still, if Wesley could not preach in a church, he would take to the churchyard, and if excluded from that there was the village green. The Established Church gave him no encouragement or consideration. The church in which his father, his brother Charles, and he himself were ordained was closed against him. At Epworth Church, sacred to John, the curate would not allow him to enter the building where his father had ministered. "Tell Mr. Wesley I shall not give him the sacrament for he is not fit." With this refusal Wesley put up a notice in the graveyard saying that he would preach there at six, and a crowd assembled as he stood on his father's grave and preached. Afterwards he wrote, "I am well assured that I did far more good to my Lincolnshire parishioners by preaching three days on my father's tomb than I did by preaching three years in his pulpit." Closed churches could not check the rising tide of revival. Such opposition only forced it into new channels, and Wesley feared none save God, his determination being—

> By all Hell's host withstood:
>   We all Hell's host o'erthrow:
> And conquering them through Jesus' blood,
>   We on to victory go.

His Triumphant Death

In spite of his rigid, disciplined life, exposure to all kinds of weather, and unceasing trials and persecutions, he reached his eighty-eighth milestone on the pilgrimage of life. To the very last he preached and wrote daily. On his deathbed he called out, "Where is my sermon on the love of God? Take it and spread it abroad. Give it to everyone."

His life from 1703 to 1791 almost covered the century; he had lived to see the Methodist body pass through every phase of its history before he sank into his grave. As he reached his eightieth year he remarked that he could remember to have felt lowness of spirits for one quarter of an hour since he was born. "By the grace of God, I never fret; I repine at nothing; I am discontented at nothing." And he died, even as he had lived, calm and content. In the week of his death, he rose at 4 A.M. each day, preached and traveled as usual until the Wednesday when he preached for the last time at Leatherhead, Surrey. On Friday symptoms appeared which left little doubt as to the end, and the next four days were mainly occupied by him in praising God. Around his bed were gathered his leading preachers and his last word to them and to the world was, "The best of all is, God is with us." At ten on Tuesday morning, March 2, 1791, he heard the divine voice say, "Come up, hither," and God took His valiant servant home. After lying in state in his ministerial robes at his chapel in City Road, London, he was buried there on March 9.

The burial of John Wesley was in keeping with his conviction about service to others. He had said that men could call him a robber if he left more than ten pounds at his death. He had drawn up instructions as to his burial and these were carried out to the letter. He was buried in nothing more costly than wool, and whatever money remained in his box or pockets was to be given to his followers. As a protest against needless funeral expenses, he had ordered that no hearse be employed and that six poor men in need of work, be hired at one pound each to carry his body to the grave. It was reckoned that over ten thousand of his followers gathered to say farewell to their honored leader.

Although the church had closed her door against him, at his end, Wesley was an honored figure throughout the British Isles, and today on the wall of Westminster Abbey you will see the medallion of his face and that of his brother Charles, the one the most successful popular gospel preacher, the other the sweetest poet of their generation. Below the medallion are three sentences expressing the spirit of John Wesley and embodying his faith—

"I look on all the World as my parish."
"God buries His workmen, but continues His work."

Then the last words which broke from his lips in death—

"The best of all is, God is with us."

At Wesley's death, there were Methodist Societies all over Britain, three hundred traveling preachers, seventy-two thousand members of Societies and about five hundred thousand adherents. About two-thirds lived overseas, especially in America, where membership continued to grow at a far more rapid rate than in Wesley's homeland. For many years those following Wesley's teachings were known as Wesleyans. They were members of the Nonconformist Church he founded about 1739. The main lesson of Wesley's life was "Be Earnest! Be Earnest." And what an intense devotion was his! "No single figure influenced so many minds: no single voice touched so many hearts." With all his consecrated heart John Wesley believed that

> 'Tis not in man to trifle, life is brief,
>   And sin is here.
> Our age is but the falling of a leaf,
>   A passing tear.

Scores of able writers, Methodists and others, have described the marvelous expansion of Methodism since Wesley's day. It only remains for us to say that all the voluminous literature on Wesley and his work is the preeminent testimony to his exemplary life and prodigious labors. He still lives in the religious community which, under the Spirit's power, he brought into being. A wise man of the world remarked, "When Mr. Wesley drops, all this is at an end." But Wesley himself replied, "So it will, unless before God calls him home one is found to stand in his place."

When he was called home there were many godly and able men ready to take his place and carry the torch forward. Certainly, they were not of the same caliber as John Wesley, for when God made him, He broke the mold, but the three hundred preachers he left behind were singularly blessed of God in spreading the flame, until now, over 180 years after Wesley's death, there are some eighteen million members of the Methodist Church scattered over the world, with an unofficial membership or constituency of more than forty million persons. In Great Britain there are about a million members, but in America the Methodist Church boasts nearly ten million members, and three large Negro Methodist bodies with about two and a half million members. Altogether, there are twenty-six separate Methodist bodies in the United States, of which the Methodist Church is numerically the strongest, with its numerous churches, universities, colleges, schools, hospitals, and homes for the aged. It holds property worth more than 3,000 million dollars. But the influence of this prominent Protestant denomination cannot be read in its statistics. In the main, the evangelistic passion for conversion, righteous living, and social welfare, so characteristic of Wesley's long ministry, still operate in the religious society he founded, causing it to be a mighty spiritual factor in a world of sin and need.

One cannot meditate upon the life and service of John Wesley without being deeply impressed with what God is able to accomplish through a man so utterly yielded to Him as was this consecrated clergyman. Believing that a loving God had every claim upon his time and talents, he dedicated them entirely to Him for the accomplishment of His redemptive plan for a lost world. By the grace of God may we be found following the stirring example of John Wesley!

18

Charles Haddon Spurgeon
The Prince of Gospel Preachers

King Solomon, who warns us that the name of the wicked will rot, also reminds us that the name of the righteous is as ointment poured forth. A name retaining its fragrance throughout the last century is that of Charles Haddon Spurgeon, who was one of the most popular and prolific preachers in an age of great preaching, and who will always remain one of the most outstanding figures among evangelical heralds. In the days of his flesh, his ministry was nothing short of a marvel, and his influence abides in the perennial publications of his gospel-drenched sermons. His picture in the portrait gallery of God's ministers is one of first order. The person who approaches it sympathetically is always repaid.

His Godly Heritage

Like so many renowned preachers, Spurgeon came of Christian stock. His grandfather was a Congregational minister greatly used in the salvation of souls. His father also was a minister of this denomination. C. H. Spurgeon was one of eight children. He was born in Kelvedon, Essex, on June 17, 1834. His mother was an uncommonly earnest Christian, who took great pains in the shaping of the character of her children. An aunt, whom Spurgeon called "Mother Ann," loved him tenderly and fostered him as her own child. After his conversion, he left the Independents and joined the Baptists. His mother was sad over his change, and told him that she had prayed earnestly for his salvation, but not that he should be a Baptist. Spurgeon replied, "Well, dear Mother, you know that the Lord is so good that He always gives us more than we can ask or think."

The name *Spurgeon* suggests his origin. He sprang from Flemish Hugenots, driven from their native country by persecution and finding refuge in the flat lands in the eastern part of England. It would seem as if his ancestry shaped his theology, for while he must have been familiar with John Wesley's writings and work, he went back further—to the Puritans of Europe, and in his doctrine and preaching he was essentially Puritan. Without doubt he was steeped in Puritan literature, and thus delighted to proclaim grace—free, sovereign, unmerited grace. Toward the end of his ministry, Spurgeon said, "I have been thirty years in one place, but I do not believe I should have been thirty months in one place if it had not been for the gospel."

Yet, although he had the privilege of a Christian home, and at the age of six delighted in reading Bunyan's *Pilgrim's Progress* and his other works, Spurgeon was not saved—"I had heard of the plan of salvation by the sacrifice of Jesus from my youth up but I did not know any more about it in my innermost soul than if I had been born and bred a Hottentot. The light was there, but I was blind. The eyeballs of the soul were not sensitive to the divine beams."

As a child he manifested evident self-possession, strong passions and will. His education was somewhat limited, being confined chiefly to a private academy at Colchester, run by a local Baptist. Later there came a year at an agricultural school in Maidstone. His parents were most eager for him to go to Cambridge, but he refused because he felt called to an active life. Educationally, Spurgeon is a fitting example of God taking the things which are not to bring to nought the things which are.

His Radical Conversion

For one so young, Spurgeon had great distress of soul over his spiritual condition. This conviction of sin lasted for about five years. He seemed to have a remarkable consciousness of sin and of the justice of God. Later on in life, referring to this flowing of heart and conscience, he said, "When I was in the hands of the Holy Spirit under conviction of sin, I had a clear and sharp sense of the justice of God." What a lack of this conviction there is today! God spoke in two ways to the young, troubled heart of Spurgeon. "Once God preached to me by the similitude in the depth of winter," he said. Looking upon the black earth he thought of sin, and in the white snow falling upon it he saw the Saviour, and was reminded that although his sins were scarlet, he could be made as white as snow.

Then there was the vision he had of a murdered friend, and the search for the murderer, with the pursuers hot on his trail. Relating this experience, Spurgeon said, "At last I put my hand upon my breast: 'I have thee now, said I: for lo! he was in my own heart, the murderer was hiding within my own bosom." Overwhelmed with guilt, he wept.

> 'Twas you my sins, my cruel sins
> His chief tormentors were:
> Each of my crimes became a nail
> And unbelief a spear.

In order to find peace Spurgeon read good books explaining a God-provided deliverance from sin—Baxter's *Call to the Unconverted;* James's *Anxious Enquirer;* Doddridge's *Rise and Progress of Religion in the Soul*—but he failed to find relief from his burden of sin. He wandered from church to church, but found no message to chase the dark night of sin away. Then one Sunday morning, unable to reach the church he had meant to visit because of a severe snowstorm, he turned in to a very small country Primitive Methodist

Chapel. About fifteen people were present that cold, bleak morning, and the minister who was to preach was held up by the storm. After consultation of the two or three leaders "a thin looking man, a shoemaker or tailor, went up into the pulpit." To Spurgeon, he seemed to be both stupid and uninstructed. When he came to his sermon he gave out a text, but could not read it properly. It was Isaiah 45:22, "Look unto me, and be ye saved." But he did not stick to his text; he could only fasten on the word *Look!* and said, "Now looking don't take a deal of pains. It ain't lifting your foot or your finger, it is just—look! *Me*—look not to yourselves, not to the Spirit working, not to your neighbours, but to Me!" Then the crude, unlettered preacher went on to urge the few worshipers before him to look to the drops of blood from the cross, and to Christ risen and ascended. After about ten minutes he seemed to be at the end of his tether, then fixing his eyes upon young Spurgeon sitting under the gallery, the poor substitute for the minister said, "Young man, you look miserable. You will always be miserable in life and miserable in death. Young man, look to Jesus Christ. Look! Look! Look!"

In giving his testimony as to what happened on that Sunday morning, January 6, between 10:30 to 12:30, in the year 1850, Spurgeon says, "At once I saw the way of salvation. Oh, I looked until I could almost have looked my eyes away. I looked at Him, He looked at me, And we were one forever." The psalmist says, "They looked unto him, and their faces were made radiant" (34:5, R V). This was the immediate and radical experience of Spurgeon: "I thought I could dance all the way home. I could understand what John Bunyan meant when he declared he wanted to tell the crows in the ploughed land all about his conversion. . . . I thought I could have sprung from the seat in which I sat and have called out with the wildest of those Methodist brethren who were present, I am forgiven! I am forgiven! A monument of grace. A sinner saved by Blood."

D. L. Moody said that on the day of his conversion it seemed as if all the birds of the hedgerow sang blither songs. G. Campbell Morgan testified that on the day of his spiritual crisis, the leaves of the trees appeared to be more beautiful. It is always so when a guilty soul looks to Jesus and is saved.

> Heaven above is softer blue,
>   Earth around is sweeter green;
> Something lives in every hue
>   Christless eyes have never seen:
> Birds with gladder songs o'erflow,
>   Flow'rs with deeper beauties shine,
> Since I know, as now I know,
>   I am His, and He is mine.

From the very outset of his conversion Spurgeon had a clear understanding of what it meant to be saved as these paragraphs prove—

> There is a power in God's gospel beyond all description. In my conversion the very point lay in making the discovery that I had nothing to do but to look to Christ and I should be saved.
>
> When I was anxious about the possibility of a just God pardoning me I understood and saw by faith that He who is the Son of God became man and in His own blessed Person bore my sin in His body on the tree.
>
> The Holy Spirit so enabled me to believe, and gave me peace through believing that I felt as sure that I was forgiven as before I felt sure of my condemnation.

The blessed assurance was his that he knew whom he had believed and by the power of God, Spurgeon became the means of leading countless numbers into the same assurance of faith.

His Pastoral Spheres

After his unmistakable conversion at the age of fifteen, Spurgeon became deeply interested in baptism. He consulted his Congregationalist father about the matter, who, like his mother, was possibly not favorable to the idea. But, convinced that he should be immersed as a witness to his faith in Christ, he walked seven miles from Newmarket to Isleham on May 3, 1850, and was baptized by Pastor Cantlow. At the time, he was tutoring at Mr. Leeding's school. It had been at New Market where he had been a scholar but now had been removed to Cambridge. It was here that young Spurgeon became a member of the Baptist Church in Saint Andrews' Street where Robert Hall, the renowned Baptist preacher, had so long been pastor.

This church had a "Lay Preacher's Association" for the supply of thirteen small, neighboring churches with preachers, and Spurgeon became a member of it. So commenced his preaching career, and he preached his first sermon in a cottage at Teversham. Quickly his fame spread, and crowds gathered to hear "The Boy Preacher," as he became known. The Baptist Church at Waterbeech, a village of about thirteen hundred at that time, called him to be pastor, and at eighteen years of age, he began a pulpit ministry that was to become famous for almost forty years. After his first sermon in this village an aged voice quavered out, "Bless your dear heart, how old are you?" The sense of quiet humor saved young Spurgeon, for his solemn reply was, "You must wait till the service is over before making any such inquiries. Let us now sing."

The fame of this youthful preacher with his buoyant exhilaration quickly spread. When it reached London it led to an invitation to preach at the New Park Street Chapel in 1853. When but nineteen years of age, he succeeded many Baptist worthies with their long pastorates in this notable church which, by this time, had become almost empty. His ministry was an instant and remarkable success, and he sprang to the highest rank in the preaching world. Within a year the church, proud of its past, was far too small for the crowds eager to hear the exceedingly eloquent young preacher. From then on he was destined for almost forty years to hold a prominent position among English preachers.

Because of the utter inadequacy of the New Park Street Chapel to hold the crowds that flocked to hear Spurgeon, the building of a very large center in the metropolis was decided upon, and while the Metropolitan Tabernacle, Newington Butts, was being built, several meeting places were used. Often he preached in the Surrey Gardens Music Hall to audiences of over ten thousand. His voice was so powerful that without effort he could reach as many as twenty thousand people, and that without our modern day microphones and address systems. "Its first note, while it filled with ease the largest place, was so personal that each one of his hearers seemed to be personally addressed."

In 1861, the Tabernacle, seating some five thousand, was opened, and at twenty-seven years of age, Spurgeon began a ministry that was phenomenal in every way. While pastoring a small church at Waterbeach in 1851, as he rode home one night he watched a lamplighter lighting the street lamps, although he could not see the lamplighter himself. The thought came to him—"How earnestly do I wish that my life may be spent in lighting one soul after another with the sacred flame of eternal life! I would myself be as much as possible unseen while at my work, and would vanish into the eternal brilliance above when my work is done." For over thirty years in the Metropolitan Tabernacle, London, Spurgeon was a mighty lamplighter for the Master he dearly loved and faithfully served. Eternity alone will reveal how many darkened hearts were illuminated through his ministry. Until his death in 1892, he continually attracted vast congregations, and to the last no church or hall in the land was large enough to accommodate the crowds who desired to hear his clarion voice ring forth the gospel he lived to proclaim. During World War II, the Tabernacle was destroyed by German bombs. It was finally rebuilt on a much smaller scale.

His Pulpit Ministry

Dr. Thomas Armitage wrote a sketch of Charles Haddon Spurgeon in *The History of Baptists* while the renowned minister was alive and active:

> As a preacher, he deals only in what Christ and His Apostles thought worthy of their attention; tells what he knows about God and man, sin and holiness, time and eternity, in pure ringing Saxon; uses voice enough to make people hear, speaks out like a man to men, lodging his words in their ears and hearts, instead of making his own throat or nose their living sepulchre. He fills his mind with old Gospel truth, and his mind with old Puritan thought, calls the fertility of his imagination into use, believes in Jesus Christ with all the power of his being, loves the souls of men with all his heart and acts accordingly. He carries the least amount of religion possible in the white of his eyes, but a living well of it in the depth of his soul, and the real wonder is not that God has put much honour upon him, for if his life had been very different from what it has been, even partial failure in the hands of such a man of God would have been a new and unsolvable mystery in the reign of a faithful Christ.

Spurgeon's constant theme, preached in simple and plain English, was that of a personal salvation through faith in Christ. In the pulpit he combined sincerity with natural gestures, easy delivery, skillfully told illustration, and often with humor which was always homely. He was an unashamed fundamentalist and was outspoken against the growth of modes of thought antagonistic to the purity of the faith he loved. It was because of this that in 1887, owing to his distrust of the adverse, modern criticism of Scripture, he felt compelled to sever his connection with the Baptist Union.

Spurgeon was often denounced and bitterly criticized by jealous-minded ministers, but his popularity with the masses never waned for the simple reason that he preached as one who knew that the God he knew personally was with him in the pulpit. No one could doubt his unquestioning faith. Puritan certitude was his strength. Everyone who heard him was inspired by his strong and confident faith to witness, steadfast to the end. Always and everywhere he was an evangelistic preacher, and "the common people heard him gladly." With a nature rich in sympathy, he was essentially a preacher to the people. "I am," he said, "neither eloquent nor learned, but the Head of the Church has given me sympathy with the masses, love to the poor, and the means of winning the attention of the ignorant and unenlightened. God has owned me to the most degraded and off-cast; let others serve their class; these are mine, and to them I must keep."

Short in stature, and not impressive in appearance—his redeeming facial feature was an eye at once brilliant and kindly. Spurgeon had a remarkable voice, clarion in its power to rouse the hearts of large audiences. "His ear for harmony was so perfect that each sentence was complete as it fell from his lips." A professor of Edinburgh University said, after hearing him, "I feel that it would do me good to hear the like of that, it sat so close to reality." Oratorical powers he undoubtedly had, but the orator was forgotten in the prophet, and it was because he was God's messenger in God's message that he was able to preach to eight to ten thousand persons every Sunday in the greatest city in the world. The *London Spectator* said of him, "It is evident that the great oratorical gifts which he undoubtedly possesses are accompanied by solid powers of thought, by imagination, and by humour."

His Literary Legacy

Spurgeonic literature never loses its appeal. This is evidenced by its continual appearance from evangelical publishing houses. How grateful we are that his sermons are still being printed—a phenomena of literature if ever there was one! In his lifetime thirty-eight volumes of them were issued, and interest in them has not died out. Millions upon millions of Spurgeon's sermons have been sold. He carefully revised every sermon before publication, a task occupying one full day every week. In every volume of his sermons there are discourses of rare power, and all in greater or less degree show the affluence of his mind. Dr. Robertson Nicoll, who urged preachers to soak themselves in Spurgeon's writings, said of his sermons, "Our children will think more of them than we do; and as I get older I read them more and more. He stood at the heart of things."

Among the numerous stories told of the abiding value and appeal of Spurgeon's printed sermons is the one I came across in W. Robertson Nicoll's biography of Dr. John Watson, who, under the pen-name of *Ian Maclaren*, authored some of the finest Scottish stories ever written. Describing the powerful evangelical forces in the life of Watson, Robertson Nicoll tells of the Blairgowrie farm where Watson made acquaintance with Spurgeon's sermons, and of how he related it in one of his happiest sketches, which we herewith cull from Nicoll's charming biography of his friend.

Watson tells how the Blairgowrie farmer is told by his good wife to bring home from the market town the tea and sugar, the paraffin oil and other necessities of life. "And, John, dinna forget Spurgeon." Spurgeon was the weekly number of the Metropolitan Tabernacle Pulpit. As the provident woman had written every requirement—except the oil which was obtained at the ironmongers's, and the Spurgeon which was sold at the draper's—on a sheet of paper, and pinned it on the topmost cabbage leaf which covered the butter, the risk was not great; but that week the discriminating prophecy of the good man's capabilities seemed to be justified, for the oil was there, but Spurgeon could not be found. It was not in the bottom of the dogcart, nor below the cushion, nor attached to a piece of saddlery, nor even in the good man's trousers pocket—all familiar resting-places—and when it was at last extricated from the inner pocket of his top-coat—a garment with which he had no intimate acquaintance—he received no credit, for it was pointed out with force that to have purchased the sermon and then to have mislaid it, was worse than forgetting it altogether. "The Salvation of Manasseh," read the good wife; "it would have been a fine-like business to have missed that; a'll warrant this'll be ane o' his sappiest, but they're a' gude." And then Manasseh was put in a prominent and honorable place, behind the basket of wax flowers in the best parlor till Sabbath. When Sabbath came the lads from the bothie were brought into the kitchen and entertained to tea. Then afterwards the master of the house read a sermon by Spurgeon. On that particular evening the little gathering was held in the loft because it was harvest time, and extra men were working. It was laid on the boy as an honor to read Manasseh.

"Whether the sermon is called by this name I do not know, and whether it be one of the greatest of Mr. Spurgeon's I do not know, nor have I a copy of it; but it was mighty unto salvation in that loft, and I make no doubt that good grain was garnered unto eternity. There is a passage in it when, after the mercy of God has rested on this chief sinner, an angel flies through the length and breadth of heaven crying, 'Manasseh is saved, Manasseh is saved.' Up to that point the lad read, and further he did not read. You know, because you have been told, how insensible and careless is a schoolboy, how destitute of all sentiment and emotion . . . and therefore I do not ask you to believe me. You know how dull and stupid is a plowman, because you have been told . . . and therefore I do not ask you to believe me.

268

"It was the light which got into the lad's eyes and the dust which choked his voice, and it must have been for the same reasons that a plowman passed the back of his hand across his eyes.

" 'Ye'll be tired noo,' said the good man; 'lat me feenish the sermon,' but the sermon is not yet finished, and never shall be."

It will be seen that Watson was brought up under powerful evangelical influences, and there can be no doubt that they touched him to the core of his heart. But it is right to say that his mother was of a broader school. He himself wrote in 1905: "My mother, I believe, would have gladly seen me a minister of the Established Church. She was a moderate in theology, and had a rooted dislike to amateur preachers and all their ways, believing that if you employed a qualified physician rather than a quack for your body, you had better have a qualified clergyman rather than a layman for your soul. From her I received the main principles of my religious thinking. She taught me that all doctrine must be tried by human experience, and that if it was not proved by our reason and conscience, it was not true; and especially I learned from her to believe in the Fatherhood of God and to argue from the human home to the divine family. She always insisted that as we were all the children of one Father, He would make the best of us, both in this world and that which is to come. This, however, was the theology of the Moderate school, and not of the Free Church." He also draws the contrast between the two churches as they appeared to him in early days. "The Free Church of that day was more intense, dogmatic, self-righteous, and evangelistic; the spirit of the Established Church was more liberal and humane, and possibly some would add less spiritual. I greatly honored the leading Free Church."

Another illustration of the influence of Spurgeon's printed messages can be found in Arthur Porritt's illuminating biography of Dr. J. H. Jowett, who was one of the most accomplished pulpiteers of his time. John Loosemore, one of his most intimate friends, wrote of Jowett's Saturday preparation of his Sunday services at Carr's Lane, Birmingham, and how very early on the Sunday morning Jowett would read "one of Spurgeon's sermons, for the sake of its atmosphere. Then he would arrive at Carr's Lane bearing in his mind the ordered and familiar results of a week's honest toil and in his heart the glorious purpose of the Christian redemption."

Spurgeon read widely, could gather material rapidly, and knew where to put it so as to have it at command when needed. His mind was both quick and retentive. A study of his printed works proves this. Think of his monumental expositions of the Psalms—*The Treasury of David*—without doubt one of the greatest works on the Psalter. Then we have his *Salt Cellars, Plain Advice for Plain People, John Ploughman's Talks, Commentary on Commentaries, Art of Illustration, Lectures to Students,* and his famous *Autobiography* in four volumes. Then there was the magazine he founded, *Sword and Trowel.* All of these, like his sermons have had astronomical sales.

His Beneficial Institutions

The labors of Spurgeon were varied. Not content with his herculean responsibilities as the pastor of the largest church in the land, and special preacher all over the country, and author of numerous books, he launched out for the Master in other directions in which his talent for organization and administration became evident. Already early in life he had a passion for books and this became more intense. It led him to form a "Colportage Society," made up of earnest soul-winners who, as colporteurs, went from house to house selling and distributing religious tracts and books. In this way, he scattered silent messengers of the gospel far and wide.

Then, with a heart full of tenderness for the poor neglected children of that time he founded the "Spurgeon Orphanages," and in this way extended his spiritual influence. Distressed by the plight of many old people, he instituted almshouses for them where they were tenderly cared for in the evening tide of their life.

Entering the ministry, as he did, without any theological training, out of sympathy for young men not able to pay for their lodging and preparation for church work, he created Spurgeon's College. Perhaps another motive he had for founding such a center for the spiritual and mental equipment of men for the ministry, was the way that many other theological schools then were beginning to adopt the liberal rationalistic approach to Scripture—a movement he strenuously opposed. He wanted to produce men who would revere and preach the Bible as he did, and he was successful in his purpose. Through his own preaching over the land, small churches sprang up, and the pulpits of these were filled with young men who, after sitting at the feet of this prince of gospel preachers, went out to proclaim the same evangel. This famous Baptist college still flourishes, and is, perhaps, the most conservative of Baptist colleges in England. During the last century many of the outstanding preachers in the Baptist denomination studied at Spurgeons, and their roll call is most impressive.

His Premature End

It is because the word *premature* means "a happening before the proper or usual time, or, too early," that we use it of Spurgeon who died before he was fifty-eight years of age. The psalmist reminds us that the normal span of life is threescore years and ten. Had this renowned preacher, whose influence is still felt, lived another ten years, one wonders what mightier things he would have accomplished for the cause of Christ. But in the divine counsels, Spurgeon's death was not before God's time; for He is the length of our days, whether they be few or many. Knowing that his times were in God's

271

hands, Spurgeon was prepared for his transition to glory. He was often ill, and as the shadow deepened, and often forced him to leave England in search of sunshine, he sensed that time was short. His last words in his dear Tabernacle on June 7, 1891, were as characteristic of any that he ever uttered—

> If you wear the livery of Christ you will find Him so meek and lowly of heart that you will find rest to your souls. There never was His like among the choicest of princes. He is always to be found in the thickest of the battle. When the wind blows cold He always takes the bleak side of the hill. The heaviest end of the cross lies ever on His shoulders. . . . His service is life, peace, and joy. God help you to enlist under the banner of Jesus Christ.

Commenting on these last words of Spurgeon, Professor Harwood Pattison says, "As a model of style, rich in illustration, perfect in euphony, these sentences have rarely been excelled. As a summing up of his whole ministry, the ministry of reconciliation, they are complete."

The facts of his last illness and death have been related by all biographers of Spurgeon. That he had a wonderful hold on the heart of Christendom was evident in the concern for him when he was forced to relinquish his great task. To quote Pattison again, "The Greek patriarch, princes and prelates of the Roman Church, Archbishop and Bishop of the Anglican Church, the Heir-Apparent to the British Throne, the ministers of his own and all other denominations, statesmen and merchants, with multitudes of less known but not less loving hearts were constant in the expression of their anxiety for his recovery." But it was not to be for "the time of the singing of birds had come," and for the happy warrior, the winter of his pain was about to vanish.

A long period was spent at Mentone, on the Mediterranean, to which he often retreated when illness struck, and it was while here, almost at the same time when his people at the Tabernacle gathered in a thanksgiving service for their beloved pastor's partial recovery, that word was flashed to them that on January 31, 1892, their "Mr. Valiant-for-the-truth" had "passed over, and all the trumpets sounded for him on the other side." Sorrow over his death was universal. Multitudes of consolatory messages reached Mrs. Spurgeon, the then Prince and Princess of Wales being among the first to "desire to express their deep sympathy with her in her great sorrow."

It is reckoned that over 100,000 people attended the various memorial and funeral services held at the Tabernacle where his magnetic voice would be heard no more. When the coffin, with the Bible Charles Haddon Spurgeon had long used opened at Isaiah 45:22—the verse God used in his salvation over forty years before—passed through the streets there were very many who recalled the prophetic picture he had given at the close of a sermon he had preached eighteen years before, December 28, 1874—

> In a little while there will be a concourse of people in the streets. Methinks I hear someone inquiring, "What are all these people waiting for?" "Do you not know? He is to be buried today." "And who is that?" "It is Spurgeon." "What! the man that preached at the Tabernacle?" "Yes, he is to be buried today." That will happen very soon: and when you see my coffin carried to the silent grave I should like every one of you, whether converted or not, to be constrained to say, "He did earnestly urge us, in plain and simple language, not to put off the consideration of eternal things. He did entreat us to look to Christ."

We can imagine how scores who heard and remembered that impressive sermon, and who were among the vast crowds of mourners as the remains of the beloved pastor were being carried to God's green acre, blessed God for the prince of gospel preachers who never failed to declare the whole counsel of God. It is to be regretted that the predominantly evangelistic preaching Spurgeon was so notable for has passed out of fashion. The utterances of many a pulpit today would not save a sparrow. The Tabernacle never heard sermons on current events, politics, or listened to essays on a hundred and one themes. Charles Haddon Spurgeon had only one theme, he could ring the changes on in marvelous ways—Christ crucified, and His power to save all who looked to Him in faith! That was the message that filled the Tabernacle every Sunday with almost ten thousand people for well over thirty years, and it remains the only message that will fill churches today.

Dr. Herbert Lockyer spent nearly three decades as a pastor in England and Scotland before coming to the United States, where he conducted a ten-year lecturing ministry under the auspices of Moody Bible Institute. He is the author of more than fifty books including the well-known, fifteen-volume All series.